THROUGH A
HOWLING WILDERNESS

ALSO BY THOMAS A. DESJARDIN

Stand Firm, Ye Boys from Maine: The 20th Maine and the Gettysburg Campaign

These Honored Dead: How the Story of Gettysburg Shaped American Memory

THROUGH A HOWLING WILDERNESS

Benedict Arnold's March to Quebec, 1775

Thomas A. Desjardin

St. Martin's Griffin
New York

www.stmartins.com

The maps are by the author, except for map 5 (chapter 5) and map 6 (chapter 6), which are details from *A Map of the Sources of the Chaudière, Penobscot, and Kennebec Rivers* (1761?) by John Montressor (1736–1799), in the Peter Force map collection, no. 37; call number: G3730 1761 .M6 vault; Library of Congress Geography and Map Division, Washington D.C.

Book design by Adele Regina

Library of Congress Cataloging-in-Publication Data

Desjardin, Thomas A., 1964–
    Through a howling wilderness : Benedict Arnold's march to Quebec, 1775 / Thomas Desjardin.
        p. cm.
    Includes bibliographical references and index.
    ISBN-13: 978-0-312-33905-0
    ISBN-10: 0-312-33905-4
    1. Canadian Invasion, 1775–1776. 2. Quâbec (Quâbec)—History—Siege, 1775–1776.
3. Arnold, Benedict, 1741–1801. I. Title.

E231.D37 2006
973.3'31—dc22

        2005044607

First St. Martin's Griffin Edition: November 2007

10 9 8 7 6 5 4 3 2 1

For Fern Marie Tardif Desjardin,

the one we all call "Mimi"

CONTENTS

INTRODUCTION

Napoleon Bonaparte, a soldier who saw a large ration of marching and combat himself, and who took historians along on his campaigns so as to record the events in the way he most desired, is credited famously with repeating an old saying, "What is history but a fable agreed upon?" The great emperor understood that the concept of a factual retelling of warfare was an impossible achievement and that what passed down through the ages as the history of any event was simply the version of the story that most people widely agreed was the truth. Such is the case with the story of Arnold's expedition against Quebec. All that can be said of the story assembled here is that it is what the participants on either side described about the events that most now know simply as "Arnold's march." As often as possible, I have attempted to weed out misstatements, using physical evidence, genealogy, local traditions, and other sources not connected to the expedition, but for the most part, this narrative relies very heavily on the often faulty memories of those who took part in these events and wrote about it. In short, this is the story the soldiers told.

Many of the primary sources used in this work are reprinted in other—sometimes many other—works, often with slight variations in words and usage. For clarity, I have cited these sources in their most easily obtained location, so that future researchers may find them more easily.

Translating the words of Native Americans, who had no written language of their own, through the phonetic soundings of English-speaking soldiers—who were often nearly illiterate themselves—always poses a sizable challenge. As a result, there are any number of variations on the spelling of native words, with place-names holding a particular charm. The soldiers of Arnold's expedition, for example, spelled the name of the most northerly falls that they encountered on the Kennebec River Caratuncah, Carratunkas, Carratunker, Carritunkus, and Carrytuck, among others. The modern-day name for the falls is Caratunk, so I have used this version here. The soldiers of the eighteenth century were not the only people who disagreed on how to spell a Native American word, however. Even modern scholars seem to struggle with challenges such as the name of the overarching tribe that dominated the region of Maine through which Arnold marched. The name Abenaki was once the most common label, before clever writers tried Abnaki, Abanaki, Abenaqui, Benaki, Oubenaki, and finally—as the latest fashion dictates—Wabanaki. For the purposes of this work, however, the simple form "Abenaki" will suffice. Though "Abenaki" is used to describe the wider tribe, various communities within the tribe were usually described according to geography. Thus, the Abenakis who made their home along the Kennebec River were known as Kennebecs (or Canabis, Kennebis, Kinnibiki, etc.). By the same rule, those Abenakis who dwelt at the village and falls of Norridgewock were known as Norridgewocks (or Norridgewogs, Narantsouacks, etc.).

In addition to spelling, the grammar, punctuation, and capitalization methods employed by journal writers on the expedition were nearly as varied as the writers themselves. In many cases, their clumsy usage is printed here in the text as it appeared in their writing, so the reader can get a sense of how Revolutionary-era folks wrote and spelled.

My thanks go out to a handful of people who gave great aid and comfort to the author in his search for the nearest "truthful" story possible. Kenneth Roberts not only reinvigorated interest in the expedition back in 1930 with his bestselling novel *Arundel,* he also published all of the firsthand accounts that he had discovered at that time in one volume for use by future historians. His *March to Quebec* saved the author not only endless correspondence and travel to collect these accounts, but also many long hours of eyestrain trying to "translate" the handwriting and slang of eighteenth-century soldiers. In more recent times, James Kirby Martin's *Benedict Arnold, Revolutionary Hero: An American Warrior Reconsidered* has reintroduced a heroic Arnold to the current generation, who otherwise know his name only as a synonym for "traitor." Closer to home, I am truly indebted to Frank Getchell of Vassalboro,

Maine, a direct descendant of the Getchell brothers who guided the expedition and profited handsomely from its lost coinage. Frank willingly shared with me his genealogical work, helping me better understand the early logistics of the march.

Finally, my wife, Lori-Ann, has provided no end of support and encouragement, buoying my spirits whenever needed and being always willing to help pull me through the traps that often befuddle a writer. Her own boundless interest in history and eagerness to see my description of parts of it have always been a great source of inspiration, and help to explain my boundless love and affection for her.

THROUGH A
HOWLING WILDERNESS

I

THE FOURTEENTH COLONY

*H*e came within view of his father's house a little past noon on a pleasant late-September day. Eighteen months had passed since he had left this home in Bridgewater of the Colony of Massachusetts to join the army of George Washington, and in that time he had taken part in adventures and hardships that people in his hometown only read about in novels—those that could read and had time for novels. During his service he had fought at Bunker Hill, then sailed to the Province of Maine with an army under Colonel Benedict Arnold, walked, waded, and swam hundreds of miles through the Maine wilderness to the city of Quebec.

Along the way this simple farmer watched men around him die of hypothermia, drowning, and drunken violence. Smallpox and falling trees killed his fellow soldiers. He saw friends die from exposure and exhaustion, from starvation and from eating too quickly after starvation. To survive, men ate dogs, shoes, clothing, leather, cartridge boxes, shaving soap, tree sap, and lip salve. If they survived, they suffered from gout, rheumatism, dysentery, angina, distemper, diarrhea, constipation, pneumonia, swollen limbs, and infestation.

With the comrades who survived, he attacked a naturally fortified city that contained a military force larger than their own, made up of soldiers from the most powerful empire the world had ever known. When the attack failed, he was captured and thrown into a dungeon-like British prison where he nearly perished from smallpox. He was then pressed into service on a British ship for months, until he, along with two other comrades, escaped and walked back through the Maine wilderness, hundreds of miles, to civilization. On the return trip, they encountered the bones of the men who had died on the way to Quebec the year before. Back among colonial villages, they sailed as laborers on a vessel bound for Boston, a few days walk from Bridgewater.

Now, as he approached the comforts and safety of home, he little resembled the fresh-faced teenager who had left to fight for the rebel cause just after Lexington-Concord. His trials had left him haggard, his skin pitted by smallpox, and his appearance greatly altered. Unconscious of the effect his sudden and gaunt appearance might have on his loved ones, he simply entered through the open door, nodded his head, and sat down in a chair just inside without uttering a word. His mother was across the room sewing and looked up when he entered, but, thinking he was a passing stranger stopping for rest or refreshment, she went back to her needlework without even a greeting.[1]

His young sister, not yet a teenager, took note of him next and, with the curiosity of a youngster, eyed him closely for a time. Suddenly she exclaimed "La, if there ain't Simon!"

At this his mother, who had given him up for dead months earlier, nearly fainted, and as the news of his return spread through the countryside, his father and brother came to confirm the rumor. That evening, friends from miles around came to the modest home to hear his stories of great adventure and suffering. Simon Fobes was home from the war and had a tale to tell of one of the greatest military expeditions in American history.[2]

QUEBEC CITY HAD BEEN THE HUB OF CIVILIZATION IN ITS REGION SINCE Samuel de Champlain first sailed up the St. Lawrence River in 1603. Here he encountered a native settlement on a prominent hill of solid rock that lay between the fork made by the St. Lawrence and one of its major tributaries. The Algonquins who used the site called it "Kebec," meaning "where the river narrows," and it must have struck Champlain as a natural and ideal base of operation for future exploration and colonization. The high rock slope rising from the rivers made it a site one could easily defend against attack, while the half-dozen rivers that converged into the St. Lawrence within ten miles made it ideal for transportation of trade goods and supplies to and from the surrounding wilderness. Even this far inland, the deep waters of the St. Lawrence provided easy access to the sea and Europe. In subsequent voyages, Champlain inquired about Quebec of the natives he encountered elsewhere, and he learned that its trading potential stretched nearly as far as he explored, all the way to the southern coast of Maine.[3]

Two years later, he sailed to Maine's Penobscot Bay and up the navigable length of its river to what is now Bangor. There he learned from the natives that one could reach Quebec by way of a series of lakes, "and, when they reach the end, they go some distance by land, and afterward enter a little river which flows into the St. Lawrence."[4] The following year he learned of yet another route, farther west, by way of the Kennebec River. "One can go from this river across the land so far as Quebec," he recalled, "some 50 leagues, without passing more than one portage of two leagues. Then one enters another little river which empties into the great River St. Lawrence."[5] This was the first time any white man ever heard of what would later be known as the Kennebec-Chaudière trail, though the natives apparently failed to mention the difficulties that lay along this path.

Convinced of the potential of the Quebec site, in 1608 Champlain led a group of thirty-two colonists to settle there and establish it as a trading center, primarily for furs. Only nine colonists survived their first Canadian winter, but the colony endured, and more settlers arrived the following summer. For the next century and a half, the citadel at Quebec was a focal point of fighting between the British and French empires until 1759, when the city fell into English hands after the pivotal Battle of the Plains of Abraham.

The generals commanding each side in this fight, Montcalm for the French and Wolfe for the British, died in the fighting, and the British seized the city. By 1761, fighting in the so-called French and Indian Wars had dwindled to a close, and the two European powers signed a formal peace treaty in Paris on February 10, 1763. By this agreement, France relinquished all of its claims to Canada, leaving tens of thousands of French settlers in Quebec Province subject to British rule.

Eleven years after the Treaty of Paris solidified England's authority over the province, the British Parliament passed what became known as the Quebec Act of 1774, instituting a permanent administration in Canada by replacing the temporary English-style government created

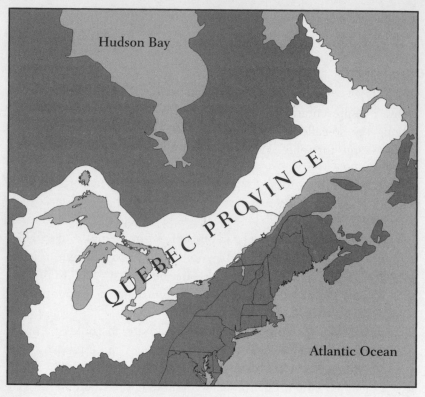

Quebec Province, 1774

When Parliament passed the Quebec Act in 1774, it made Quebec larger than Britain's other North American colonies combined. The establishment of a huge province where Roman Catholicism was dominant and practiced freely —looming over the thirteen colonies, where Protestantism dominated—led the Continental Congress to list this among the "Intolerable Acts" that led to the American Revolution.

in 1763 with a French form of civil law, while maintaining the British system of criminal law. In addition, it gave French Canadians complete religious freedom—a direct threat, as the other colonies saw it, "to dispose the inhabitants to act with hostility against the free Protestant Colonies, whenever a wicked Ministry shall chuse so to direct them."[6] Representatives of the lower thirteen colonies soon listed it among the so-called Intolerable Acts, about which they pled with King George for relief. When he ignored their plea, they turned to open rebellion.

By the mid-1770s, Champlain's Quebec had grown into a huge province stretching to the Mississippi River and including modern-day Ohio, Indiana, Illinois, Michigan, Wisconsin, and Minnesota. It was home to eighty thousand inhabitants, though only 2 percent of them spoke English. Despite its official status as a North American colony under British rule, Quebec never became a part of the coalition of colonies that eventually declared their independence in 1776. Language and religious differences set the Québécois well apart from their neighbors to the south, and when representatives of the lower thirteen colonies met at the First Continental Congress in Philadelphia in 1774, no delegate from Quebec answered the roll. As the Protestant colonies then saw it, Catholic Quebec existed "to the great danger, from so great a dissimilarity of Religion, law, and government, of the neighboring British colonies by the assistance of whose blood and treasure the said country was conquered from France."[7]

Once fighting had broken out between colonists and soldiers of the Crown, however, some in the lower thirteen began to see the advantages of enlisting the fourteenth colony to the north. Aside from alleviating the danger they felt from their northern neighbors, gaining the support of eighty thousand French, who were predisposed to British-hating anyway, could create a decided advantage in their designs against the mother country. At the very least, removing the British strongholds at Quebec and Montreal would eliminate any threat against the colonies from that region, effectively quashing British attempts to open a northern front in the newly begun conflict from which it could march an army south and cut the colonies in half.

If there was to be a fourteenth colony in the struggle against England, those in favor of it would find an obstacle in their way that would prove to be even more formidable than the high stone walls of Quebec. Governor Guy Carleton had returned to Quebec City from London in 1774 having married, become a father twice over, and seen to the passage of the act the colonists were then listing among the intolerable. Carleton's Quebec Act allowed the Québécois to worship as Catholics even though this was illegal in England itself. It also retained the French system of land tenure, and even let them speak French while serving in public offices. This was a remarkable feat for the governor, since it showed not only his understanding of his subjects and how best to placate them, but also his ability to persuade the British Parliament to go to such unusual lengths to do so. With the same stroke, Carleton had also seen his dominion of Quebec expand westward all the way to the Mississippi River.

However it was that Carleton swayed Parliament to grant him such requests, it certainly had nothing to do with his personal charm, which he seemed to lack altogether. Cold and aloof, he was, as an officer who served under him once wrote, "one of the most distant, reserved men in the world; he has a rigid strictness in his manner very unpleasing and which he observes even to his most particular friends and acquantances [sic]." Even General James Wolfe, hardly a model of good humor himself but one of the governor's closest friends, described him as "grave Carleton."[8]

Still, he was considered the very model of an eighteenth-century British officer. At fifty years of age, he was six feet tall, with a high forehead that his hairline seemed to have largely abandoned. Born in Ireland to English gentry, he joined the British Army as an ensign in 1742, during the War of the Austrian Succession. He later served as Wolfe's quartermaster general and chief engineer during the campaign that ended, along with Wolfe's life, on the Plains of Abraham, when the British seized Quebec from the French in 1759. He was wounded two years afterward, leading an assault against the French island of Belle-Île off the Brittany coast, and again the following year, assaulting Morro Castle in Havana, Cuba.

Carleton was active and energetic in his work, and King George III once wrote that his "uncorruptness is universally acknowledged."[9] Years later, a soldier under his command at Quebec would say, "There is not perhaps in the world a more experienced or more determined officer than General Carleton."[10] In 1766, with the help of his benefactor the Duke of Richmond, Carleton gained the King's appointment as lieutenant governor of Quebec and brigadier general in America. Two years later, King George elevated him to governor.

Returning from London in 1774, Carleton was well aware of the rebellion brewing in the other American colonies, and he hoped that his work with Parliament back home would pay dividends in Quebec. As a rule, prominent French inhabitants warmly received the news of the Quebec Act and its concessions to their religion and law.

In September 1774, Carleton sent two regiments to Massachusetts to help with the unrest there. This severely depleted his defensive forces at Quebec, where he found the Québécois ambivalent about the city's defense, and the French idea of employing Native Americans out of the question. Carleton winced at the brutality shown by natives toward colonists, including innocent civilians, and he "would not even suffer a Savage to pass the Frontier [into the lower colonies], though often urged to let them loose on the Rebel Provinces, lest cruelties might have been committed, and for fear the innocent might have suffered with the Guilty."[11] In addition, the boiling cauldron of insurrection in the lower colonies meant that he would get no help from London. In the summer of 1775, he wrote to a friend, "The situation of the King's affairs in [Massachusetts] leaves no room in the present moment for any consideration [other] than that . . . of augmenting the army under general Gage [in Boston]."[12]

On May 19, 1775, a month-old letter arrived from General Thomas Gage stating that hostilities had broken out in Massachusetts. The following day, a courier arrived with word "that one Benedict Arnold said to be a native of Connecticut and a Horse Jockey" had led five hundred colonists in taking British outposts at Ticonderoga and Crown Point and had even penetrated to Saint Jean, within the boundaries of Quebec Province. It was not the last Carleton would hear of this horse jockey.[13]

DOWN IN THE TROUBLED AND TROUBLESOME COLONY OF MASSACHUsetts, the shooting at Lexington and Concord had shifted the disagreements with the King from political to military in April. A growing colonial force had fought at Bunker Hill against the British in June, and though the King's soldiers could claim a narrow victory in the fight, the colonists had shown that they were something more effective than an organized mob. As a result, they held the British garrison in Boston under siege while volunteers and militia groups from as many as hundreds of miles away rushed to join the now swelling colonial ranks. Daniel Morgan marched his Virginia rifle company six hundred miles in twenty-one days, and Michael Cressap's Maryland company covered 550 miles in twenty-two days to join the rebellion. On July 3, General George Washington, carrying his appointment as commander-in-chief of the colonial forces from the Continental Congress in Philadelphia, arrived in Cambridge to take command.

Among those anxious to rally around the patriot cause was Benedict Arnold, a prominent trader and merchant from New Haven, Connecticut, who had made his fortune sailing goods from the West Indies to ports such as New York, Boston, Montreal, and Quebec. Energetic to an extreme and often impetuous, he had graying hair by 1775, giving him an air of maturity, but at thirty-four he remained a man of unusual strength and agility. He was of average height for his time, but his steel eyes, prominent nose, and a tendency to speak in a crisp and succinct manner gave those who encountered him cause to grant an instant respect. Though he had made himself one of the wealthiest men in the Colony of Connecticut, he was not of like mind with many of the "old guard" patriarchs of New Haven, who resisted the growing disagreements with the mother country. Instead, he seemed anxious not only to witness the outbreak of military action between King and colonies, but to participate in them personally, even though it meant risking his fortune.[14]

As political tensions grew, Arnold helped form, and was elected captain of, the Governor's Second Company of Guards. When he received news of the fighting at Lexington and Concord, he started for Cambridge to join the forces gathering there. Realizing that the colonials had little powder and almost no cannons, Arnold turned his attention to the British strongholds on Lake Champlain known as Fort Ticonderoga and Crown Point. He sought and received the permission and authority of the Massachusetts Committee of Safety to capture these garrisons and their military stores. Commissioned a colonel by the committee, Arnold left his own troops at Cambridge and set off for western Massachusetts with a handful of captains to recruit the necessary companies of militiamen.

Shortly thereafter, Arnold learned that some prominent Connecticut citizens had sent an emissary to the New Hampshire Grants (later Vermont) in an effort to convince Ethan Allen and his Green Mountain Boys to seize the British strongholds. Allen and his band had been in conflict with British authorities across Lake Champlain in New York for years, even to the point of prodding the Crown's representatives to place a bounty on him. Thus, the choice of using Allen's men to capture the military stores in their own region of the colonies was a logical one.

Hearing of this potential competition for the prize, Arnold raced to the eastern shore of Lake Champlain in search of Allen. When he overtook the Green Mountain Boys, Arnold claimed the authority to lead the expedition under his grant from Massachusetts; however, realizing that the men with Allen would not suddenly abandon their leader in favor of an interloper, he agreed to cooperate with Allen in leading the assault. In the dark, early hours of the next morning—May 10—the force of less than one hundred men crossed Lake Champlain, surprised the sleeping garrison, who were still unaware that fighting had broken out in Massachusetts a month prior, and seized Fort Ticonderoga. Crown Point surrendered shortly thereafter.

Though struggling to establish his legitimacy as the rightful commander of these conquered strongholds, Arnold worried that the British might launch a counterattack from Canada. Based in Montreal, British forces could move up the Richelieu River and sail down the lake to reestablish their hold over the region. Boldly seizing the initiative, Arnold made use of a schooner that the Green Mountain Boys had captured at nearby Skenesborough, and set off to invade Canada so as to raid the British outpost at Saint Jean, just twenty miles southwest of Montreal. Reports held that a seventy-ton sloop-of-war was anchored there, and by taking this vessel, Arnold could delay any British countereffort, since it was the only ship in the region large enough to carry troops across the lake. Meeting with little resistance, Arnold and his party successfully carried out the raid.

Within the span of a few weeks, Benedict Arnold had raised a company of militia, delivered it to the colonial force at Cambridge, conceived of and helped carry out the seizure of two key British forts on Lake Champlain, invaded British Canada, seized a sloop of war, and secured the Champlain region against British invasion for a season at least. With all of these credentials at hand, he paid a visit to General Washington in Cambridge in hopes of discussing his idea of invading Canada in command of a larger continental force with the goal of seizing it entirely, bringing a fourteenth colony into the war.

ON MAY 1, 1775, JONATHAN BREWER OF WALTHAM PETITIONED THE Massachusetts Provincial Congress for support in his idea to "march with a body of five hundred Volunteers to Quebeck, by way of the Rivers Kennebec and Chadier [sic]."[15] The plan never materialized, and perhaps it was just as well. Three weeks later, the Massachusetts Committee of Safety was accusing Brewer of leasing land he did not own and stealing horses from fellow officers. Then Brewer was badly wounded at Bunker Hill. The idea of seizing Canada from British forces and bringing its eighty thousand inhabitants into the American cause, however, had been on the minds of many patriots that summer.[16]

Among them was the unsung hero of Ticonderoga and Crown Point, who had already mounted his own successful mini-invasion. On June 13, 1775, Arnold drafted a letter to the Continental Congress offering both a plan and its justification. In his work at Crown Point, Arnold had communicated both with native tribes and French merchants in Canada with whom he had traded regularly. Among the natives, the intelligence was positive, indicating that they were "determined not to assist the King's Troops against us. . . ." One tribe even established a law prohibiting any of its members from assisting the British, under pain of death.[17] Among the white population, Arnold's intelligence reported that Governor Carleton had been able to raise only twenty volunteers among the British living in Quebec and was so frustrated with the ambivalence of British merchants in Montreal that he threatened to burn the city down if they did not defend it against an American attack. For their part, the Québécois—French inhabitants of Quebec—fully anticipated a colonial invasion. In fact, he explained, "Great numbers of Canadians have expected a visit from us for some time."[18] Arnold's plan involved an assault up Lake Champlain to Saint Jean, Chambly, and then Montreal that if successful would crown its achievement by marching on Quebec City itself. Doing so would not only remove the threat of a British invasion that would drive through the heart of the colonies, but would certainly get the King's attention and perhaps lead to a more serious consideration of colonial grievances.

Arnold's plan had many enticements. British ships had carried five hundred thousand bushels of wheat per year from Quebec, and an occupying American army would be able to control the lucrative fur-and-pelt trade as well. Having so easily captured Fort Ticonderoga and then commanded its ruined ramparts for a time, Arnold raised another benefit of his plan. "At least it will," he wrote, "in my humble opinion, be more advantageous, and attended with less expense, to reduce *Quebeck* and keep possession, where provisions of every kind are plenty, and a strong fortress built to our hand, than rebuilding *Ticonderoga*. . . ."[19] A successful expedition, Arnold reckoned, would require two thousand men at most and, if no one else saw fit to volunteer to command it, he had someone in mind. "If no person appears who will undertake to carry this plan into execution, (if thought advisable) I will undertake it and, with the smiles of Heaven, answer for the success of it."[20]

By early July, however, General Washington had chosen Philip Schuyler, a former British officer and wealthy New Yorker, to mount an expedition from Fort Ticonderoga up Lake Champlain to seize Montreal and Quebec. On hearing of this, Arnold relinquished his command of the Champlain forts and traveled to Watertown, Massachusetts, to settle his accounts with the Massachusetts Provincial Congress. On his way, he stopped in Albany to meet Schuyler, who had already been advocating Arnold's advancement in the nascent American military.[21]

Back in Cambridge, George Washington was accumulating all of the intelligence that he could regarding the attitudes of people living in Quebec Province. In addition to Arnold's reports from Lake Champlain, the general happily reported, "Several Indians of the Tribe of

St. Francis came in here yesterday, and confirm the former accounts of the good Dispositions of the Indian Nations, and Canadians to the Interests of America."[22] Other reports, about the natives around Montreal, were less favorable but still promising.[23]

In the first part of August, Benedict Arnold reached the patriot camp at Cambridge and reported to General Washington on the situation at Ticonderoga and Crown Point. Washington was eager to hear Arnold, particularly concerning supplies of lead and powder at the Champlain forts, since his own army around Cambridge suffered shortages of both. As they spoke, the invasion of Canada that Arnold had proposed to Congress, and which Washington had been intently organizing, became a subject of conversation; before they parted, Arnold had not only made a favorable impression on the commander, but also proposed a second arm of the expedition, through the Province of Maine, which he would lead personally.

On August 20, Washington wrote to inform General Schuyler about "a Plan of an Expedition, which has engaged my Thoughts for several Days. It is to penetrate into Canada by Way of Kennebeck River, and so to Quebeck by a Rout ninety miles below Montreal." Offering to provide as many as twelve hundred men for the expedition, Washington proposed that such a diversion would make Schuyler's job easier by distracting Governor Carleton. "He must either break up and follow this Party to Quebeck, by which he will leave you a free Passage, or he must suffer that important Place to fall into our Hands, an Event, which would have a decisive Effect. . . ."[24] Schuyler responded by saying that he "only wished that the thought had struck you sooner."[25]

The presence of a water route through Maine to Quebec had been the subject of interest since Samuel de Champlain had encountered native people along the Maine coast who told him of the passageway. At the time, Champlain's ideas were of commerce, linking vast areas of potential trade together by water. In the time since, the route by way of the Kennebec and Chaudière Rivers had been an avenue for natives from Quebec Province to slip down upon the colonist communities of Maine to attack British settlers, either of their own accord or on behalf of their French trading partners and allies. It had also provided a route through which French Jesuit missionaries working

among the native tribes could communicate with Catholic establish-
ments in Quebec Province. In 1761, just after fighting ceased in
the Seven Years' War between colonial Britain and France, a British
officer and engineer named John Montressor had made use of the
Kennebec-Chaudière trail, mapping it and creating a journal of his
travels.[26]

One of the patriots who lived along this route, a shipbuilder named
Reuben Colburn, who was a member of the Committee of Safety up
in the Province of Maine, happened to be in Cambridge in mid-
August and met with General Washington. Having lived for more than
a decade along the Kennebec, Colburn was in a position to provide
highly useful intelligence about the region and its native inhabitants,
some of whom he had introduced to Washington. Washington, who
had decided that sending an additional force through Maine to act in
concert with Schuyler was at least something to consider seriously,
gave Colburn money to saw planks "for the purposes of building bateaus
for the use of the Continental Army" and sent him to meet with Benedict Arnold.[27]

Colburn then traveled to Watertown, where he received more detailed instructions from Arnold, who now held a commission as colonel
in the Continental Army. There Arnold instructed Colburn to find out
how long it would take to build two hundred bateaux "capable of carrying six or seven men each, with their provisions and baggage (say
100wt. to each man) the boats to be furnished with four oars, two paddles, and two setting poles each." Thorough as he was, Arnold wanted
Colburn to be sure he could obtain enough nails for the building, and
discover the amount of fresh beef he could purchase on the Kennebec.
He asked that Colburn scout any British vessels in Newburyport on his
way back to Maine, and then any that might be on or near the Kennebec. He wanted to know the length and number of portages on the
route to Quebec, how deep the water was at this season, and any other
intelligence that Colburn could gather.[28]

Returning to Maine at the end of August, Colburn sought the knowledge of Samuel Goodwin of the Kennebec region, who had been "traveling, surveying, and settling this part, ever since the year 1750."[29] With
three weeks to prepare them, Goodwin supplied Arnold with a chart of
the Maine coastline, including the passages into the Kennebec River, as

well as a map and journal describing the route up the Kennebec and Dead Rivers to "Ammeguntick Pond" (Lake Megantic), including the falls and carrying places. Colburn also dispatched a scouting party of local patriots and a native guide to travel this route up the Kennebec River to its western branch, called by the natives the "Dead River" because of its slow current, and then on to the lake that made up the headwaters of the Chaudière River. Once he had made preparations back home, Colburn returned to Cambridge one last time. After he had reported the latest news to the general, Washington made the decision to go ahead with the expedition. He sent Colburn back to Maine with orders to engage a company of twenty men to build bateaux for the trek and "to assist in such service as you and they may be called upon to execute." In addition, he needed Colburn to acquire "five hundred Bushells of Indian Corn all the pork and flour you can from the inhabitants . . . sixty barrells of salted beef of 220lbs each Barrell. You are to receive Forty Shillings lawful money for each Batteaux, with the Oars, Paddles, and Setting Poles included. . . ."[30]

As plans for the invasion neared completion, General Washington was reassured of the disposition of at least some of the native tribes on the route. On August 30, he wrote to General Schuyler that a native chief named Swashan had come to Cambridge promising to aid in the invasion. "Swashan says he will bring one half of his tribe and has engaged 4 or 5 other tribes if they should be wanted. He says the Indians of Canada in general, and also the French, are greatly in our favor, and determined not to act against us." Though he had little use for the offer of large native war parties—the Continental Congress had decided against involving natives in the conflict—Washington must have welcomed the reassurance as he plotted this first military expedition in United States history.[31]

2

TO QUEBEC AND VICTORY!

September 5 dawned, a pleasant morning in the wake of a long storm. Having wallowed in the inaction of Cambridge for two months since he took command of the colonial forces, George Washington must have relished the opportunity to act against the British almost as much as he dreaded the possibilities of failure that might fall along the path to Quebec. He was acutely aware that Arnold's expedition was already weeks behind schedule and that the cold season was relentlessly approaching.

On that same day, an increasingly ill General Schuyler and his western invasion force—smaller than he had hoped, at just one thousand patriots—arrived at Saint Jean and met the enemy. Rather than a substantial force of British regulars, however, the colonials encountered a band of armed Native Americans, who killed a sergeant, a corporal, and six privates. The engagement signified that Schuyler, hoping to attract enough Canadian inhabitants to his command to seize Montreal, was well under way, but that the native inhabitants of Quebec might not be as disinterested as previous intelligence had led patriot leaders to believe. Neither of these two facts boded well for Arnold, whose mission was to work in tandem with Schuyler but who had yet even to assemble his troops.[1]

In his general orders for the morning, still unaware of Schuyler's initial engagement with enemy forces in Quebec, General Washington called for volunteers from among the soldiers in camp for a secret mission under command of Colonel Arnold. He needed 676 privates, the attendant cadre of officers, and three whole companies of riflemen. All of these volunteers, Washington cautioned, should be "active

Woodsmen, and well acquainted with batteaus; so it is recommended, that none but such will offer themselves for this service."[2]

This done, Washington drafted an "Address to the Inhabitants of Canada," which Benedict Arnold could carry to the Québécois along the route. In an eloquent, perhaps overly optimistic political statement, he explained the reasons that the lower thirteen colonies had been drawn into war with the Crown and met with surprising success. "We have taken up Arms in Defence of our Liberty, our Property; our Wives and our Children," he declared. "We are determined to preserve them or die." Announcing that he had detached Schuyler and Arnold into Canada "not to plunder but to protect you," Washington, though he did not suggest that they take up arms and join Arnold, asked that they provide the men of his expedition with all that they could: "I invite you therefore as Friends and Brethren, to provide him with such supplies as your Country affords. . . ." And, in case the cause of liberty alone did not motivate them, Washington offered money: "I pledge myself not only for your safety and security, but for ample Compensation."[3]

ON SEPTEMBER 6, WASHINGTON AND ARNOLD CHOSE THE MEN FOR the expedition, dividing them into three battalions. Two of these were made up of regular Continental troops who volunteered for the mission and carried standard muskets as weapons. The third was a collection of three companies, one from Virginia and two from the Pennsylvania frontier, all of whom carried rifles.

Arnold gave the command of his first battalion of musketmen to a forty-six-year-old former British officer from Connecticut named Roger Enos. Enos was not only an experienced soldier, but was familiar with Canada, having served there during the 1759 campaign and five years later on an expedition against Indians. His service also included campaigns in the West Indies and Havana. In 1775, he received a commission in the Continental Army as lieutenant colonel of the 22nd Regiment.

Enos's major was Return J. Meigs, a thirty-five-year-old Connecticut merchant. Though unusual in most eighteenth-century households, Major Meigs's first name was not at all out of place in his own. His father had also been named Return, and his relatives included

Church, Recompense, Mercy, the twins Silence and Submit, Thankful, Wait-still, Mindwell, and Concurrence. Prior to Lexington-Concord, Meigs had been a captain in the Connecticut militia.[4]

Henry Dearborn, a twenty-four-year-old New Hampshire physician, commanded one of the companies of musketmen in Enos's battalion. He was an ardent patriot, as evidenced by his reaction to the news of the fighting at Lexington and Concord. A few hours after word of the fighting reached his hometown, he set off marching to Cambridge with the company he had drilled that winter—even though his wife had given birth to a daughter that morning. He fought along the famous rail fence at the Battle of Bunker Hill before being detached, together with his company, to Arnold's command. On this trip he brought along one of the few dogs that traveled with the expedition, this one a large Newfoundland.[5]

The second battalion of musketmen fell under the command of Lieutenant Colonel Christopher Greene, the thirty-eight-year-old cousin of Brigadier General Nathanael Greene. A Rhode Islander, he had served in the state legislature and was appointed by that body as a major in the "Army of Observation" in 1775. Reporting to Cambridge with a company in tow, he was appointed by Washington to march with Arnold. In this endeavor he brought along his wife's brother, Captain Samuel Ward, the nineteen-year-old son of Rhode Island's governor, who had graduated from Rhode Island College (later Brown University) at age fifteen.

Second in command of the battalion was thirty-five-year-old Major Timothy Bigelow of Worcester, Massachusetts, who was a blacksmith at the outbreak of the Revolution. He had led a company of militia that marched to Cambridge at the news of Lexington-Concord and so distinguished himself through the discipline of his company in Cambridge that General Washington promoted him to major and assigned him to Arnold's expedition.[6]

Among those also in Greene's battalion was, in Arnold's words, "a young gentleman of much life and activity . . . with great spirit and resolution," whose name was Aaron Burr. Years later, he would fall a single vote short of becoming President of the United States, a prize that he instead agreed to relinquish to a Virginian named Jefferson. Still just nineteen years old in 1775, Burr was the son of the second president of the College of New Jersey (later Princeton University) and grandson of both its third president and Jonathan Edwards, whose preaching is said to have been instrumental in launching the religious movement known as the "Great Awakening." Though orphaned at two years of age, and despite a difficult childhood under his uncle's care, Burr was brilliant as a youngster, applying for admission to Princeton at age eleven. He was rejected, but tried again two years later and was admitted, then graduated with distinction at the ripe old age of sixteen. At Cambridge, Burr and his friend Mathias Ogden sought commissions from George Washington; despite their letter of recommendation from Continental Congress President John Hancock, Washington declined, so the two volunteered to join Arnold's expedition to Quebec.[7]

The third battalion was actually a combination of the three rifle companies assigned to the expedition by Washington. These men carried "Long Rifles," which were more accurate but more difficult to load than regular muskets. As a result, they were deadly at a distance where aim was critical, but less effective at close range, where rapid firing was an advantage. Thirty-nine-year-old Daniel Morgan led the Virginia rifle company, all six feet two inches and two hundred pounds of him. His substantial frame had stood him in good stead during the many brawls in which he is said to have engaged and emerged victorious. Born and raised in New Jersey, he ran away from home to Virginia when he was seventeen. As an adult, he served in the British Army during the Seven Years' War, was commissioned an ensign, served briefly in Pontiac's War, and led a company of militia after the war in Virginia, where he became a prominent citizen. At the outbreak of the Revolution, the Virginia Legislature appointed him captain of one of the two rifle companies from that state. He then set an example of patriotism and exertion when he led his company on a march of six hundred miles in just three weeks to reach Cambridge.

The other two companies of riflemen came from the Pennsylvania frontier. One marched under the command of Captain Matthew Smith, whom one of his men described as "a good looking man with the air of a soldier, (who) was illiterate, and outrageously talkative."[8] The other was led by Captain William Hendricks, "tall, of a mild and beautiful countenance. His soul was animated by a genuine spark of heroism."[9]

Having served in the brief war as complete units, and transferred to Arnold's command as such, the rifle companies had an esprit de corps that not only bound their members together but set them apart from the other soldiers in the expedition. The men of these companies had a distinct personality, based largely on an elitist confidence in their abilities, and it showed outwardly. In addition to their rifles, each man carried a tomahawk and a long "scalping knife." Uniformed in gray hunting shirts, leggings, and moccasins, they resembled Native Americans in dress: "It was the silly fashion of those times for riflemen to ape the manners of savages."[10]

In his morning orders for September 8, General Washington provided the military details for the formation of Arnold's expeditionary force.

> The Detachment going under the Command of Col Arnold, to be forthwith taken off the Roll of duty, and to march this evening to Cambridge Common; where Tents, and every thing necessary, is provided for their reception. The Rifle Company at Roxbury, and those from Prospect-hill, to march early to morrow Morning to join the above detachment. Such Officers and men, as are taken from Genl. Green's brigade, for the above detachment, are to attend the Muster of their respective Regiments to morrow morning at seven O'Clock, upon Prospect-hill, when the Muster is finished, they are forthwith to rejoin the Detachment at Cambridge.[11]

With the exception of detailed instructions he would draft the following week, Washington had done all he could to organize the eastern prong of the Canadian invasion. From this point forward, he could do little to aid in its accomplishment, for he had other issues bearing on his abilities. A commander's duties regarding the haphazard collection of patriots that was then besieging the British Army in Boston forced his constant attention to the drunkenness, desertion, spies, orders, instructions, rumors, dispatches, chronic shortages of everything, visits from dignitaries, and letters to Congress that seemed ever-present. On the day Arnold chose his men from the army around Cambridge, for example, Washington had to deal with everything from sending a ship to Bermuda, in an effort to seize British powder that was stored there, to a soldier's letter asking to be dismissed from the army to attend to his injured wife. Among the mostly idle men under his command, drinking had become rampant and resulted in "the Troops being continually debauched, which causes them to neglect their duty, and to be guilty of all those crimes which a vicious, ill habit naturally produces." In addition, with reports of ships arriving in Boston Harbor and boats running back and forth from Boston to Charlestown almost hourly, he had to keep a close eye on the enemy. Clearly, the success or failure of the expedition would have to be entirely up to Benedict Arnold.[12]

THE TOWN OF NEWBURYPORT, ON THE NORTHERN COAST OF MASSAchusetts, was then serving as a sort of homeport for patriot operations in the region, and it was from here that the expedition would board the ships that would take them up the coast to the Kennebec. When they did so, they would become not only a part of the first major military expedition in the history of the nation they were forging, but also its first naval-borne invasion force. It was hardly a navy worthy of such historical import, however. One soldier described the eleven vessels gathered for the mission as little more than "dirty coasters and fish boats," but they were seaworthy and available.

On Saturday, September 16, the army was assembled and ready but the winds were onshore, preventing a timely departure. The greatest danger to the expedition in the next few days would be the vulnerability they would endure aboard ships at sea. If any British warships were to discover the fleet, they would have little difficulty seizing or sinking the vessels, ending the grand scheme before it even reached the Kennebec. With this in mind, Arnold dispatched three small boats along the route that his fleet would take, asking them to return with any intelligence they could gather about British naval activity. Contrary winds resumed on Sunday, and bad weather added to the delay. On Monday morning, the men finally boarded the ships and set off to clear the head of the harbor. Before they could gather and start up the coast, however, a schooner in the fleet named *Swallow* ran aground on some rocks, and after waiting impatiently for the tide to free the ship, Arnold finally ordered the soldiers aboard to transfer to other ships, and the *Swallow* and its crew, with its stores of provisions, to follow the fleet whenever the tide allowed. Though the soldiers had boarded the ships at seven that morning, it was well into the afternoon before the fleet turned northeast and sailed for Maine.

A few hours into its journey, the fleet came upon two fishing schooners that could provide no intelligence as to the possibility of British vessels in the area, but their lack of knowledge at least meant there was no enemy in the area they had come from. By late afternoon, a fog closed in on the fleet, then wind and rain. The seas tossed the vessels about until the men, especially those who were not sailors in their civilian lives, suffered greatly. "During this short voyage I became very seasick," explained one soldier, "and *such* a sickness, making me feel so lifeless, so indifferent whether I lived or died! It seemed to me that had I been thrown into the sea I should hardly have made an effort to have saved myself."[13] Dr. Isaac Senter was a bit more elegant in his description of the seasickness when he wrote that the wind and swells "occasioned most of the troops to disgorge themselves of their luxuries so plentifully laid in ere we embarked."[14] Finally, at midnight, Arnold's lead ship reached the islands at the mouth of the Kennebec, and he decided they should anchor to ride out the weather. When daylight illuminated the still-stormy seas the following morning, it revealed that only eight of the original eleven ships had arrived safely.[15]

For most of the soldiers in the expedition, it was their first look at the great river Kennebec, a waterway that had served as an essential artery for food, trade, and transport for Native Americans for thousands of years. In more recent times, it had become an important passageway for European explorers and settlers as well. Just in the leeside of the sharp peninsula that juts out to protect the headwaters from the Atlantic lay the ruins of an English colony established in 1607. Funded by Sir John Popham, this sister colony to Jamestown seemed a marvelous idea when folks back in the British Isles looked at their maps, noticed that Maine's latitude was equal to that of the south of France, and reckoned that its weather must be as well. After becoming the first tourists to discover the harshness of a Maine winter, the surviving colonists were so eager for home that they set to work constructing the first ship ever built in North America—and sailed it back to England.[16]

In 1604, Samuel de Champlain sailed through these waters, but even his exploring crew may not have been the first white men to see the Kennebec. Not far over the ridge that shadowed the failed Popham Colony lies the aptly named Spirit Pond, where, in 1972, a man with an inflatable boat and a keen eye discovered rocks carved with what appeared to be Norse runic writing. Those who have tried to translate these figures say that the stones were left by Vikings as early as 1010 A.D. An archaeology team dispatched in search of further evidence found two sod houses with charcoal that dates as far back as 1335 A.D. Still other scientists dismiss the notion of early Viking landings altogether.[17]

Arnold's men were not even the first army ever to navigate these waters, though they were as much as ten times the size of any that had preceded them. For nearly a century ending just twelve years earlier, British settlers endured a near-constant state of war with the French and their native allies to the north and east. To protect the King's settlements along the river from the savage raids launched against the tenuous English hold on the region, the colonial government of Massachusetts had seen to the construction of several forts, small and large, reaching sixty winding miles upriver. Seldom housing more than a few dozen soldiers at best, these garrisons served as defensive structures during attacks and as trading centers around whose protective influence communities grew. On occasion, when the settlers had borne enough of the fear and carnage, they banded together with the soldiers to launch their own strikes against native outposts and villages well up the Kennebec.

None of this historical precedent likely entered the mind of Benedict Arnold when he ordered his ships, still hampered by the storm, up the river. A few miles along, near a place known as Parker Flats, Arnold spied a group of armed men along the shore—a coastal watch keeping out an eye for tyrannical British ships. He hailed them and inquired about a pilot to guide the ships through the sometimes narrow channel of the river, and, seeking a respite from the wobbly voyage, Arnold and others went ashore for "refreshments."

The area where they landed was known locally as Georgetown, after one of the islands that divided the Kennebec from the Sheepscot

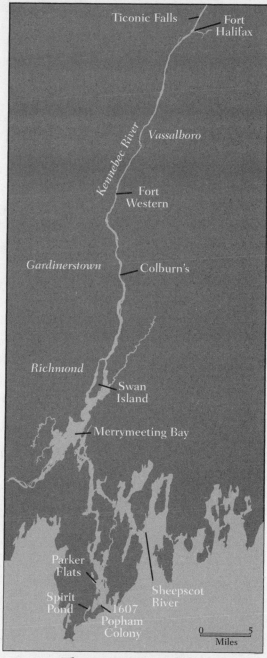

The Lower Kennebec

River. Another of these islands, known as Arrowsic (pronounced to rhyme with "cow sick"), was quite well populated and included "a handsome meeting-house, and very good dwelling houses."[18] One of the residents of the island was there to meet the expedition with a group of local volunteers, the first that the expedition would take on while en route. In April 1775, in response to the alarm of Lexington-Concord, Samuel McCobb, who was both the town clerk in George-town and a delegate to the Massachusetts Provincial Congress, raised a company of local men and marched to Cambridge in just six days. In June, his company was attached to Colonel John Nixon's regiment, and McCobb commanded these men behind the famous rail fence at Bunker Hill. When Washington detached men to accompany Arnold through Maine, McCobb volunteered, but his company was twenty men short of its necessary strength of sixty-four. Apparently as ener-getic as he was patriotic, McCobb sped home to Arrowsic, persuaded more of his neighbors around Georgetown to volunteer, and was wait-ing with them on the Kennebec, ready to join Greene's second battal-ion of musketmen, when Arnold arrived.[19]

Back in their boats, Arnold and his men must have been relieved when two of the lost ships came sailing out of an arm of the Sheepscot River and rejoined the flotilla. A few miles onward, the expedition nav-igated a narrow passage known locally as The Chops, and reached the site where six rivers collide to form the largest freshwater bay on the Eastern Seaboard. Merrymeeting Bay is a nine-thousand-acre body of water bounded by marshy flats that teem with fowl and game. Looking at this fertile land, the men of the expedition must have thought that the barrelfuls of provisions they had stowed aboard their ships would be entirely unnecessary. Surely this river region would provide nour-ishment aplenty.[20]

At the northern end of the bay, the river forks to stretch around ei-ther side of a four-mile-long island. Swan Island, as it is known, housed a small settlement across the river from one of the protective forts and its accompanying town, this one known as Richmond. There is navigable water on both sides of the island, but only an experienced pilot, sensing the influence of the tides and currents, can coax a siz-able sailing vessel past. Apparently, the ship carrying Henry Dear-born's company lacked such a pilot, for it ran aground in the shallow flats. It was late by then anyway, and soon after the anchor dropped, Dearborn went ashore with some other officers to spend the night on *terra firma*. In the morning, the ship was again under way, passed the courthouse and jail at Pownalborough, just above Fort Richmond, and sailed the final few miles to an area of Gardinerstown known as Colburntown, after the family of Reuben Colburn. Here they found their bateaux lying on the shore awaiting service and noticed "a Liberty Pole Erected, 2 Saw mills, and a Number of very good Dwelling houses on the right of the river."[21]

The size and shape of the bateau (the French word for "boat") varied in the colonies, but each was higher and pointy at the ends with a flat bottom for navigating shallow water. In Maine, these were generally smaller than in more southern colonies, standing just three feet tall at the bow and stretching twenty-two feet from prow to stern. While they were rugged and durable, they weighed hundreds of pounds each, which made them a poor choice of vessel for an expedition that would be carrying them often. On land, as few as four men could transport them on their shoulders, but not without great exertion.

By now, even the *Swallow* had freed itself from the rocks at Newburyport and overtaken the fleet. Either the crew had learned from their experience, or the removal of the ship's cargo of soldiers had lightened it so that its keel rode higher, because it sailed safely past Swan Island and the two other ships still stuck aground there including Dearborn's. When the *Swallow* reached Colburn's shipyard and offloaded its cargo of provisions, Arnold sent it back to help bring the other two upriver. When these three finally anchored at Colburn's, all of the ships that had left Newburyport had safely reached their destination at the highest navigable point on the river.[22]

THOUSANDS OF ISSUES MUST HAVE WEIGHED HEAVILY UPON ARNOLD'S mind as he set to work getting the men off the ships and into the two hundred bateaux that Colburn had managed to assemble in just two weeks. Arnold described the bateaux as "smaller than the directions given and very badly built." Though he did not mention it specifically, Arnold must have been keenly aware that, given the short notice and lack of available seasoned lumber, Colburn's men had constructed the bateaux out of green wood, which meant that they were much heavier—

an important factor, given the many portages over which his men must carry them—and would likely be less reliable in the water. Another problem that plagued the near-impossible task that had faced Colburn's craftsmen was the shortage of nails for such a large number of boats. Even if they had the raw materials and enough blacksmiths on hand to forge the nails in the one-by-one fashion of the day, creating enough for a huge fleet of bateaux in just a fortnight would have been a monumental feat. Instead, the builders simply shirked on nails, using fewer on each boat than would have been advisable under normal circumstances. Further, to make up for the smallness of their size, Arnold asked Colburn to build twenty more bateaux in time for his departure in two days. With remarkable patriotic fervor, Colburn not only saw to the construction of the twenty extra bateaux, but he also assembled a company of two dozen craftsmen to accompany the expedition at least as far as the Dead River, to help repair the boats and carry the provisions over the portages.[23]

Another important issue causing fret in Arnold's planning was that of intelligence. Colburn helped ease this somewhat when he gave Arnold a written report from the local scouts he had sent upriver in the weeks prior, to explore the route as far as Chaudière Pond. The scouts encountered no great obstacles in the way of the expedition except a Native American named Natanis who lived in a cabin up on the Dead River. What they had learned upon reaching his cabin was that the wily Carleton was already one step ahead of Arnold's plan. "We got intelligence of an Indian that he was stationed there by Govr. Charlton [sic] as a Spy to watch the motions of an Army, or Spies, that was daily expected from New England: that there was spies on the Head of the Chaudière River, & down the River some distance there was Stationed a Regular Officer and six Privates."[24]

The report also stated that Natanis had threatened to alert the British if the scouts traveled farther up the Dead River. Undaunted, they had continued another thirty miles before turning back. While they were absent from the camp, one of their native guides who had remained behind encountered a native woman who gave them more information about the inhabitants of the region. According to the woman, all of the young natives in the area had gone west to trade, under a commission from Governor Carleton. At Sartigan, however—a region consisting of the southernmost settlements on the Chaudière—a great number of Mohawk Indians had gathered, and Natanis fully expected the arrival of three canoes full of warriors at any moment. Despite the potential for conflict with Indians, British outposts, or both, Arnold must have taken some solace in the fact that this group of scouts had traveled both quickly and safely to the Chaudière River and back, over the route his men were about to traverse.[25]

As September drew near a close, Arnold knew he was about to move his army up the Kennebec weeks later than he had hoped, and well past the date when the weather would allow for an easy, comfortable expedition. For three days, he concentrated on getting his men and their provisions off the ships, into the bateaux, and up the river a few miles, to what was once Fort Western, the largest and most important trading and military outpost in the region for two decades, and site of a key British trading post known as Cushnoc dating back to the 1620s. He would use the old fort as his jumping-off point, sending his men off in four divisions, each a day apart.

A few hundred miles to the west, General Schuyler's Lake Champlain expedition against Montreal had been under way for a month, and an advance group under Ethan Allen had already made a poorly planned and unsuccessful attack on the city. Arnold's expedition was far behind schedule and had yet to face its first obstacle or realize that the route was twice as long as they had conceived—or planned.

3

SCOUTING PARTY

With the eastern side of the Kennebec bustling with activity from Fort Western to Colburntown, Colonel Arnold set about, in his usual manic way, putting his plans for the journey ahead into action. The first of these would involve sending a small party of men forward, up-river, to mark the Indian trails and carrying places that the remainder of the army would need to use on its march. At the same time, this group could scout the countryside for signs of natives—hostile or friendly—British spies, or anything else that would be of interest. To lead the party, Arnold chose thirty-five-year-old Archibald Steele, a lieutenant in Smith's company of riflemen. Steele then singled out five members of his own company—Robert Cunningham, Thomas Boyd, John Tidd, John McKonkey, and sixteen-year-old John Henry—to accompany him, along with Jesse Wheeler, George Merchant, and James Clifton from Morgan's rifle company. Two men who lived just upstream in Vassalboro, John Getchell and a gray-haired Irishman named Jeremiah Horne, would serve as guides.

John Getchell was a veteran of the colonial militia and member of a quintessential family of Maine settlers. The Getchells had moved to the wilds of the Province of Maine from Massachusetts and settled the town of Vassalboro, just upriver from Fort Western. As a group, they were talented explorers, woodsmen, and guides, and were well acquainted with Native Americans in the region. Earlier in the year, the selectmen of Falmouth (now Portland) had sent John along with Remington Hobby, a leading Quaker in Vassalboro and its delegate to the Provincial Congress, to visit with the natives and gain intelligence about a rumored army of Indians from Canada that they believed might be descending on the settlements. John's brother Dennis Getchell, a veteran of the colonial British Army, served as first selectman of Vassalboro and was one of the guides whom Reuben Colburn had sent up the Kennebec a few weeks prior. A third brother, Nehemiah, was also with the army and would serve as a guide for the main body.[1]

These eleven men left Fort Western on September 24 in two light birchbark canoes, each loaded down with a barrel of pork, a bag of meal, and "two hundred weight" of biscuit or flour. In his journal for that day, Arnold explained that Steele's mission was "to reconnoiter, and get all of the intelligence he possibly can from the Indians who, I am informed, are hunting there."[2] The first division of the army, consisting of the three rifle companies, would follow the next day.

Arnold's choice of Smith's company as the pool from which most of his scouts were drawn was significant, given the background of both Smith and many of the men under his command. Captain Matthew Smith was a native of Lancaster County, Pennsylvania, and had been one of the ringleaders of the so-called Paxton Boys—or Paxtang Boys, after the township many of them inhabited—a mixture of rough Scots-Irish frontiersmen with a violent history toward Native Americans.

The end of the colonial struggles between Britain and France known as the French and Indian Wars twelve years earlier had left in the Ohio Valley Native Americans who had previously been allied with the French and were now chafing at the idea that the victors in this conflict expected them to accept British rule. This uneasiness resulted in the conflict known as Pontiac's War, after the Ottawa chief who led the natives, and it included numerous attacks on colonial settlers on the Pennsylvania frontier.

The Paxton Boys were an organized mob that had formed in anger over what they perceived as neglect from a colonial government that had failed to protect their frontier region adequately from these attacks. Stirred by their passions, the boys raided the nearest native village, which just happened to be a peaceful and unthreatening community of Conestoga Indians of the Iroquois Nation. They killed six natives in the attack and then marched on the Lancaster jail, where they killed fourteen more who had fled there for protection. Governor John Penn issued warrants for the arrest of the Paxtons but was unable to bring them to justice, thanks to the sympathetic leanings of other frontier families in the region.

The Boys next turned their attention to a group of peaceful Moravian Indians living in Bethlehem, but word reached the village soon enough that the natives were able to flee to Philadelphia, which was then the capital, and to the protection of the British garrison there. Outraged that the colonial government, made up largely of pacifist Quakers, would expend resources to protect Indians but not frontier colonists, the Paxtons began to march toward Philadelphia. By now the gang had grown to include several hundred angry frontier folk, and the unlikely vision of pacifists arming themselves to defend Philadelphia became a reality. Before the mob could reach the capital, however, a delegation that included Benjamin Franklin met its leaders and negotiated an end to the crisis.[3]

Although it is not clear how many men of Smith's company were either members of or sympathetic to the Paxton Boys back in Pennsylvania, their hostility toward Native Americans likely pervaded the ranks. Ironically, the natives that the scouting party was most likely to encounter on the upper reaches of the Kennebec, and would need to gain useful intelligence and cooperation from, were members of the Norridgewock tribe that had suffered a fate similar to that of the natives of Paxton country. A half-century earlier, British settlers and soldiers from Richmond, Maine, paddled up the Kennebec and attacked the Norridgewock village near the main forks of the river, virtually destroying the tribe. This had been such an unusually brutal attack that it made even Massachusetts authorities uneasy.

The Norridgewock brutality had taken place under British rule and thus kindled a hatred of the Crown among Native Americans in the Upper Kennebec region. Since the natives and colonials now shared a mutual enemy, Arnold may have assumed that whatever natives the scouts encountered would be cooperative. Nevertheless, given the army's need for useful intelligence, it does not seem it was the best of ideas for him to have sent forward a small party of men who must have held deep apprehensions, if not outright hatred of native people. Further complicating this problem was the fact that Arnold ordered Steele and his men to kill Natanis, one of the last surviving Norridgewock Indians, at whose cabin Reuben Colburn's scouting party had rested a few weeks before. This order resulted from Natanis's boast to those scouts that he was a paid spy for the British.[4]

ON THE THIRD and fourth days the party paddled upstream, the gradual shift from inhabited countryside to ominous wilderness became more noticeable, so that by the time they approached the scene of the Norridgewock village and massacre their apprehension was already heightened. Along the water's edge, they noticed an unusual bluish rock that was "scalloped out" down to its waterline. According to one of the guides in the party, it was a place where Native Americans obtained their points for arrows and spears.[5]

In the afternoon, the party crossed to the west side of the falls, searched out the carrying place around them, and marked the path for the army. Near the falls was a large natural meadow, and as one of the party hunted near it for deer, he met two white men mowing the wild grass. Finding them friendly, the party traded some of their salted pork for two fresh beaver tails for stewing.

Above the falls the party took to the water again, and, leaving the last of the white settlements behind, they delved into a foreign wilderness inhabited primarily by Abenaki Indians. The only orders they had regarding the natives concerned Natanis, whom they were to shoot on sight. Colonel Arnold had come to believe that Natanis would warn the garrison at Quebec of the approach of any colonial force passing through these trails. To avoid discovery by the British or an attack by native warriors, the men of the scouting party were obliged not to fire their guns or make any substantial fires at night. These rules only increased their apprehensions. John Henry, the teenager in the party, remembered, "We frequently saw ducks, &c. and many moose deer, yet we discharged not a gun; in truth we had been made to believe that this country had numerous Indians in it."[6]

Several days into their journey, the scouting party reached the point on the river where carrying their canoes overland was easier and faster than paddling the river course. Upstream several miles ahead of them by water, the river forked to east and west. The western or left leg, which would take them on their chosen path, bent southward again at the forks, so that it wound to within twelve miles by land of where they now stopped. Rather than continue against the current, encountering many rapids, falls, and portages, the natives had created a trail over land that measured twelve miles to the nearest point of the western branch of the Kennebec, the Dead River. To this twelve-mile trail, crossing several ponds and a wide bog, the natives gave the appropriate name the Great Carrying Place.

Having reached the outer limit of the area that their guides had previously traveled, the party would now have to wander into territory completely unknown to them except by a few sparse words of direction from Colonel Arnold, given as they departed Fort Western. They soon found the trail westward and made it more easily recognizable by slashing trees with their tomahawks and leaving other distinctive signs for those who would follow. Near nightfall, they reached the shore of the first pond, which they guessed to be about a half-mile wide, and camped for the night. To their delight, they discovered both that the pond was full of trout and that James Clifton of the party had a knack for catching them.

The next morning, with full stomachs, the party made plans for their foray westward and decided that it would be wise to leave two men behind at this place, along with half of their provisions, so that when the remainder of the group returned this way, presumably in eight or ten days, they would have food and supplies to sustain them. Though he resisted greatly, James Clifton was chosen as half of the stay-behind party, since he was the oldest and some of the younger men had sensed that he was tiring. As his comrade, the group had little difficulty choosing John McKonkey, whom the others had found obnoxious and unreliable. True to his reputation, McKonkey was delighted to forgo the dangerous journey that lay ahead.

Having chosen the men who would continue, Lieutenant Steele divided up the provisions in the manner of "Whose shall be this?" In this process, one member of the party would turn his back while the lieutenant placed his hand on one of the portions. At this the lieutenant would ask, "Whose shall be this?" and the man with his back turned would reply with the name of one of the party, to whom that portion would be given. This would continue until the portions were divided; the men considered it the fairest means of division.

The following morning, the main force of the party headed off to the west and the Dead River. Skirting the pond to the south, they hauled their boats and provisions over land to a second pond, about a mile past the first. Here they loaded the canoes, pushed from the shore, and paddled its half-mile width. In all, this journey of only two miles, partly by water and partly over land, had taken the entire day—much of it spent carrying their boats and provisions while marking the trail for the army that followed. The primary reason for their slow slog, however, was not the horizontal distance but, rather, the vertical. The western shore of the Kennebec, where the men left the river at what is now called Carrying Place Stream, is roughly 450 feet above sea level. The place where they now halted was more than eight hundred feet higher.

When they set up camp at the far side of the second pond, more conscious than ever of their isolation in a hostile wilderness, they had no way of knowing that they rested within a half-mile of what would, more than a century after them, become known as the Appalachian Trail. Nor could they have understood that the expedition of which they now formed the lead body would become so well known in history that the ponds they were crossing would eventually bear the names of East Carry, Middle Carry, and West Carry Ponds in the Great Carrying Place Township of Maine.

Two miles of carrying—the first of it more than two hundred feet upward and the last of it more than 150 back down—another mile of paddling across the third pond, and yet another three on foot, first up two hundred feet and then down that and more, and the little band finally reached what appeared to one of them "a beautiful plat of firm ground, level as a bowling green, and covered by an elegant green moss."[7] Burdened by their loads, they headed off across this fine stretch of land, relieved to be walking in a level direction for a change. No sooner had they reached the edge of the bowling green, however, than they encountered an entirely different source of fatigue. Rather than firm ground, the party had reached a thick, deep bog. "Every step we made," remembered John Henry, "sunk us knee-deep in a bed of wet turf. My feet were pained and lacerated by the snags of the dead pines, a foot and more below the surface of the moss. . . ."[8] With great difficulty, they crossed the mile-wide bog to reach the shores of the Dead River.

After a night's rest, some of the group, following the advice of their guide Getchell, sought out small pouches bulging beneath the bark of

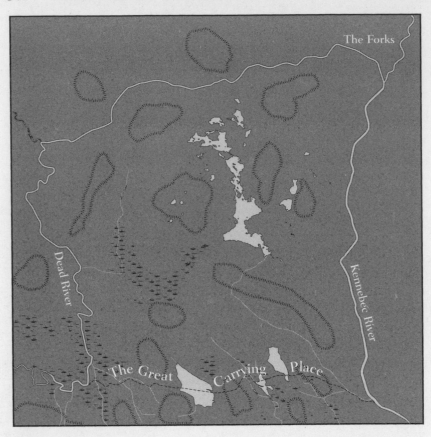

The Great Carrying Place is a twelve-mile overland trail that allows travelers to move between the Kennebec and Dead Rivers while avoiding the falls and rapids they would encounter by water.

balsam-fir trees that grow plentifully in Maine. By laying a broad knife across the bottom of one of these bark bubbles, they slit the bottom so as to let the sap drain across the blade to where their mouths awaited. The result, said John Henry, "was heating and cordial to the stomach, attended by an agreeable pungency." More than its momentary pleasure, the sap-sucking seemed to have a lasting benefit as well. "This practice, which we adopted, in all likelihood contributed to the preservation of health—for though much wet weather ensued, and we lay often on low and damp ground, and had very many successions of cold atmosphere, it does not now occur to me that any of us were assailed by sickness during this arduous excursion."⁹

Getchell probably learned of the medicinal powers of balsam-fir resin from area natives who used the resin externally as an important ingredient of healing salves for treating cuts, wounds, and burns. The Malecite Indians of New Brunswick, Canada, used the resin effectively as an application for treatment of frozen limbs. Various folk-medicine traditions hold that the sap can be used as an antiseptic healing agent applied externally to wounds, sores, and bites, and as an inhalant to treat headaches; a tea made from the leaves is a remedy for scurvy. Taken internally, the sap is said to treat coughs, colds, fevers, and sore throats. It has also been used against afflictions of the urinary tract, ulcerations of the bowels, and as a treatment for gonorrhea, diarrhea, bronchitis, cancers, corns, warts, dysentery, and rheumatism.

THIS LAST DAY of September, the party resolved not only to ration their pork and biscuit but also to reserve the beginning and end of the day for eating. In this way, they reckoned they could speed the accomplishment of their mission. Their evening meal, then, consisted of half a biscuit and a half-inch-square piece of raw pork. Despite their fatigue, and the drift of snow that had turned the hills around them a winter white, they set off up the Dead River, happy to be using their arms again and resting their legs as they pushed upriver as many as thirty miles, and in surprisingly good spirits. Having covered such a considerable distance made their decision to rest for the night all the easier when they reached the foot of a set of rapids that gave them reason to begin questioning the name "Dead River."

In the morning, two men set off in each canoe while the remainder of the group walked the shoreline marking the carrying path around the rapids. Though the men on the water soon learned that the rapids were about three times longer than they appeared from the bottom, they cleared them within the span of an hour. For the next few days, this rhythmic schedule continued as the party made fairly good time between the rapids and falls, then divided over the portages, rested, and put back into the river to paddle, once again, upstream. With each day, however, the fatiguing work drained their bodies of energy that their small diets could not replenish.

During one evening's respite, Sergeant Boyd noticed that the water was colder and that there was low ground across the river. Sensing some meaning in this, he stole across, disappeared for an hour, and returned with a dozen trout. These creatures fascinated John Henry, who thought them of "extraordinary appearance, long broad, and thick. The skin was of a very dark hue, beautifully sprinkled with deep crimson spots." Though Henry had never seen them before, these may have been lake trout, sometimes called "togue," which in Maine can grow to lengths of nearly three feet and weigh ten pounds. These fish continue to attract anglers to this region from around the world more than two centuries later. Henry contrasted them with those they had caught previously. "The river trout were of a pale ground, with pink spots, and not so flat or broad." In all likelihood, these were the smaller brook trout, the only other native trout species still swimming in Maine waters. Though the trout supplemented the men's diet, neither type of fish, by itself, was providing the nutrition necessary to fuel their wearying bodies, as they provided protein but not the carbohydrates needed to keep up their exertions.

As the party was making camp the following night, one of their guides informed them that the next day's journey would bring them to the cabin of the Indian named Natanis. When the scouts were about three miles below, the party pulled the canoes out of the water, leaving two men to guard them while the rest headed on foot to the cabin. As they came to a clearing in the woods, the men saw the cabin placed twenty yards back from the river's edge on a bank about twenty feet above the water.

When the first settlers reached Maine in the early seventeenth century, one of their first chores was to clear what they called a "bowshot" around the site where one planned to build a home. This essentially meant clearing the trees and brush away in a radius that equaled the distance that an Indian's arrow could fly. In this way, the occupants of the house were safe from anyone in the woods who might fire an arrow without first stepping into the clearing and exposing himself. Natanis's bowshot reflected the advance in technology brought about by European settlement, in that his clearing reached farther out, to cover the distance of a musket shot.

From two hundred yards away, the men saw smoke coming from the chimney, and, with their apprehension rising, they spread out to cover any escape route Natanis might take from his cabin. Rifles loaded and ready, they bolted from the woods, crossed the clearing, and descended upon the cabin. To their surprise and relief, they found it empty and no fire burning—the smoke had been a figment of their imagination and fear. The coals within, however, had been burning within the previous week, and there were items inside that the group presumed no Indian would permanently discard; their fear of encountering savages before they completed their trek was only compounded.

Back in their canoes and farther upstream, they encountered more signs of recent native activity. Reaching a fork in the river and uncertain which direction to take—they had no map or chart to follow—one of the party noticed a stake driven into the ground on the shore. It caught his eye partly because of a piece of birch bark folded neatly into a fork in the stake in such a way that it must have been left intentionally by human hands. When they retrieved the bark and opened it, they discovered that this was a map showing the river in both directions from the fork, including marks that seemed to indicate Indian camps in the area. This left no doubt that they were in the midst of the Indians' territory. "There were some lines," John Henry recalled, "in a direction from the head of one branch to that of another, which we took to be the course of the paths that the Indians intended to take that season."[10] Assuming this was the work of Natanis, or his brother Sabatis, they nonetheless used its accurate depiction in choosing the eastern fork, which kept them on the Dead River. Since the river along that branch was shallower and held many rapids, it is likely that the group would have abandoned this course and wasted time and precious energy trying the western fork, if not for the birchbark guidance.

In time they reached the first pond that makes up the headwaters of the Dead River, and with it a welcome treat. On a tiny island they discovered "a delicious species of cranberry, entirely new to us."[11] The taste of the berries must have been a rich reward for men who had been subsisting on pork, flour, and fish for more than a week, but, more important, it gave their bodies the first sugar they had consumed in many days of fierce and continuous exertion. Soon after the first pond came a second, and then a third, with the land on each side becoming more and more mountainous and the streams between ponds less and less navigable, even in light birchbark canoes. At the end of this chain of ponds was the height of land that separates the waters of Maine from those of Canada.

"My wardrobe," recalled John Henry years afterward, "was scanty and light. It consisted of a roundabout jacket, of woollen, a pair of half-worn buckskin breeches, two pairs of woollen stockings, (bought at Newburyport,) a hat with a feather, a hunting-shirt, leggins, a pair of mockasins, and a pair of tolerably good shoes, which had been closely hoarded."[12] The weather was getting colder, and Henry noticed that he paddled with more energy in order to stay warm from the exertion.

Another day of traveling brought them to the last pond in the chain, one that today bears the name Arnold Pond, in memory of the expedition. What they could see from this lake may have given members of the party reason to forget about the cold and hunger for a time, for it was from here they got their first glimpse of the mountain range that Native Americans simply called the Height of Land. "It made an impression upon us," Henry later testified, "that was really more chilling than the air which surrounded us."[13]

Actually an extension of the Appalachian Mountains, this ominous bank of hills divides the water that pours into Quebec's Saint Lawrence River from that which fills Maine's two great rivers, the Kennebec and the Penobscot. It took a mile of hiking upward to reach its summit— eight hundred feet higher than its base—then three more miles across its plateaued crest before the last mile back down. More desolate than any other portion of their trek, it was without game, fish, berries, or any other sustenance. Finding a poorly marked trail left by natives who occasionally found the courage to pass over it, the party, now more intent than ever on hurrying their task, hauled their canoes ashore, buried them under brush and leaves, and headed up into the mountains, knowing that the completion of their duties lay just beyond—the banks of the Chaudière River.

Summoning the strength to make quick work of the journey, they reached what they believed to be the river's edge on the far side of the Height of Land, though they were actually still a great distance short of their intended goal. Much relieved, they could now return to the army, with its safety and its food. Before turning to reverse their course over the Height, however, Lieutenant Steele decided they should take one extra measure and get a view as far northward, up the river, as they could. Finding a tall pine tree, Steele asked who was the best climber in the group. At this, Robert Cunningham stepped forward, and though the tree had no branches on the first forty feet of its trunk, he was up and in its canopy in no time. Getting a clear view of the river's course, Cunningham signaled down to the men that he could see smoke in the distance, a sign that a native hunting party was uncomfortably close.

As soon as the climber got back on the ground, the party headed back along the trail over the Height of Land. It was nearly dusk by then, but the sky seemed clear as they progressed single-file in a hurried fashion, each being as careful as speed would allow to walk in the tracks of the man in front, so as not to leave any clear evidence of the size of their party. Being second-to-last in the van, John Henry noticed that John Getchell, behind him, was using his feet to brush away their tracks as best he could.

Heightening the sense of fear and mystery the Height of Land presented, the clear skies that the men of the party had looked up to as they began their return journey now filled with clouds and the feeling of impending rain. This awful place seemed to summon the rain, which soon fell in "tremendous torrents" while snuffing any light that may have shone from the night sky. Hustling along in the dark and barely able to sense the presence of the man before him, John Henry caught his foot on something on the ground as they descended the ridge, fell headfirst some twenty or thirty feet, and lay stunned by the fall. So stifling was the rain and darkness that Getchell, close at his heels, did not notice the absence of his friend a few feet in front of him. Henry eventually recovered his wits and somehow managed to find the trail and continue on, arriving an hour later than the rest of the group. When they reached the stashed canoes, the party erected a shelter of branches and bows that did little to hold back the rain. Soaked, cold, and exhausted, they tried to sleep.

When morning came, it was evident that the rain had raised the water level of the pond four feet overnight, and it was still raining. The only advantages were that all of the energy of this water was now pushing them in their intended direction, down the Dead River, and that they could easily paddle over areas where shallowness had forced them to carry their canoes and supplies on the trip up. Down to only two of their biscuit–and–half-inch-of-pork rations, they ate one for breakfast and started back down the chain of ponds. When they reached the fourth pond in the chain, several of the men simultaneously spotted a wayward duck within shooting distance. A number of them fired their rifles, but it was later agreed that Jesse Wheeler's ball had hit the mark, and to shouts of approval the duck was scooped up into one of the canoes to await the dinner hour.

After a long day's paddle, the little band pulled ashore for the night having traveled as many as forty miles down the swollen river. Here Boyd and Cunningham managed to light a fire against a fallen tree, and the group huddled around for warmth and to plan their dinner menu. Each man had only the last half-inch of pork for his rations, but the duck would have to be divided as well. After a discussion, they decided that the best way to extend the benefits of their otherwise meager provisions was to boil both the duck and the pork into a broth, which would serve for dinner; the duck meat would have to do for breakfast. Each man skewered his pork on a stick marked distinctly as his own, and the strange stew was cooked. In the morning, the duck was divided according to the usual "Whose shall be this?" method. John Henry took special note that, despite their fatigue and hunger, no one raised any argument over the division, not even Cunningham, whose paltry share turned out to be the feet and head. "My appetite," recalled Henry, "was ravenous as that of a wolf, but honor bound the stomach tight."[14]

Through the rest of that day and all of the next, they worked their way downriver with empty stomachs and growing fatigue. Buoyed only by the belief that in a day or so they would again come upon the rest of the army, they paddled in mundane silence. Hope and relief flashed in the minds of the men on the following morning, when they saw a plume of smoke in the distance—large enough, they reckoned, that only the encampment of an army could be its source. Pressing ahead with added vigor, the men dug hard with their paddles in hope of speeding their relief. But before they could cover much distance, the men in the larger canoe felt a shudder and heard a horrible, terrifying sound. A branch of a tree nearly buried under the risen water had thrust its point through the bark walls of the canoe, tearing a gash its entire length and opening a hole through which poured icy river water.

There are times when the lives of men in treacherous circumstances are saved by instinctive reaction, and surviving the canoe's damage took the reflexes of every man in it. If the boat had turned over and any of them had been lucky enough to avoid drowning or hypothermia in the icy water, they most certainly would have perished along the river's edge within a short time, being without transportation. What saved each of them from a watery grave was the impulse to lean to one side just enough to raise the gash in the canoe above the waterline while balancing so it did not flip entirely in the other direction. Performing this precarious balancing act, and paddling gently to preserve it, they called to the two men in the first canoe, who pulled ashore. Several hundred yards downriver from where the tree had torn the bark from their vessel, the teetering canoe also made it safely to the shoreline.

As much as the scouts might have felt justified in breathing a great sigh of relief at safely reaching dry land, the sight that now presented itself made that difficult. The smoke whose source they had now reached was not the army after all, but what must have seemed a miraculous forest fire. A few days earlier, the party had camped on this site and built a fire that had little more than smoked at the time. Despite the torrential rain and wetness of the season, the remnants of their campfire had burrowed under the ground and found purchase among roots and moss before raging to cover half an acre.

Exhausted from their near-death experience and without a morsel of food, the men looked on their ravaged canoe with great dismay.

Gone were the pitch and bark they might have used for repairs, for these had seen duty patching previous holes, and the men began to question whether the army was even within miles of them. They also began to wonder if Arnold and his troops had turned back and were just then sitting, warm and fed, before a campfire in Massachusetts. Through the bleakness came the calm voice of John Getchell, who gave instructions to collect birch bark, cedar roots, and pitch from the plentiful pine trees. Having consumed all their pork, the men realized that they had no fat with which to convert the pitch to its proper consistency, until it occurred to one of the party that the bag that had held the pork still lay in the bottom of the canoe. Scraping against the sides of the discarded sack, they managed to gather half a pint of lard. Thanks to the woods-wise Getchell and the warmth of the fire, the canoe was ready to bear service again within two hours.

Once they had eased it back into the water, the crew held close to shore in anticipation of a failure somewhere along the new repair work. About five hundred yards along, just as the men began to feel the seal might hold, the canoe raked over the top of another branch hiding just below the water. This time the branch punctured the bottom of the canoe, and the disheartened lot put back to shore and set to the repair work again.

It was a smaller hole and a shorter job, thanks in part to their swiftly growing experience at field repairs, and within an hour the canoe was once more ready for the water. As the group prepared to resume their challenge of the river, Sergeant Boyd grabbed the bow of the smaller canoe and began to set it gently down the bank into the water. But his footing failed on the steep bank, and the canoe fell hard, its bow and stern wedging between the top and the bottom of the bank. Except for the wooden gunwale that ran around the very top of the canoe's sides, the entire vessel had broken in two.

At this third calamity, the despair in the minds of the men found new depths, stirring thoughts that something greater than coincidence or bad luck was at work. "A thought came across my mind," recalled John Henry, "that the Almighty had destined us to die of hunger in this inhospitable wilderness. The recollection of my parents, my brothers and sister, and the clandestine and cruel manner of my deserting them, drew from me some hidden, yet burning tears, and much mental contrition."[15]

Faced with yet another challenge, John Getchell met it with the calm determination with which he had guided the group through all others that had come before. He dragged the canoe to the fire, sewed the two halves together with cedar root, and buried the new seam in a mound of pitch. On top of this he placed more bark, sewing it in place before adding more pitch. For good measure this time, he added the pork bag as an extra layer of material. The repair sessions had taken most of the day, but, thinking with their stomachs, the group decided to take again to the water and push on through darkness, hoping to reach the army at last.

They had paddled some time when the smaller, lead canoe rounded a bend in the river a few hundred yards ahead of the other boat and out of view. Soon after it left their sight, the crack of a rifle came billowing back from below the bend; then another crack, followed by a shout. The men of the rear canoe dug deeply into the water with their paddles to reach their friends ahead, now under attack by some unseen enemy. As they rounded the bend, they saw the men of the lead canoe pulling hard for the shore to their left. The rear men lifted their eyes to the top of the bank to see what kind of enemy had befallen them, and were astonished to witness the last moments of a large moose as it fell dead a few feet from the water.

Moose spend much of their day belly-deep in water, grazing on the plant life that grows on the bottom of lakes and streams. While rounding the bend, the first canoe had surprised the beast, which instinctively plodded for the shore and the cover of trees beyond. Lieutenant Steele had fired first, hitting it in the flank, but the blow seemed to have no effect as the animal trotted up the bank. Just as it reached the crest of the shoreline, Wheeler, ever the sure marksman, fired a ball that pierced the moose's heart. With energy they would not have believed they still possessed, the men of both canoes got ashore and lit a fire; almost before the flames could emerge, Jeremiah Horne, their gray-haired Irish guide, cut off the nose and lip of the animal and had them searing. They spent that entire night butchering the beast and cooking the choicest parts in every way that one can over an open fire in the wilderness. Toward morning, they slumbered, at last secure in the knowledge that they were back in a region where food would no longer be scarce, and that they had left the threat of any large Indian parties well upstream. They had cheated death in many forms and had managed to hold it in abeyance.

As the refreshed crew set about their morning duties, George Merchant suddenly came bounding back from a trip to the river, grabbed his rifle, and headed back from where he had come. Others in the group snatched up their own rifles and followed him, soon to be confronted by another bull moose. "The enormous animal was coming towards us," remembered John Henry, "and not more than fifty paces off, his head and horns only above water. The sight was animating."[16] Shots from a number of rifles rang out, but apparently none found their mark, even though the usually sure-shooting Wheeler was among those who fired. The beast was so large that one in the group even pondered whether some of the shots had found their mark but failed to penetrate its thick skull. Slowly the moose changed course and swam for the opposite shore. Waiting for his enormous body to present itself as a target when he climbed the far bank, the party fired again. This time John Henry was sure his ball had struck the moose in a fatal spot, but the animal only plodded about indecisively for a moment before wandering off again. Taking to one of the canoes, Wheeler and a party of pursuers followed a trail of blood, but to no avail. The hardy moose was gone.

Having loaded their belongings, including enough moose meat to force the sides of the canoes deep into the water, the group returned to their river course downstream. Miles along their route, they came across a large gray wolf sitting above the shore too far away for their rifles to reach accurately—though they tested this anyway. A little farther downstream, they came upon a small moose—some three hundred pounds, they estimated—swimming toward an island. Vulnerable as it was, they quickly shot it, only to find that they had apparently interrupted the wolf preparing his dinner: the ears and sides of the young moose were badly torn. Even though their canoes were nearly overflowing with meat, their memories of near starvation were still fresh enough that they butchered the best parts of the young animal, leaving the remainder so that the wolf would get his dinner after all.

The following day, the men of the group began to recognize a puzzling paradox. Though they were overburdened with fresh moose meat, they felt their strength waning. When they stopped to camp for the night, they found themselves too weak to drag their canoes up the banks of the river. Years afterward, John Henry tried to explain their predicament as a lack of oils in their diet.

One who has never been deprived of bread and salt, nor known the absence of oleaginous substances in his food, cannot make a true estimate of the invaluable benefits of such ingredients, in the sustenation of the bodily frame; nor of the extremity of our corporeal debility. . . . Though we might have killed more [moose] deer, the vigor of our bodies was so reduced that we were convinced that that kind of food could not restore us to our wonted energy, and enable us to perform so rugged and long a march as that to the frontiers of Maine.[17]

One hundred ninety-seven years before Dr. Robert Atkins published his revolutionary theories on dieting, the members of Arnold's scouting party, though completely unaware, had discovered the weight-loss capacities of a low-carbohydrate diet. Five days had passed since they had eaten the last of their small rations of flour for biscuits, the only carbohydrates that their diet had provided save the berries they had discovered near the Height of Land. The tremendous exertions that they undertook each day only worsened their physical condition; since they all had little body fat on their frames to begin with, the increasing weight loss caused by the absence of sugar, or carbohydrates to convert to sugar, was rapidly depleting their strength.

As their desire to exert themselves physically in their canoes waned considerably, the party found their last reservoirs of optimism failing as well. "The non-appearance of the army," recalled John Henry, "and our distress induced a conclusion that we were deserted and abandoned to a disastrous fate, the inevitable result of which would be a sinking into eternity for want of food."[18]

Realizing that they did not have the strength to tote the canoes up the riverbank, much less over the Great Carrying Place, the group decided that their only hope of survival was to find strength enough to walk over the route back to the cache of supplies that they had left at the first pond in the care of Clifton and McKonkey three weeks earlier. To prepare for the journey back toward the Kennebec River, they set up a rack of sticks about four feet above the fire and laid meat in thin strips across the rack. By tending a smoky fire beneath the rack for nearly a week, the men could dry and smoke—or jerk—the meat into a state that would preserve it for long periods, even in wet weather.

While the jerking station was being prepared, Lieutenant Steele, along with the guide Getchell and Wheeler the sharpshooter, would continue on foot over the twelve mountainous miles of the Great Carrying Place and return with provisions, either from the army or their cache. The remaining men would tend the jerking fire and rest at their latest campsite. By the time Steele and his companions had been gone for four days, however, the patience of the remaining men was waning almost as fast as their strength. "Having neither bread, nor salt, nor fat of any kind," one of them recalled, "every day we remained here we became more and more weak and emaciated."[19] Finally, on the morning of the fifth day of waiting, Sergeant Boyd, the hardiest of the group at the beginning of their journey, and John Henry, the youngest, decided to follow Steele over the Great Carrying Place, rather than sit along the riverbank waiting until they simply withered to death.

Boyd and Henry traveled by canoe to a creek that got them closer to the first pond on the carry, then set off on foot, shuffling along, so that the slightest obstruction in their path caused them to fall. After a time, they reached the edge of the huge, knee-deep bog over which they had passed with great exertion nearly three weeks prior, when they were still far from the desperate condition in which they found themselves now. Looking out over the mile-wide mossy thicket was more than either of them could stand. Boyd fell first, landing against a log, certain he would not again rise. Seeing the collapse of his friend, who less than a month before had been perhaps the strongest man in the entire expedition, John Henry fell after him, trying in vain to encourage him onward.

"The debility of his body had disarmed his courageous soul," said Henry of his friend Boyd. "Every art in my power was exercised to induce him to pass the bog. He would not listen to me on the subject.

Melancholy, of the deepest kind, oppressed me. Convinced that the army had retreated, a prognostication fastened on my mind, that we should all die of mere debility in these wilds."[20]

After sitting an hour against the log, the two somehow found the energy to stagger back to their campsite and the men they had left by the jerking fire. Seeing their two comrades again within a few hours of their departure raised the spirits of the men at the campsite, who took the rapid return as a sign that some good news returned with them. This temporary delight was quashed by a deep gloom when the truth returned to the fire with their friends. Borrowing mental strength from one another, the group determined to rest through the night and then attempt together one last effort on the trail to preserve their existence.[21]

In the morning, they rode their canoe as far as the creek and then passed afoot the same route that Boyd and Henry had taken the previous morning. In due course, they arrived at the log on which Boyd had fallen prostrate, and here a markedly different emotion suddenly overtook them. Looking out across the deadly bog, they saw the figures of men swinging axes and laying logs across a pathway. They quickly realized these must be the pioneers of Arnold's expedition sent ahead to prepare a road through the wilderness. The weary group found relief and an enthusiasm they had not felt in weeks. Passing over the bog with what little strength they had left, they reached a surprised group of axmen, who were startled by their pitiful appearance.

"Our wan and haggard faces," remembered the youngest of the group, "and meagre bodies, and the monstrous beards of my companions, who had neglected to carry a razor with them, seemed to strike a deep sorrow into the hearts of the pioneers."[22] In addition to their sorrow, the pioneers shared with the scouting party the first food they had eaten in ten days that did not come from a moose. This encounter, however, could not have been as joyful for the pioneers as it was for the scouts, for inherent in their discovery of the wretched condition of their comrades was a recognition that they were about to encounter the same wilderness and deprivation as the poor souls who had just staggered toward them. It must have struck hard on their minds that within a week or two they might well be in the same condition as these poor creatures were now.

Emboldened by a rest, the rations, and the news that the advance guard of the army was just down the trail at the next pond, the scouts gathered themselves up once again and hurried along as well as they could. John Henry, the Pennsylvania teenager, was the first of the scouts to reach the first campsite of the army, where he collapsed at the fireside of Major Febiger. Confounded at the sudden arrival of a sixteen-year-old boy from out of the Maine wilderness, a bewildered Febiger inquired who Henry was and where he had come from. When Henry had explained himself, the major quickly handed him a canteen that was thought to contain the last liquor in the expedition. Henry took a swig just as Cunningham stumbled into the campsite, "the most ghastly and way-worn figure in nature."[23] When the rest of the ragtag scouting party had reached the fire, Febiger offered them all a share of a stew that was made up largely of pork and dumplings—including the carbohydrates that their bodies had been craving.

As soon as the scouts had rested and recuperated a while, they returned to the path, sought out their companies, and returned to their proper places in the army, more than three weeks after striking out from Fort Western. Back among familiar faces, they learned why they had been so long without aid. Lieutenant Steele, along with Getchell and Wheeler, had met the army on the Kennebec side of the Great Carrying Place. Shortly afterward, while helping to move supplies up the steep slopes from the river, Steele had fallen and sprained his shoulder. Nevertheless, he ordered some men to carry supplies to the relief of his fellow scouts, but for reasons not discovered, these had never arrived. The group also learned that Clifton and McKonkey had abandoned most of the supplies that the scouting party had left with them at the first pond, carrying off what they could.

John Henry attributed this last event to "the dastardly vices of the latter [McKonkey] prevailing over the known courage, good sense, and sedate age of the former. Nothing occurs to me contributory to the fame of these men afterwards. The first was an invalid, the latter a caitiff coward."[24]

Now that both their anger and their hunger had begun to subside, the scouts turned north again as guides for their respective companies, leading them back across trails and carrying places they had discovered and marked. To hear young John Henry describe his feelings, their awful experience and the possibility that they might soon be reimmersed in it had not left them entirely disillusioned. "We now found ourselves at home, in the bosom of a society of brave men, with whom we were not only willing, but anxious to meet the brunts of war."[25]

4

CHALLENGING THE KENNEBEC

On September 21, the day after most of Arnold's sailing ships reached the Kennebec River, George Washington wrote to the Continental Congress to inform them of the expedition. "I have detached Colonel Arnold," he wrote, "with 1000 men to penetrate into Canada by way of Kennebec River and if possible to make himself master of Quebec." Washington justified the diversion of this number of men from his task around Boston by saying that the many deserters from the British Army had repeatedly revealed that the Redcoats had no plans to leave the city before being reinforced, and were actually building barracks in preparation for a winter encampment there. Though the patriot army was so poorly provided for that "they may be deemed in a state of nakedness. Many of the men have been without blankets the whole campaign," Washington argued that the possibility of success was worth both the risk and the expenditure of provisions.[1]

Two days afterward, Arnold's army was spread along the Kennebec River between Reuben Colburn's shipyard and Fort Western in an effort to get the men and provisions assembled at this starting-off point. As if Arnold did not have enough regular matters to attend to as commander of the expedition, internal problems now began to set upon him as well. First, the men of the rifle companies raised a fuss about who would be their superior officers. Arnold had devised a plan that included dividing his army into four divisions, to depart Fort Western on consecutive days. These divisions, he reckoned, would be better off if they included men from both the musket and the rifle companies, so as to give each division the benefit of each type of weapon in an emergency. To this the captains of the rifle companies objected, saying that General Washington had promised that they would fall directly under the command of either Daniel Morgan or Arnold himself. Rather than create further uneasiness within the ranks at such an early stage, Arnold agreed to send the rifle companies forward as a single division under command of Captain Morgan, though he wrote to Washington about the matter and the general replied to Morgan in a somewhat scolding matter on the subject some time later. The second unexpected matter that beset Arnold resulted in the first casualty of the expedition.[2]

As the soldiers gathered around Fort Western, they took up residence in any available accommodations. Since 1769, the fort had been the property of James Howard, Esquire, a prominent and influential trader and landowner. Apparently, the Howards were not put out by the invasion of fifty score of ruffians, since the expedition surgeon referred to their hosts as "an exceeding hospitable, opulent, polite, family."[3] Some of the soldiers tented or built board cabins on the fort's parade ground, a few hundred took lodging in the main building of the fort, more took over the blockhouses. The least fortunate served among the companies that had no shelter, forcing them to sleep outdoors despite the rainy, cold weather. Perhaps the best accommodations fell to those who imposed on local residents to stay as guests in area homes. John Topham and Simeon Thayer, both captains in Greene's battalion of musketmen, were sleeping in the bedroom of one such house when a ruckus arose among the soldiers in the main rooms and one of them asked Captain Thayer to come and settle the argument. Thayer obliged and ordered the drunken quarrelers to settle down and get some rest. This might have been the end of the trouble, and appeared to be, until Thayer passed by the front door and saw the flash of a musket's priming pan from outside. Fortunately, this gun did not discharge, but Thayer called out to Captain Topham, who came to his aid just as a shot rang out from another musket in front of the house.[4]

In the darkness, it was impossible to see who had fired the shot or what had been the intended target, if any; with drunken soldiers everywhere in the area, there could be any number of relatively innocent explanations for the firing of a musket, so Topham and Thayer returned to bed. A short while later, the men in the main room heard the sound of the front latch as the door flew open and a musket fired at close range. In the confusion that followed, they discovered that the ball had struck Reuben Bishop, a sergeant in Captain Thomas Williams's company of musketmen who had been lying in front of the fire. The wound in his abdomen did not kill Bishop instantly but, rather, left him to suffer for twelve hours, bleeding internally, after which he "died in great horror and agony of mind at the thought of going into eternity and appearing before his God and judge."[5]

Topham and Thayer rose again and with more determination to discover who was behind the shot they seized a man named Ryder as a suspect among the drunkards in the house, but soon found they had grabbed the wrong man. A search ensued throughout the area all night, but to no avail. The following morning, a sergeant across the river from the fort stopped a soldier and questioned him, suspicious that he was deserting. When the sergeant brought him back to the army, it became clear that "the circumstances of his being out all night, and his guilty looks and actions, were pretty convincing proof against him."[6]

The captured villain, a private from Captain William Goodrich's musket company named James McCormick, was from North Yarmouth, Maine, a village about fifty miles to the southeast. He had been serving in Captain Jeremiah Hill's company of Colonel James Scamman's regiment at Cambridge when he was transferred to Arnold's expedition. His comrades found him generally a simple and quiet man when he was sober.

The following morning, Arnold ordered a court-martial to convene and try McCormick for murder, which it promptly did. Despite the guilty verdict, McCormick maintained his innocence even as soldiers constructed the gallows for his execution and the army's chaplain, Reverend Samuel Spring, "conversed with him respecting his crime, the awful punishment he was soon to suffer, and the more awful and never ending punishment that would await him in the eternal world if he did not repent." The next day, Arnold had the condemned taken to the gallows and, after a time atop the hanging stand in close proximity to a noose, McCormick confessed that he had been in a violent quarrel the night before the killing, with Captain Goodrich, and intended to kill the officer but, in his drunken state, had inadvertently shot Sergeant Bishop instead.[7]

Arnold took pity on McCormick, granting a reprieve from execution, and instead sent him under guard back to Cambridge, where General Washington could deal with him as he saw fit. In his letter to Washington he added, "The criminal seems to be very simple and ignorant; and in the company he belonged to, had the character of being a peaceable fellow." As it turned out, Washington would not have to carry out McCormick's sentence. The condemned man died in prison before his execution.

Despite having shown some leniency, Colonel Arnold had to address the drunkenness and establish discipline within the ranks. The expedition was heading into a dangerous wilderness, where strict adherence to discipline would be essential to their survival and success. Beginning that afternoon, and in the days that followed, Arnold set a harsher tone. First, he had a soldier with the untimely name of Love struck thirty-three lashes and drummed out of the army for stealing. Three others were likewise whipped and a fourth punished for letting one of the thieves escape. The following day, yet another soldier suffered thirty-three lashes for theft.[8]

September 24 was a Sunday, and the day Lieutenant Steele and his scouting party set off up the river. Later in the afternoon, Arnold dispatched a second exploratory group, this one led by Lieutenant Church and sent "with a surveyor and pilot to take the exact courses and distances to the Dead River." Plotting his course on the river was important to Arnold's thorough, detail-oriented mind, and he had reason to doubt the information available to him. As it turned out, he actually had a highly accurate description of the distances between significant points on the route, though this did not take into account the roughness of the terrain or how the weather this late in the season would slow his men. In his letter informing Congress of Arnold's expedition, George Washington included a description of the route that was remarkably accurate, considering the lack of precise measuring devices available at the time; it was probably drafted by the surveyor Samuel Goodwin, who also provided Arnold with maps and journals, at Colburn's request. Arnold may have had reservations about Goodwin's data, for he was known to be something of a Tory, but the surveyor appears to have been keeping in good graces with both sides at this early stage of the Revolution. As far as their knowledge and experience extended, local settlers who had traversed at least part of the route, such as the Getchell brothers, might have verified Goodwin's distances.[9]

In addition to Goodwin's work, Arnold had a copy of the journals of John Montressor, the British army engineer who had explored and recorded his observations of the region in 1761. Though Montressor's work provided a good description of the Kennebec–Chaudière route, it was a military document, with, in order to render it less useful to the enemy, blank spaces where most of the distance and direction figures should have been recorded. Still, Montressor made his journey to Lake Megantic, the hardest portion of the trek, in about eleven days, but with a relatively small party, not an army in excess of one thousand men. In a letter to Washington as the divisions were departing from Fort Western, Arnold reckoned, "We shall be able to perform the march [to Chaudière Pond or Lake Megantic] in twenty days, the distance about 180 miles." His estimate of distance was off by at least fifty miles, and his mistake in the number of days was even more significant.[10]

THOUGH DISCIPLINARY PROBLEMS among the men seemed to have abated now that the activity of the march eliminated their idle time, other issues now set upon the commander. There was the squabble with the rifle companies over who would command them; although Arnold reported to Washington, "There is at present the greatest harmony among the officers." Then, within a day of departure, the health of many of the soldiers began to deteriorate. They had recovered from their seasickness, but the change in diet and constant exertion were beginning to exact a toll, so that the expedition doctor reported, "Several of our army were much troubled with the dysentery, diarrhea, etc."[11]

So poorly outfitted were many of the soldiers that cold, wetness, and disease were sure to follow. Aaron Burr wrote to his sister from Fort Western the day the advance parties set off, and he described the haphazard nature of his clothing, most of it borrowed.

To begin at the Foot—over a Pr. of Boots I draw a Pr. of Woolen Trousers of coarse Coating. A short double breasted Jacket of the same, over this comes a Present from a Southern Gentleman—a short Shirt after the Rifle fashion—curiously fringed, with a Belt as curious. By Way of Hat another Present—A small round Hat with the Brim turn'd up—on the Top a large Fox Tail with a black Feather curld up together—the Donor I suppose meant to help my Deficiency in Point of Size. My Blanket slung on my Back, as that's a thing I never trust from me. To these add a Tommahawk, Gun, Bayonet, &c. and you .have your Brother Aaron—And pray how do you like him?[12]

With the two advance parties under Lieutenants Steele and Church on their way, the three rifle companies under Captain Morgan departed with forty-five days' worth of provisions and orders for the riflemen to clear a wide road through the woods for the divisions that would follow. A day later, Lieutenant Colonel Greene and Major Bigelow led the second division, made up of three musket companies (Topham's, Thayer's, and Jonas Hubbard's); the following day saw the departure of Major Meigs with four more musket companies (Oliver Handchett's, Dearborn's, Ward's, and Goodrich's). Lieutenant Colonel Enos commanded the balance of the troops (Williams's, McCobb's, and Scott's companies), who carried a greater share of provisions, since they would have an easier time traversing country already made passable by those traveling and toiling ahead. Colburn's company of boatbuilders would bring up the rear, carrying provisions and making seaworthy any boats that failed or fell behind. With them went Colonel Arnold, who procured a birchbark canoe so that he might move swiftly and overtake the advance parties within a few days' travel. He had gone only eight miles, however, when his canoe proved too leaky for service, so he stopped in Vassalboro to acquire a dugout canoe known as a pirogue.[13]

THE SECOND DAY of travel brought the expedition to the point where the Sebasticook River emptied into the Kennebec. Here, in 1754, Massachusetts Colony officials had built Fort Halifax, a post similar in size and shape to Fort Western, designed to defend the lower fort's trading center and the river settlements below. Whereas Fort Western governed the highest navigable reaches of the Kennebec, Fort Halifax dominated the confluence of two rivers while sitting just downstream from the Kennebec's first major obstruction, Ticonic Falls. Given the relationship between these two outposts, a rough road connected them through the woods, stretching eighteen miles along the east bank of the river. Many of the expedition's men had rowed bateaux upstream, but others took to the road bearing loads at least a portion of the way and tackled the distance on foot or with the help of local settlers with teams of oxen or other means of easing a burden. Arriving at the northerly fort, they soon discovered that they would have even poorer quarters than at Fort Western.

The remains of Fort Halifax had become the home of Ephraim Ballard, whose wife, Martha, would join him in this region of the Kennebec two years later. After her arrival from Massachusetts, Martha quickly became essential to the community as a midwife of remarkable skill. From 1777 to 1812, she guided local women through nearly one thousand births, losing only five children—a rate of infant mortality that modern medicine would not achieve in the United States until the 1940s. By all accounts, Ephraim was a "rank Tory" but not altogether undesirable. One soldier described him as "an honest man, of independent principles, and who claimed the right of thinking for himself." He added that they exchanged a barrel of salmon with Ballard for one of pork "upon honest terms."[14]

Across from the fort, the men encountered their first carrying place, which led to and above Ticonic Falls. In the few days of travel above the falls, the men remained upbeat despite falling temperatures and an increasing need to carry their boats and provisions around places in the river where paddling was impossible. One soldier happily reported, "Eate Broiled Salmon for Supper—and slept comfortably about 13 hours . . . All in Good Spirits none Dismayed." Although they had begun the grueling work of moving their loads on their backs, most often making several trips across each carrying place, the Kennebec River Valley supplemented their rations providing all the nourishment they needed to regain their strength each night. The river "abounds in fish of many sorts," and they saw plenty of beaver, otter, and mink. The men added to their provisions by shooting rabbits, partridge, hawks, woodcocks, even a ferret, though this last morsel probably did not fill many stomachs. In all, they were traveling in "Pretty Pleasant Country."[15]

Ever diligent, Colonel Arnold was sending orders back and forth among the companies, making arrangements for any eventuality. He ordered some of the provisions remaining at Fort Western sent up to Fort Halifax, where they would be left under the care of Mr. Howard, who agreed to go there and look after them. The supplies that had remained at Colburn's when the last bateaux departed would be stored there until "the event of this expedition is known." As hopeful as he was of success, Arnold was making contingency plans in case of failure. If the expedition turned around short of its goal, there would be something for the men to eat when they again the reached the Lower Kennebec.[16]

IN THE SPRING of 1771, Joseph Weston and Peter Heywood, along with three of their sons and a small herd of cattle, reached the Falls of Skowhegan, thinking it a rich and fertile place to settle and create new lives for themselves. Their families joined them the following spring and became the first settlers of Canaan, later Skowhegan, Maine. Thrifty with their exertions, they took advantage of an old campsite that natives had cleared on an island near the falls, planting their first crop without the toil of clearing the land, and used the blown-down path of a hurricane as a ready-made pen for the cattle. Between farming the virgin soil, raising animals, and trapping furs to make clothing and to trade at Fort Halifax for their other needs, the small group fairly prospered, so that by 1775 a half-dozen families made up the settlement three miles below the falls.[17]

Those who were building new lives in this region were either patriotic or willing to share their comforts and labors in exchange for something of value to them. One soldier found them willing to profit from the army's passage. "The people are courteous and breathe nothing but liberty. Their produce (they sell at an exorbitant price) consists of salted moose and deer, dried up like fish. They have salmon in abundance."[18]

To get around Ticonic Falls and a few miles beyond, Arnold hired the ox team and services of a Mr. Crosiers. He then got a meal at the Westons', below Skowhegan Falls. In addition to the hospitality, Arnold gained the services of his host, Joseph Weston, and two of his nine children, sons Eli and William, who agreed to accompany the expedition for a time, helping muscle and maneuver the bateaux through shallows and rapids and over the carrying places. With the fall harvest put to rest and a few weeks' respite before the winter woodcutting-and-trapping season set in, being able to hire themselves out to the army must have seemed a lucky turn. Within two weeks, however, the Weston boys were back at the settlement, nursing their father, who had developed a fever wading in the frigid waters. The fever worsened until October 15, when Joseph Weston became the second fatality of the expedition, leaving his wife and nine children to fend for themselves at the edge of the Maine wilderness.[19]

AT SKOWHEGAN, REUBEN Colburn had taken advantage of the energy exerted by the falling water and built a sawmill on an island there, though it was, by one soldier's estimation, "the worst constructed I ever saw." The island was the same upon which Peter Heywood had settled, taking advantage of land the natives had cleared. This rock-based piece of land divided the river into two streams just at the falls and provided a small area of slow water on its downstream shore. This pool of relative stillness, however, was but a calm between two storms. Just after the falls, the river narrows considerably while taking a sharp right turn that creates a triple whirlpool. High banks on either side left the men of the expedition with no alternative but to push their bateaux up through the intense current, driving for the lee created by the island. Once they arrived here, however, their battle with the falls was barely half won. The carrying place that enabled them to avoid the falls passed directly over the top of the island, and the first few yards of the bank mirrored that of the ledge over which the river fell. Here the men had to drag their boats up a steep incline of more than twenty feet—an exhausting enough chore for men who had not just surmounted the heavy current to reach the shore. It is no wonder, then, that the soldiers later exaggerated their descriptions of this feat. "We had to ascend a ragged rock, near on 100 feet in height and almost perpendicular," one of them recalled. "Though it seemed as though we could hardly ascend it without any burden, we succeeding in dragging our bateaus and baggage up it."[20]

When he had gotten above Skowhegan Falls, Colonel Arnold spent the night in a log home known in the area as the Widow Warren's house.

The widow had moved back to Massachusetts the year before, and it was available to him because of an event that helped strike home the danger of the river on which he was now conducting an army. Like the Getchells of Vassalboro and the Westons of Canaan, a small group of Massachusetts men had come to this area known as Norridgewock to take advantage of the virtually free land lots in Maine given to a few settlers in each region by the landowners—known as proprietors—to encourage wider settlement on their lands. In 1773, William Fletcher, James McDaniels, William Warren, and a man named Lamson, along with their families, began setting up farms beside the river, and had gotten a good enough crop of wheat in the ground that by spring of the following year their yield was worth a trip down to the flour mill near Fort Halifax. All four men packed themselves and their wheat into a canoe and headed downriver, hoping to make a return trip with flour for the coming year. Not far downstream, the canoe struck a rock and overturned. After he had reached the shore, William Fletcher faced the unenviable task of reporting back to the village that not only would there be no flour this year, but the entire adult male population, save himself, had drowned. Fletcher thus went down in history as the town's first permanent settler, while the stone that had killed his neighbors became known as Death Rock.[21]

As the settlers had discovered too late, traveling down this stretch of the river was perilous. Arnold's men came to see that trying to move northward against the current was a herculean task. Using setting poles, they stood inside the boats and shoved them forward a few feet at a time while others struggled in the water to keep them moving. When strong rapids or falls made this miserable method of transportation impossible, they switched to an equally exhausting method. "On arriving at one of these falls," one veteran remembered, "we pushed as near to the shore as possible. Those of the detachment whose turn it was to march up the bank came to our assistance. Then we got out into the water, placed our handspikes under the bateaux and carried out. Our progress under these immense burdens was indeed slow, having to lay them down at the end of every few rods to rest. The bank in general being high, and especially that part of it opposite the falls, we of course seldom failed to have a considerable hill to climb."[22]

Even when they were moving through currents too rapid to paddle against, the work was exhausting. Often the men waded waist- or chest-deep hauling the boats by rope. "While one took the bow, another kept hold of the stern to keep her from upsetting, or filling with water. Thus our fatigues seemed daily to increase." If the cold temperatures of the season and the water did not create misery in the ranks, the fear of a watery grave did. "The water in many places being so shallow," one soldier recalled, "that we were often obliged to haul the boats after us through rock and shoals, frequently up to our middle and over our heads in the water; and some of us with difficulty escaped being drowned."[23]

The stretch of river that ran past the Falls of Skowhegan and Norridgewock was particularly difficult. "Not once in the whole course of the passage from Fort Halifax to the head of the Kennebeck, was there an occasion for rowing," lamented one soldier. "In pulling the bateaux through the rapids, shoals and shallows, it frequently happened that some of the men plunged over the head into the deep bas[i]ns formed by the concussion of the water against the large rocks, and with difficulty escaped drowning, especially those who could not swim."[24]

At times, all of this work to get the boats safely upstream against the current must have seemed a wasted and futile effort, given the deteriorating condition of the vessels. "By this time," wrote the expedition's surgeon, "many of our bateaux were nothing but wrecks, some stove to pieces, &c." At carrying places, "the carpenters were employed in repairing them, while the rest of the army were busy in carrying over the provisions." Henry Dearborn recalled that, at each of the two falls, "We hall'd up our Batteaus and Caulk'd them, as well as we could they being very leaky, by being knocked a Bout a Mong the Rocks, and not being well built at First." More and more men were now walking along the shores rather than paddling boats that had become "little better than common rafts."[25]

Unaware that the exigencies of the expedition had left Colburn and his builders without the time to acquire enough seasoned wood or forged nails, the soldiers blamed them for the condition of the boats. "I would heartily wish the infamous constructors," one unhappy soldier wrote, "who, to satisfy there [sic] avaricious temper, and fill there purses with the spoils of their country, may be obliged to trust to the mercy of others more treacherous than themselves, that they might judge the fear and undergo the just reward of their villainy." Another soldier: "Could we have then come within reach of the villains who constructed these crazy things, they would have fully experienced the effects of our vengeance. . . . Avarice or a desire to destroy us, perhaps both, must have been their motive." None of the men who blamed the condition of the boats on the greed of their builders could have known at the time, but Reuben Colburn would go to his grave many years later having never received payment from the government for his bateaux save a small advance to cover the sawing of planks. Moreover, many of these angry laments aimed at the builders must have been written many years after the expedition, since those who built the boats marched alongside the soldiers, carrying, pulling, and repairing the vessels as they went, and there is no record of any conflict over them.[26]

The failure of the boats and the roughness of the water led to still greater problems for the expedition. The constant effort wore even healthy men down, so there were fewer and fewer of them to be found. The men were wet constantly, and dropping temperatures took a toll. The first frost fell on the last few days of September, while the head of the army was between the falls. Within a few days, the morning chills had become a source of great discomfort. Men awoke, if they slept at all, with their wet clothing frozen "a pane of glass thick." "Our fatigues seemed to daily increase," remembered one soldier, "but what we most dreaded was the frost and cold from which we began to suffer considerably." Another soldier reported, "Last night it froze so Hard as to freeze our wet clothes that we did not Lie upon."[27]

While moving between the falls, the surgeon reported, "Several of our army continued to be troubled with the dysentery, of which disease, Capt. Williams, a gentleman from Connecticut, came nigh to lose his life." At this point, officers began ordering the worst cases to return downriver in the best way they could, so as not to remain a burden to the rest of the army. This became increasingly important, since the situation with the bateaux had also reduced the army's provisions to a dangerous level.[28]

Water constantly assaulted the boats, over the sides and through the cracks. "The bread casks not being water-proof, admitted the water in plenty, swelled the bread, burst the casks, as well as soured the whole bread. The same fate attended a number of fine casks of peas." Then they realized that the beef was unfit for consumption as well, "being killed in the heat of summer, took much damage after salting, that rendered it not only very unwholesome, but very unpalatable." All of this took place as the army left the rich, fertile region of the Lower Kennebec and moved higher into hilly, more desolate country, where the local settlements and wild game that had been supplementing their provisions became more scarce.[29]

How the men of the expedition endured these trials is difficult to imagine, though one of them offered an optimistic if not idealistic explanation: "Soldiers used to manly toil, know not the pains of indolence. Great as their sufferings often are, they are never doomed to endure the miseries of those terrible spectres, spleen and melancholy, the usual companions of idleness. Their school is the school of fortitude. Their heroic labor, their love of glory, their steady attachment for each other, constitute their health and their happiness, keep up a constant glow of soul, which the indolent and luxurious never feel."[30]

AT SKOWHEGAN FALLS, the Kennebec turns southwest for six miles and then takes a right turn, heading northwest for another eight, after which it tumbles over Norridgewock Falls. At the point where the river makes that turn lies the present-day town of Norridgewock, but the settlers who founded the area were centered much nearer the falls of the same name, which today separate the towns of Madison and Anson. They did so to take advantage of the remains of what had once been a substantial Native American village, sometimes called Narrantsouak. The village had been the domain of Father Sébastien Râle, a Jesuit priest who had set up his mission there in 1689. A year after his arrival, Râle began writing a dictionary of the Abenaki language, which had grown to five hundred pages by the time of his death. Râle possessed a true gift for his work and had managed to "Christianize" a substantial number of natives, forming them into a devoted community at the village.

In 1724, an army of English settlers from Fort Richmond set out to destroy the village. Jeremiah Moulton, the leader of the party that attacked Norridgewock that August, had decidedly personal reasons for his hatred of the Indians. On a snowy January morning in 1692, natives of the same region, spurred on by a different Jesuit priest named Thury, had attacked his hometown of York, Maine, an event that became known as the Candelmas Day Massacre. The natives killed dozens of inhabitants and burned forty of the forty-five houses to the ground. Among those slain was Moulton's father, who was scalped—a butchery Moulton is said to have witnessed, though he was only three years old. The natives spared Moulton and his brother but took them prisoner, then returned them some time later. Jeremiah went on to become a prominent member of the provincial militia, and he might have been forgiven if his life experience made him overzealous thirty-two years later at Norridgewock. Under his command, the settler raiding party shot Râle repeatedly, scalped him, and mutilated his body. Still worse, they slaughtered women and children.

Half a century after that, white settlers from Massachusetts made use of the remnants of cleared land at Râle's old village to resettle the area. By the time the expedition passed over the part of the river between the falls of Skowhegan and Norridgewock, the foundling village had managed to survive the drowning of nearly all of its adult men, and about a dozen settler families were working the land. All that remained of the native village was the foundation of Râle's old church, ruins that appeared to Arnold's men to be a fort, and a marker at his grave. The site of the village was in such a preserved state that Arnold thought it had been "destroyed by the English ab't 10 years since" rather than the fifty that had actually passed. The villagers, however, had not fared so well. White settlers told Arnold, "The whole tribe, we are told, are extinct, except two or three."[31]

The carrying place around Norridgewock Falls—more a run of heavy rapids than falls, actually—stretched just over a mile, and, to lessen the fatigue of the men, two teams of oxen slowly dragged the boats and provisions over the carrying place on sleds. Never has an ox been known to break a land-speed record, but the pace of these two teams was even slower than usual, thanks to the steep slope of the land and the poor quality of the road, all of which was complicated by a drenching rain. Supervising the work kept Arnold at the falls for seven full days, but it did not keep him idle.[32]

When the last bateaux slid back into the river above the falls, the expedition had seen its final glimpse of civilization until they reached the settlements up on the Chaudière River. With the exception of Nata-nis's cabin on the Dead River, they would travel that far before they en-countered so much as a trapper's hut or a native campsite. The next major obstacle was the most powerful waterfall on the Kennebec, in terms of water flow. Caratunk Falls—from a native word for something rough or broken—was a much shorter carry and less time-consuming than Norridgewock, but they represented the visual and geographical passage from the fertile lowlands of the Kennebec Valley to a more mountainous, desolate region—a fact that most of the men who kept journals noted. From here, the western shore of the river rises imme-diately into the foothills of the region, making it impassable for an army on foot. On the eastern bank, however, there were stretches where the men had to walk as much as a half-mile inland, keeping to the river course, in order to find ground and forest that would accom-modate them. This would continue until the upstream march brought them to an overland passage from the Kennebec to its western branch, the pathway the natives called the Great Carrying Place.

On October 11, the day he had predicted to General Washington that his expedition would rendezvous at Chaudière Pond, Arnold reached the eastern terminus of this passage. He was still at least sixty rough wilderness miles, and countless days of exhausting toil, short of his goal.

ON OCTOBER 5, WHILE ARNOLD WAS FRETTING OVER THE SNAIL'S PACE of the portage around Norridgewock Falls, colonial privateers seized a ship sailing from Quebec to Boston and discovered several letters on board, which they sent to General Washington at Cambridge. Among the intelligence he gleaned from these was the belief that Governor Carleton had sent all of his troops to Montreal, leaving Quebec City without any regular British soldiers and with a population more dis-posed to the American cause than to their British overseers. In addi-tion, the letters indicated that the city held "the largest stock of ammunition ever collected in North America." They also revealed that the Québécois, especially those pressed into service by Carleton, were not likely to fight against the colonists: "It's generally thought here that if the rebels were to push forward a body of four or five thousand men, the Canadians would lay down their arms, and not fire a shot." At this news, George Washington's eyes must have widened. Not only did

Quebec hold the military stores his army at Cambridge so desperately needed, but it had been left virtually unguarded, and the expedition he had sent to seize the city was now, according to the estimate in Arnold's most recent letter, just three weeks away from capturing it all without opposition.[33]

5

THE RIVER DEAD

*I*t is difficult, even today, to explore much of the remote parts of Maine's northern wilderness without eventually coming upon an example of the strange knobby-kneed creature known as the moose. Perched atop long spindly legs, these enormous animals can stand seven feet at the shoulders and often exceed one thousand pounds. Male moose can carry a rack of antlers that spread beyond five feet across and weigh sixty pounds, leaving a person who spies one for the first time to wonder how they hold their heads up. To survive, they must eat as much as fifty pounds of vegetation each day, and prefer the weeds that grow in ponds and streams, so one often encounters them belly-deep in the water, grazing along the bottom. For most of the men in the expedition, the moose—or moose-deer, as they called it—was a foreign creature, and their first encounter with one was not soon forgotten.

The first moose killed by anyone in the expedition—aside from the men in Steele's advance party—was a paltry two hundred pounds, but the animals began to make themselves known between Norridgewock and Caratunk Falls, just as both provisions and other types of game were growing scarcer. Before long, the army had moved deeply into the animals' domain, until they became so common that one soldier declared, "We could scarcely travel fifty yards without coming upon their tracks." Either the noise and activity of the army made them skittish or the majestic Maine moose has lost much of its agility in two centuries, for, whereas one soldier declared, "It is seldom they can be shot, being so swift that they disappear in an instant among the thickets and swamps," today about 80 percent of the hunters who get a moose license in Maine take home a trophy.[1]

*   *   *

Now IN THE domain of the moose, the divisions of the army began to arrive at the Great Carrying Place, that overland bypass that enables those traveling up the Kennebec to avoid the rough water that today supports a thriving whitewater-rafting industry—one that travels exclusively *down*stream. Twelve miles of carrying, broken up in three places by ponds, brings upstream toilers to the west branch of the Kennebec, known to natives as the Dead River. Though this water gained its label from the absence of movement of its usually slow current, the stretch was linked to death in any number of ways. It was, in the eyes of those in the expedition, a more desolate place than any other segment of their march, representing a long stretch of river separated at each end from human inhabitants by an exhausting overland carry. It was here that Lieutenant Steele's scouting party was just about now coming perilously close to starvation before it finally reached safety among the lead elements of the army at the western end of the Great Carrying Place. Before they could meet the Dead, however, soldiers in the expedition had to endure their longest and most exhausting work, first carrying their bateaux the twelve miles, then heading back for a barrel or cask full of provisions, and then making a third trip for military supplies. More often than not, they did this piecemeal, covering the route from the Kennebec to the first pond several times before moving to the second pond, then the third—back and forth, back and forth—and finally reaching the Dead River. When not crossing one of the ponds, each bateau made the trip upside down on the shoulders of four men who struggled as they chafed under the sharp edges of the boats' gunwales. Each barrel, too, required the strength of four men, who hung it by ropes from two poles and walked while trying not to entangle their feet.[2]

One soldier looked back on his experience and declared it "perhaps the most prodigious march ever accomplished by man. The oppressive weight of our bateaux, the miry state of the earth from the rain, the thickets, hills and swamps were difficulties which were surmounted with an alacrity that would have astonished the most extensive imagination."[3] The unusually wet fall season had made an already difficult portage into a nightmare. "The rains had rendered the earth a complete bog; insomuch that we were often half leg deep in the mud, stumbling over old fallen logs, one leg sinking deeper in the mire than the other, then down goes the boat and the carriers with it."[4]

When the men straightened their backs long enough to take in their surroundings, they began to notice hieroglyphics carved in the trees. Created by the area natives, these were mostly animal figures "such as Moose otter Deer Musquash Sable and Beaver—and birds of Several Sorts which we Concluded must represent the Number of Beasts and Birds they catched and killed. We Discovered a Great Number of their Characters but Could not explain but few of them."[5] These were not the only messages left along the trail, however. While he kept a careful log of the course of both the river and the land passages connected with it, John Pierce—a member of Lieutenant Church's surveying party, which had followed Lieutenant Steele's scouting party up the river ahead of the main body of the army, left written "advertisements," as he called them, at each of the carrying places. An example: "1st Carrying Place W 23° N. 9 perches on the Left hand the river Please let this Paper Stand that all may Know the Course and Distance and you'll oblige Gentleman Yours to Serve. *Jno. Pierce Surveyor.*"[6]

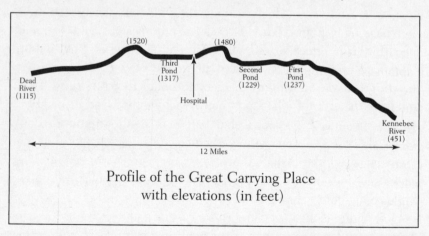

Profile of the Great Carrying Place
with elevations (in feet)

The rains not only made the traveling more grueling, they also made it difficult to recover from the exertion when night came. "Our encampments these two last nights were almost insupportable; for the ground was so soaked with rain that the driest situation we could find was too wet to lay upon any length of time; so that we got but little rest. Leaves to bed us could not be obtained, and we amused ourselves around our fires most all the night." A few of the riflemen in McCobb's company, suffering in the rain from having "no shelter but the Heavens," built a fire against a tree to try and shield the flames, and perhaps themselves a bit, from the rain. No one mentioned whether the fire weakened the tree or the wind gave it a heavy shove, but, whatever the cause, the result was the same: the tree toppled onto a soldier named Buck, who shortly thereafter became the expedition's third fatality.[7]

Despite their miserable condition, the soldiers of the expedition found time to amuse themselves. As their fatigue increased, they tried to cope through good-natured taunting and melodramatic play-acting. One of them remembered this fondly years afterward. "The lovers of the drama too, could they have witnessed our performances and fancied a wilderness for a theatre, might have had a plentiful entertainment, both of the tragic and comic exhibited, not by proxy but in real life; for such were our performances."[8]

During the first night on the carry, two soldiers let a quarrel get away from them and before long were savagely beating each other. Captain Hubbard came upon the altercation and quickly separated the two, but not before one of them, in his rage, could grab the captain. Hubbard's response would make for a good campfire story. "The Captain laid the fellow down carefully by the side of a log, and held him there until he begged his pardon and promised reformation. Captain Hubbard being a large man, and good natured as he was stout, came in laughing and told what he had done." The first pond on the carry also proved to be a trout fisher's paradise that amply rewarded those who stopped to fish. Even Arnold remarked, "Nothing being more common than a man's taking 8 or 10 Doz. in one hours time, which generally weighed half a pound a piece." The fishing in this region is still quite pleasant, but modern anglers no longer brag of catching a half-pound lake trout every thirty seconds.[9]

Though getting there was an easier march than to the first, the second pond on the carry was far less attractive as a resting place. The trees around it were dead and moss-covered; the water was muddy, so that it "makes as desolate an appearance as the first does bountifull." Dr. Senter described the lake as "low, surrounded with mountains, situate in a low morass." Worse, the dirty water was the soldiers' only means of drinking and cooking, and with heavily salted meat and fish making up most of their diet, the men drank in large quantities. "No sooner had it got down than it was puked up by many of the poor fellows." All of this fatigue, bacteria, and poor diet conspired to weaken the men until too many of them had fallen ill to ignore. At the second pond, Arnold ordered Goodrich's company to build a log blockhouse in which the expedition could leave behind the sick with provisions, so that they might recover enough to return to the villages down the Kennebec. The men gave the crude building the name "Arnold's Hospital."[10]

Not far from the hospital was an even cruder hut made of brush in which Morgan's division had left behind a lieutenant named Matthew Irvin. Though raised in Philadelphia as a physician, he was not in the hut to care for the sick—he was the sick. Troubled by dysentery from the start of the march, Irwin had neglected to do anything about it. Wading chest-deep in the Kennebec pushing a bateau when not sleeping on cold wet ground each night had not improved his health any. Dr. Senter observed that it "kept him in a most violent rheumatism I ever saw, not able to help himself any more than a new born infant, his extremities inflexible and swelled to an enormous size." Two other soldiers in much the same condition accompanied Irvin in his misery. When his comrades moved on, they left three men behind to help him as best they could, keeping his fire warm and rolling him over occasionally—little comfort, for he was covered with lice and completely helpless.[11]

Some of the sick were more fortunate than Irwin in that, though they could not continue, they had at least enough strength to return. A rifleman in Captain Hendricks's company described their departure.

> . . . unceasing fatigue began at length to make a deep impression on some of us. Several sunk under the weight of it. Their strength was exhausted; grew sick; and as our provisions were vanishing away, it was deemed proper to send them back. Who could not have been touched with pity and admiration for these brave men, struggling with ruthless toil and sickness and endeavoring to

conceal their situation? When any of their comrades would re-
mark to them that the[y] would not be able to advance much farther, they would raise up their half-bent bodies and force an
animated look into their ghastly countenances, observing at the
same time that they would soon be well enough. But their pitiful
case was no longer to be concealed. Daily they grew worse and
worse, became burthensome to the army, and in consequence
were compelled to return. We parted with them with that fellow
feeling, that benevolent affection which never fails to pervade a
soldier's breast. They returned with heavy hearts.[12]

When he had a few moments to think of Quebec, Arnold drafted a
letter to merchants in the city with whom he had done business before
the war. Addressing himself to a lawyer and merchant named John Dyer
Mercier, or two others in his absence, Arnold asked for any information
he could get on the disposition of the Québécois, the merchants in Quebec, and the British forces, including any ships that might then be in the
vicinity of the city. With a stroke of his pen he doubled the size of his
army, telling Mercier he was marching with two thousand men and informing him that his mission was to work with General Schuyler's invasion force to the west in order to "frustrate the unjust and arbitrary
measures of the ministry and restore liberty to our brethren of Canada."
Sending this letter was a substantial risk, since it was possible that the
information would end up in British rather than friendly hands, but the
intelligence he sought would be critical to his success. To carry the message through, Arnold chose Frederick Jaquin, a settler who had joined
the expedition as it passed his home ten miles above Fort Halifax, and
two of the Saint Francis natives, Eneas and Sabatis. He then sent them
ahead with orders that Lieutenant Steele give them the company and
services of John Hall, who spoke French. Once they reached the inhabitants, Hall would employ a local villager to accompany the natives to
Quebec City and deliver their message, then return to Chaudière Pond
with news of the Québécois's feelings toward the expedition and any
guidance he could provide on traveling down the river.[13]

Having taken care of the issues ahead of him, Arnold turned his
attention to the difficulties mounting around him at the second

pond and wrote to Washington with news that the expedition was about one hundred men smaller than when it left Cambridge. Though he tried to put a positive spin on his circumstances, assuring his commander that the men were in "high spirits," the condition of the expedition had clearly deteriorated. He informed Washington of his decision to forward the spare provisions to the Great Carrying Place "to secure our retreat." On the shore of the Kennebec, where the trail to the first pond begins, Captain Dearborn's division built a log house to serve as a depot for these stores. Arnold's decision to establish this forward base was part of a careful plan to deal with the growing possibility of failure. He noted that he was confident the current provisions they carried would get them back to this place if they were forced to turn back in the coming days; the spare barrels would then allow them to survive long enough to head down the Kennebec and hope that the army at Cambridge could send provisions to their relief. At the same time, he believed that the provisions they carried with them would be enough to get them to the French inhabitants on the Chaudière. At that point, both the success of the expedition and the lives of its members would depend entirely on the good will of the Québécois.[14]

At about this time, Lieutenant Steele returned from his scouting trip, reached Arnold's headquarters, and reported that the route up the Dead River reached Chaudière Pond (Lake Megantic) in another eighty miles, with a handful of carrying places, and was free of any natives, including the loathsome Natanis. Still wanting all of the intelligence he could acquire, Arnold sent Steele and Lieutenant Church with twenty ax men up the Dead River, over the Height of Land, and down the Chaudière River to near the Québécois villages. Steele would reconnoiter the Chaudière, making note of the falls and other hazards, while Church continued his survey. Both would rendezvous with the army back at Chaudière Pond and report to Arnold there.[15]

The following day, Arnold sent orders back to his second-in-command, Lieutenant Colonel Enos, with a more ominous message. He told Enos to hurry the rear elements of the expedition on to Chaudière Pond. There he hoped to receive intelligence from Hall about the Québécois, hold a council of war with his officers, and "be able to proceed or return as shall be thought best." Except for his warning to Washington, this was the first time he mentioned the very real possibility of turning back, and he planted in Enos's mind the idea that a council of war would make this decision, which meant by a vote of the officers. Arnold would soon regret having made this suggestion—to Enos in particular.[16]

From the second pond, the trail worsened. Arnold recorded that the going was "extremely Bad, being choaked up with Roots, which we could not clear away, it being a work of time." The end of this toilsome path rewarded the soldiers with a view, at least: "very noble, a high chain of mountains encircling the pond." Over all of this loomed the sight of the snow-covered mountain that Montressor had labeled "Tiaouiadicht" on his map but that would later gain the name Mount Bigelow, because of a legend regarding one of Arnold's majors who was supposed to have climbed it. The summit reached a vertical half-mile higher than the Dead River. At the pond, a blustery wind delayed some of the soldiers, preventing the safe passage of bateaux across. This gave at least some in the expedition a day's respite from the toils of carrying boats and baggage.[17]

The carry from the third and last pond to the brook that leads into the Dead River was five miles. It began with an abrupt climb, then turned to a long downward slope before reaching the great bog at which two members of Lieutenant Steele's scouting party had nearly perished. One of the soldiers who marched in the rear division, after the rest of the army had made the trail as passable as they could, described the first three and a half miles of this carry as a "very bad way" and the last mile and a half "a hundred times worse." Adding to the misery, a cold rain fell, soaking the men from without and making the depth of the bog mud as much as knee-deep, while a layer of ice had formed over the top of the moss.[18]

Late at night on his first full day after leaving the Great Carrying Place, Arnold caught up with Colonel Greene's division and found that they had nearly used up the flour that had not spoiled or sunk while on the river. Topham's and Thayer's companies dropped to half-allowance, only to discover the next day that they had only five or six pounds of flour left, with sixty men to feed. To supplement the depleted rations, Arnold ordered Major Bigelow to take one bateau and

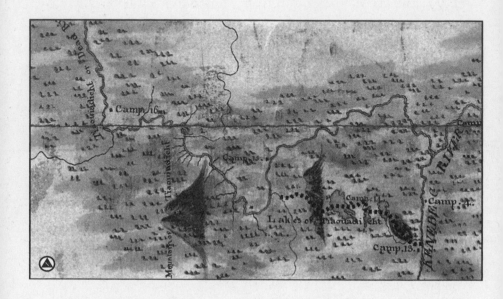

The Great Carrying Place from the Kennebec to the Dead River, as depicted in Montressor's map. The dotted line (enhanced here for viewing) shows the twelve-mile overland route taken to avoid the longer upstream paddle through shallow water with numerous falls and rapids. The largest mountain is now known as Mount Bigelow, after Major Timothy Bigelow of the expedition, who climbed it in hopes of seeing the spires of Quebec City.

thirty-one men from each company back to the ponds, where they could find Enos's division and carry back some of the excess stores that the rear guard had been carrying for the rest of the army. All was not completely bleak, however: Arnold recorded catching "a Number of fine Trout on the River," and two men in Lieutenant Church's surveying party killed a yearling bear cub, but not without somehow breaking both of their rifles in the effort.[19]

Two days later, Major Meigs ordered a squad of men to kill the two oxen that had somehow survived and surmounted the Great Carrying Place. Five of the beef quarters went forward to the men on the Dead River; the other three remained under guard for Colonel Enos's men. As large as an ox might seem, the stomachs of a thousand-man expedition are much larger, and though some soldiers undoubtedly enjoyed the fresh meat, there was hardly enough to offset significantly the dwindling nature of their provisions.[20]

Late in the evening of October 19, Arnold caught up with the lead division, the riflemen under Captain Morgan, who had set up their tents in a poor campsite but were more concerned with escaping the rain and getting some rest. Though it had rained steadily for most of the two previous days, the river's current was still fairly calm and the portages were relatively easy, especially compared with those they had previously surmounted. Cold, wet, and exhausted, Arnold continued upriver another mile before he found better ground on which to spend the night. When he awoke the following morning, he found a new enemy had beset his expedition. Still recovering from the fatigue of the Great Carry and nearly out of provisions, Morgan's division was in no mood to continue their slog through the rain when every mile they made put them farther ahead of the food that the rear divisions were bringing toward them. It would be four days before the riflemen took another step northward.

A few miles downriver, Greene's division was faring no better. Having filled spare casks with the cartridges Arnold had set them to making, they finally took up the march again, after lying idle nearly six days, but their energy and spirits had plummeted. The entire division, save those who accompanied Major Bigelow on his mission to retrieve desperately needed provisions, had remained stationary, consuming precious food while getting no closer to the Québécois villages on the

Chaudière. Nearly a week passed before their spirits brightened, upon Bigelow's return, but this upswing in mood was short-lived. Enos had surrendered only two barrels of flour, not even enough to sustain the detachment that had gone to retrieve it. Greene's division was now completely without rations or hope of getting any before reaching the inhabitants—an event still a week or more away.[21]

FOR THREE DAYS now, rain had been falling on the expedition, adding to their discomfort and misery. October 21, the third day of heavy rain, brought with it an ominous increase in wind as the men of Greene's division finally got moving again. As nightfall approached, they made camp and tried to get as warm and comfortable as the conditions would allow. John Henry, the teenage rifleman who had been part of the scouting party, would remember the unusual events that followed. The rain had added significant volume to the river, so that the water was running a few feet higher than normal, and to be safe, the men "encamped on a bank eight or nine feet high." As it turned out, eight or nine were not enough. "Towards morning we were awakened by the water that flowed in upon us from the river."[22]

A few miles downstream from the riflemen, Colonel Arnold had stopped traveling late, and in the darkness could make only a basic camp. It was eleven o'clock before those in his party could dry their clothes and turn in for the night, finally resting comfortably under their blankets. Five hours later, the water woke them up as well, "rushing on us like a torrent." To reach them, the river had risen eight vertical feet in as many hours, and it reached their campsite before any of them had time to gather their belongings. Snatching their baggage from the rising water, the men were fortunate to discover a small hill nearby; they managed to retrieve their supplies and equipment, but it took all of the next day to get everything dried. "This morning presented us a very disagreeable prospect," Arnold recorded in his journal after surveying the damage done by the flood. The water level had risen to such a height that it became nearly impossible to find the curving course of the river, and if they could have found it, the current racing down toward them made it impossible to paddle, pole, or push the boats onward.[23]

In twenty-eight years of life, Ephraim Squier had never seen a more windy or rainy day. The wind blew so ferociously that the men with him in Lieutenant Colonel Enos's rear division sought out clearings rather than risk being in the woods, with the falling limbs and trees. The men struggled to get a campfire burning, but got little comfort from it before the flood reached it around midnight. By morning, the water stood four feet deep where the fire had been. In all, Squier reckoned that the water had reached an amazing twelve feet higher than the previous day.

The storm subsided around midnight, and the expedition spent the remainder of the evening cold, wet, and fretting over their losses. At first light, they began to move again, and quickly discovered that the Dead River had come to life. Most of the army had been marching by land along the riverbank, and as they tried to resume their progress, they also discovered that the rain had displaced the river's banks as much as a mile inland while swelling all of its tributaries to an impassable degree. To move onward, the men in the bateaux lay on the bow and grabbed at bushes and trees, pulling the boat ahead hand over hand; others waded alongside, holding the sides. At one set of falls, the river's now driving current swamped and sank five or six bateaux. Losing the scant provisions and powder that these vessels held was hard on the expedition, but the loss was all the harder to bear because one of the barrels held hard currency—gold and silver coins intended as pay for the men. No doubt the soldiers, watching the heavily laden barrel sink below the rapids, thought the loss a great waste of money. What none of them could have known at the time, however, was that it would not go entirely to waste.[24]

As guides for the expedition, John and Nehemiah Getchell were among those who witnessed, or at least heard about, the sunken payroll. Living several days' canoe-paddle downstream on the Kennebec, they were familiar with the region. This put them in a position to profit from the expedition's loss, and four years later, these two woodsmen suddenly, and quite remarkably, became land barons. In 1779, the two brothers purchased three lots along the Kennebec, filing one deed for the three at the county courthouse. According to the deed, they came into ownership of the land "in consideration of the sum of four thousand dollars of the present circulating currency of North America, and the further sum of one hundred and five pounds and five shillings." The seller of the deed recorded the transaction with one additional note not at all common in such records, perhaps leaving a clue about how two simple farmers from the edge of the Maine wilderness might have come upon such a sum. He described the form of payment as being "in gold and silver coin to me in hand paid by John and Nehemiah Getchell both of said Vassalbourough."[25]

WITH EVERYTHING ELSE going wrong, Captain Henry Dearborn recorded in his journal, "A very unlucky accident happen'd to us today." The river where his and Meigs's divisions camped had risen eight feet because of the storm, and with every tributary swollen by the rain to two and three times normal size, it became hard to determine whether various streams were wrong turns or the main course of the river. Consequently, most of Dearborn's men had followed a swollen stream up the wrong route and were now miles off-course, wasting energy that could only be replenished by their now precious provisions. When he realized the error, Dearborn sent some men up the stream in his bateau to get them. About four miles up the errant course, the searchers discovered a fallen tree and determined that the lost marchers had used it to cross over the stream. Hoping that this was a sign that the wayward men had discovered their error, the men in the bateau returned to the main river, and all of Dearborn's men reunited at a carrying place around some falls upstream.[26]

Arnold took stock of his miserable situation—low provisions, lost powder and arms, sick men departing south, no intelligence from Canada, and the ever-present fear that the Québécois would be unwilling to provide any aid when they reached the villages—and finally ordered a council of war to discuss the rapidly failing condition of the expedition. By decision of the council, he sent twenty-six men from the rifle companies and another forty-nine from the second division back toward the Kennebec under command of Lieutenant Elihu Lyman, who accepted the assignment reluctantly. According to the Lyman family history, his reluctance was well placed. "He finally succeeded in [his mission], although many times in the homeward march his life from them was in great peril. But when, on one occasion, there was every indication of mutiny, his decision and courteous manner towards them completely subdued them." With Lyman and the sick moving rearward, Arnold dispatched Captain

Oliver Handchett and about fifty men in the opposite direction, hoping they could reach the villages at Sartigan and return to the army with supplies.[27]

The next morning, Arnold wrote to inform Lieutenant Colonel Enos of the council of war and its decision, ordering him to provide three days' provisions to each member of the group that was heading back to the Kennebec. This would be enough to get them back to the log hospital on the Great Carrying Place and then over to the log storehouse that Colonel Farnsworth would have filled with provisions by now. He also made Enos aware that the flood had reduced the twenty-five days' provisions down to just two weeks, with at least four days of exertion still ahead before reaching Chaudière Pond, much less the settlements well beyond. It would take, by his estimate, fifteen more days to reach the safety of the inhabitants—assuming the Québécois would be friendly to his invading army—and Enos was to send forward all of the men still able to continue, as long as he could supply each with enough food for that length of time. Those he could not supply, including the sick, were to return to the Kennebec. To add weight to his orders, Arnold expressed himself plainly. "I have no doubt," he wrote Enos, "you will join me in this matter as it may be the means of preserving the whole detachment."[28]

Having attended to these necessities, Arnold and the riflemen set off again up the swollen river at around noon. At one or two of the usual carrying places, the river was so high that the boats could actually pass right over the top of water that would normally be far too turbulent for passage. Near nightfall, however, almost unbelievably, the rain began anew. At this, the expedition's surgeon exclaimed to his journal, "Every prospect of distress now came thundering on with a two fold rapidity." Within a few hours, what had been falling as rain turned to snow, which continued until a blanket six inches deep covered the ground. This latest dilemma had as profound an effect on the psyche of the men as it did on their physical ability to continue. "The continual snow aggravated us more, and left [us] in a situation not to be described," recalled a captain of one of the companies in the middle division. "Besides bad walking by land; the men are much disheartened and Eagerly wish to return—however, I am certain that if their bellies were full, they would be willing eno' to advance."[29]

But they were not full; quite the contrary. Despair had set in as deeply as the pangs of hunger, and the prospect of relief was remote at best. Game was so scarce that one man found it worth mentioning when his comrades had shot a robin and a ferret. Men boiled candles down and mixed the wax with gruel; others boiled pieces of leather that they had brought along to repair and replace shoes. Those that had any stores at all mixed small portions of salt and flour in water, then buried these under the ashes of a campfire to make crude cakes. A Rhode Island captain summed up his fears succinctly when he wrote, "We are in An absolute danger of starving."[30]

With despair growing in the ranks of his division, Lieutenant Colonel Christopher Greene took to the river and headed upstream to find Arnold. It was necessary not only to inform his commander of the dire condition his division was in, but also to seek out any provisions that might be available among the division of riflemen or from Meigs's musket division. Greene soon found that Arnold was too far ahead to reach, and when he returned to his divisional camp around noontime, Greene found Enos and most of his officers waiting for him. The leaders of the fourth division had traveled ahead of their men to ask that Greene and his officers meet with them in a council of war to discuss the possibility that both divisions should turn back and give up on the expedition. Those against returning—all from Greene's division—argued that they had received no permission, much less any orders from Arnold, to return to the Kennebec. In fact, his last letter back to them had ended with the plea, "Pray hurry on as fast as possible." Those in favor of returning pointed out that Arnold's orders required sending forward only those men that they could provide with provisions for fifteen days. The fourth division had perhaps eight days' rations remaining, and now had to supply about 150 invalids from other divisions. Thus, following Arnold's instructions, no men at all should continue forward.

When the votes were cast, the differences lay clearly between the two divisions. Greene and his men—Major Bigelow, and Captains Thayer, Topham, and Hubbard—who had now less than two barrels of flour left to sustain them, voted to continue on toward Quebec, while the officers of Enos's division—Captains Williams, McCobb, and Scott, along with an adjutant named Hyde and a lieutenant

THE RIVER DEAD   81

named Peters—voted to return to the Kennebec settlements. Faced
with a deadlock in the voting, Enos was left to decide the issue. He
knew that the lesser-provisioned men of the other division had heartily
argued for continuing, and cast his vote against his own officers, agree-
ing with Greene's that the whole must continue as ordered save those
too sick or weak to do so.

Barely a few minutes had passed before Enos's officers gathered
again outside the circle of Greene and his men, and held another, less
formal council. Unanimously, they voted that the fourth division
should return at once toward the safety of the Kennebec and the provisions at the blockhouse beyond the Great Carrying Place. In deference
to Greene's division, they promised to hand over four barrels of flour
and two of pork, but when Captain Thayer arrived in his boat to retrieve them, Enos's officers would part with only two barrels of flour. At
the same time, Enos told Greene's men that, though he was willing to
go forward, he felt his duty lay with his division. "Col. Enos advanced,
with tears in his Eyes," recalled Captain Thayer of Greene's division,
"wishing me and mine success, and took, as he then suppos'd and absolutely thought, his last farewell of me." Thayer was unconvinced of
Enos's sincerity, for he went on to write, "It is surprising that the party
returning, professing Christianity, should prove so ill-disposed toward
their fellow brethren and soldiers . . . especially when we observe our
numerous wants and the same time they overflowing in abundance of
all sorts and far more than was necessary for their return."[31]

Isaac Senter, the doctor for the expedition, observed these events as
they transpired. Describing Enos and his men, he later wrote, "Here sat
a number of grimacers—melancholy aspects who had been preaching
to their men the doctrine of impenetrability and non-perseverance.
Col. Enos in the chair." What most irked Senter was a clear advantage
given to Enos's men in the manner in which Arnold had organized the
divisions back at Fort Western. "The advantage of the arrangement
was very conspicuous, as the rear division would not only have the
roads cut, rivers cleared passible for boats, &c., but stages or encampments formed and the bough huts remaining for the rear. The men being thus arranged, the provisions were distributed according to the
supposed difficulty."[32] Despite this imbalance of provisions, and the
harder work falling to those now continuing forward against the river's

current and a greater distance to the nearest inhabitants, Senter was furious to find that those turning back would not share their stores. Enos, despite the "expostulations and entreaties" of Greene's men, refused to order his men to relinquish their provisions, for they were "out of his power, and that they had determined to keep their possessed quantity whether they went back or forward." By two o'clock that afternoon, the fourth division, now around 450 men in all, turned downstream under orders from Enos and abandoned the expedition. Colonel Arnold had lost one-half of his men.[33]

THAT AFTERNOON, MAJOR Bigelow, who had voted to continue, took the opportunity to write a brief letter to his wife. With unusual candor, he described the bleak situation that he and his comrades now faced while he bade his family a thinly veiled farewell.

October 26th, 1775

On that part of the Kennybeck called the Dead river, 95 miles above Norridgewock

Dear Wife. I am at this time well, but in a dangerous situation, as is the whole detachment of the Continental Army with me. We are in a wilderness nearly one hundred miles from any inhabitants, either French or English, and but about five days provisions on an average for the whole. We are this day sending back the most feeble and some that are sick. If the French are our enemies it will go hard with us, for we have no retreat left. In that case there will be no alternative between the sword and famine. May God in his infinite mercy protect you, my more than ever dear wife, and my dear children, Adieu, and ever believe me to be your most affectionate husband, Timo. Bigelow."[34]

6

THE KING OF TERRORS

On October 24, 1775, the day that the violent rainstorm fell upon the expedition and revived the Dead River, General George Washington wrote a letter informing Congress of an ominous problem. While Arnold's expedition had been laboring over the Great Carrying Place, the port city of Falmouth (now Portland), one hundred miles due south of them, had been in flames. British ships intentionally burned the town and made it clear to its leaders that they had orders to do the same down the Atlantic coast as far as Boston. Washington now feared that Portsmouth and Newburyport would be the next targets. As news reached Cambridge, men from Falmouth were rapidly leaving the army to go home and find some form of shelter for their now homeless families, just as the harsh Maine winter approached. In answer to pleas from the citizens of Falmouth to send a detachment of troops for their protection, or at least powder with which they could defend themselves, General Washington replied that he had none to spare and could only offer his condolences and lament, "I can only add my wishes and exhortations that you may repel every future attempt to perpetrate the like savage cruelties."[1]

The task of maintaining the American army suffered from greater threats, however, than the departure of some Falmouth troops. The Continental Congress had sent a "Committee of Conference" consisting of Benjamin Franklin, Benjamin Harrison, and Thomas Lynch to Cambridge, and they were in camp gathering information on how this new army should best be arranged. What they learned did not bode well for the future defense of the colonies. The colonial army had formed largely as an impulsive reaction to the outbreak of armed conflict at

Lexington and Concord and had remained in place around Boston, bottling up a British force since then. As the months passed without any further outbreak of violence, that initial sense of urgency seemed to wane, and the enlistment periods for which many of the soldiers had signed on were approaching expiration. The challenge for Congress was to increase the size of the army and to maintain it indefinitely, and as the committee discovered, this would be no simple task. It was with great difficulty, for example, that they could persuade Connecticut troops to enlist only for the month of December, much less any period beyond. Leaders of the colonies were learning that resisting the combined arms of the most powerful empire in the world was no easy task.[2]

One optimistic note may have brightened General Washington's mood at least slightly in these troubling times, however. In the last communication he had from Benedict Arnold, the expedition's leader expected to be in Quebec "in a fortnight," which meant that he should now be within a day's march of the walled fortress. If Arnold could seize the city, or at least aid Brigadier General Richard Montgomery's efforts against Montreal by distracting the British on a second front, the colonists' goal of seizing Canada might soon be accomplished.

AT TICONDEROGA, GENERAL SCHUYLER WAS HAVING TROUBLES WITH his troops as well, while he struggled to keep the western arm of the invasion of Canada on track. The invading army, which he had placed under Montgomery's command, had reached and besieged the British outpost at Saint Jean, but Schuyler found it a struggle to send reinforcements to further the invasion. A regiment of soldiers under General David Wooster was then with him at Ticonderoga and ready to join Montgomery, but a gale had stoked the wind on Lake Champlain and prevented their departure. During the delay, Schuyler became aware of a strong sentiment among Wooster's men that, with winter coming on, the lake would soon freeze over, preventing a return passage by boat. To Congress, Schuyler described the perplexing situation: "Most of the men apprehend being detained in *Canada* all winter; that they will perish with cold or with sickness." Thanks to the untiring zeal of a parson who managed to convince 350 men to move northward with Wooster, they finally sailed for Saint Jean the following afternoon, but "with the greatest reluctance."[3]

Four days later, at the exact hour that Enos's division turned around, Schuyler received a letter from Montgomery with good news. Fifty Americans had threatened the British outpost at Chambly when its garrison of three hundred Canadians and eighty-three Royal Fusiliers proposed terms of surrender—of their garrison. The counterproductive behavior of the Canadians toward the British had apparently rendered the outpost untenable. By accepting, the Americans took possession of the fort, its six tons of powder, and other provisions, along with the Fusiliers, whose "number of women and quantity of baggage is astonishing," according to Montgomery. The victorious general closed his communication to Schuyler with a plea, "Let us have rum, my dear general, else we shall never be able to go through our business," and an ominous note, given Arnold's now desperate reliance on the inhabitants of Sartigan: "Some of the prisoners (*Canadians*) are dangerous enemies, and must be taken care of."[4]

On the day when Enos's division performed its about-face on the Dead River, inhabitants of the fortified Canadian city on the Saint Lawrence learned from the morning edition of the *Quebec Gazette* that an annoying embargo was extended at least nine more days. Beginning on September 28, Governor Carleton had proclaimed that no ships be allowed to leave the Province of Quebec until the danger posed by the rebel invasion near Montreal had passed. Carleton had taken such a step in order to prevent the departure of the crews serving on board these ships, who might be pressed into service defending the city if needed. The governor had then moved over to Montreal as soon as Montgomery's expedition began to threaten the region, and in his absence, the lieutenant governor—a man with the distinguished-sounding name of Hector Theophilus Cramahé—now extended the embargo well into November. This was not only an inconvenience to the crews, captains, and owners of these vessels, but also a great disappointment to the merchants of Quebec and their customers, since no ship was likely to enter the province knowing it would then be prohibited from leaving.[5]

This last point was particularly displeasing to the citizens within the city's walls, because it compounded a growing problem. Governor Carleton had declared martial law in the province in order to grant himself the authority to force the French inhabitants to take up arms in defense of it. Without enough British troops to enforce these measures, however, Carleton had little success persuading the Québécois to fight with the British against a colonial invasion. To the contrary, fear of being pressed into such service was keeping inhabitants of the countryside from venturing into the city, so the goods they would normally bring to market never breached the city walls. If the colonials were to set up a siege of Quebec City, starving the inhabitants into surrender would thus take little time.[6]

On October 28, John Dyer Mercier, a merchant and lawyer in Quebec, was walking through the city when the town sergeant stopped and apprehended him, taking him into custody by order of Lieutenant Governor Cramahé. The following morning, guards transferred him to a sloop-of-war in the river, an act that so alarmed his fellow citizens that they sent a trio of emissaries to Cramahé for answers. The lieutenant governor dismissed them, saying that he "had sufficient reasons for what he had done, which he would communicate when and to whom he should think proper." As the townspeople stirred with accusations of tyranny against one of their own, Cramahé called together his militia captains and informed them that he had arrested Mercier because of a letter, intercepted on its way to the city and addressed to him, whose contents were reason enough for detaining the attorney.[7]

With the discovery of this letter, Arnold's expedition had been revealed. The correspondence addressed to Mercier was the letter that Arnold had given to Jaquin and the two natives (Eneas and Sabatis) on the Dead River weeks prior. In it, Arnold claimed to be leading two thousand men to Quebec on the same day he wrote to Washington that he had 950 men with him. Either Arnold hoped to recruit a thousand or so Québécois to his force, or he had adjusted his figures for just the sort of eventuality that came to pass. Either way, the authorities in Quebec were now aware of his approach.[8]

Back in the Maine wilderness, the two halves of Arnold's expedition pushed on, one south toward the Kennebec settlements and the other north toward Canada, with increasing misery and difficulty. Those still intent on Quebec were struggling to finish off the last stretch of the Dead River, at the end of which they would leave the Province of

Maine and enter that of Quebec. With Enos, his men, and their provisions heading downstream in the opposite direction, food became an even scarcer commodity. "Our bill of fare for last night and this morning consisted of the jawbone of a swine destitute of any coverings. This we boiled in a quantity of water, that with a little thickening constituted our sumptuous eating."[9]

The day before his two rear divisions held their impromptu council of war, Arnold had left the detachment behind and sped forward with a few men in an effort to reach the Québécois and send food back along the route, so that his men would meet it sooner. For the next two days, he struggled against the last obstacle that the Dead River could put up. The river is fed from its northern reaches by a series of swamps and ponds that drain southward through mountainous country, forming a chain of water with streams connecting the ponds; it is still known today as the Chain of Ponds. This would have been a tiresome route to traverse in 1775, even when the water was within its normal banks, for it consisted of an interminable number of carrying places followed by stretches of pond. At each pond, the boats would go back into the water and a few men would paddle their length while the rest waded along the shore through one morass after another to keep to the same general route. The rain of the previous week had made this already difficult task insufferable, for the flooding thoroughly disguised the main channel of the river, adding to their struggles the challenge of finding the correct path in the midst of a flooded landscape.

As the men of the expedition struggled over these numerous carrying places, word began to reach them of Enos's betrayal. Captain Henry Dearborn no doubt spoke for many of the men in the forward divisions when he wrote, "Our men made a General Prayer, that Colo: Enos and all his men, might die by the way, or meet with some disaster, Equal to the cowardly dastardly and unfriendly Spirit they discover'd in returning back without orders, in such a manner as they had done."[10]

The reward for finally reaching the headwaters of the Dead River was a steep climb over the snow-covered Height of Land, the mass of hills and mountains that separates Maine from Canada. This extension of the Appalachian Mountains not only divides two nations at this geographic region, but also marks the separation between waters that flow southward through Maine to the Atlantic and those that flow northward to the Saint Lawrence River. With rations dwindling and their exertions growing daily, the Height became an enormous obstacle to overcome. Rifleman George Morison remembered that his company "forced a passage, the most distressing of any we had yet performed. The ascent and descent of the hill was inconceivably difficult." For rested, well-fed soldiers, it would still have posed a tiring challenge, but given the physical state of the men of the expedition at that point, it was unusually daunting. "Besides we were very feeble from our former fatigues and short allowance of but a pint of flour each man per day for nearly two weeks past, so that this day's movement was by far the most oppressive of any we had experienced."[11]

The men of the expedition felt they were achieving a symbolic victory when they could shift from a struggle against one river's current to a more leisurely ride in flow with another. It was a mean obstacle to overcome, but once across the Height, down its northern slope, and across a stretch of flatter land, they would be able to put their boats into Chaudière Pond, paddle across it to the river of the same name, which it feeds, and be done with the murderous Kennebec and its branches.

ON OCTOBER 26, the expedition's surveyor, John Pierce, and his party crossed over the Height of Land and reached Chaudière Pond an hour before sundown. Following an old trail made clear by the travel of generations of natives, and blazed further by Steele's, Church's, and Handchett's advance parties, the party reached a natural encampment. In the midst of the thickest wilderness most of them had ever seen, they abruptly came upon a beautiful meadow of grass alongside a stream that led in their intended direction. With daylight fading, they took advantage of the suddenly comfortable environs and made camp. As they settled into the meadow for the night, Pierce and his men were startled by the appearance of a dog without the slightest hint of where he had come from. Soon afterward one of the party saw smoke drifting up from the base of a nearby mountain, so they turned in for the night—skipping their usual dinner ritual, for there was nothing to cook or eat—having posted sentries around the campsite to watch for danger. In his journal Pierce noted that the men were "faint and weak" from the lack of food, so he thought it best that he "kept the dog with us" and ominously recorded this fact in his journal. The following morning, they awoke to find the smoke still drifting menacingly in the distance, but were soon much relieved to discover that it was from the campfires of the advance party under Captain Handchett, which Arnold had sent ahead to the inhabitants for provisions. The two groups then walked the remaining distance together to the Chaudière River, where they met the advance party of Lieutenants Church and Steele.[12]

With the two lieutenants they also found Jaquin, the man whom Arnold had sent forward with the ill-fated letter to John Mercier. Jaquin had left the inhabitants four days earlier and carried—along with some fruit sent to Arnold by a woman among the inhabitants— the news that the Québécois were friendly, even rejoicing at hearing of the expedition's approach. In his trip forward, he learned that Governor Carleton had gone to the defense of Montreal, met Montgomery's army at Saint Jean, and lost nearly five hundred men for his trouble. As a result of Montgomery's invasion, there were virtually no British troops in Quebec, and only one frigate in the river there.[13]

This welcome news was important to Pierce's men, on whom that day's march to the river had been very hard. They had waded much of the way, "water up to our middles," and were suffering from the cold as the sun began to set. Finding a small piece of high ground in the swampy landscape, they built five fires and were beginning to recover some warmth when two of the party swam across the river in search of a boat to help hasten their excape from the swamp. With great difficulty the two wandered about before they came upon Colonel Arnold, who sent some bateaux to retrieve the wet and stranded parties of Church, Steele, and Pierce. It took four trips with the bateaux to get all of the stranded men to the pond, and it was near midnight before the feat was accomplished. Reunited with their commander, the group made camp, shot twelve partridges, boiled them into a soup, and divided it at a ration of one pint per man.[14]

That night, with the intelligence from Jaquin in hand, Arnold wrote a letter to General Washington, giving him the latest, though unhappy news of the expedition's progress. He also tended to the men behind him, knowing of the dangerous possibility of getting lost in the swamps on this side of the Height of Land. Pierce and his party, along with

most of Handchett's group, had all come upon a stream as they descended from the Height of Land and naturally followed it, believing it
would lead them to Chaudière Pond. This the stream did, but they had
no bateaux, so the path beside the stream forced them to wade through
quagmires for as much as two miles, only to end up stranded in the
swamps. Traveling by boat with his party, Arnold had moved with relative ease down the stream to the lake, stopping occasionally to clear
a fallen tree from the path. Still, Arnold could see what a mess the
region was for troops on foot, a fact heartily confirmed by Pierce and
Handchett.[15]

Realizing the disaster that would follow if the divisions behind him
were to make the same mistake as Pierce's surveying crew, Arnold
drafted a letter to their officers with clear directions on how to reach
Chaudière Pond by an easier route. "By no means keep the brook," he
warned them, "which will carry you into a swamp, out of which it will
be impossible for you to get." He instead ordered the divisions to bear
slightly northeast, along the higher ground at the base of the Height of
Land, thus avoiding the swamps that surrounded the stream. With
only the journal and map made by Montressor twenty years before,
and whatever insight Sam Goodwin's maps and directions could add,
Arnold had no idea he was directing his men into a fatal, horrible trap.
Montressor had traveled by boat as well, and had failed to explore the
area beyond the southeastern shore of Chaudière Pond. If he had, his
map would have shown that the path directed by Arnold led to even
thicker swamps, crisscrossed by numerous streams, all of which led to
two lakes that, though far smaller than Chaudière Pond, were impassable on foot unless frozen solid. Following this route would add days of
miserable marching to the journey, an addition to their toils that would
tax the little strength and provisions that many of the men had left.

Completely unaware of his error, Arnold sent the directions rearward, and, to be certain the message was clear to the divisions behind
him, he sent along one of the Kennebec settlers, Isaac Hull, in order to
"pilot them up." Hull carried the message from Arnold back to the
meadow, where he met some of the rifle companies under Morgan.
Captains Dearborn, Goodrich, Smith, and Ward, with their companies,
had already moved on, though Hull had not passed them in the woods,
and they were denied the presumed benefit of Arnold's guidance.

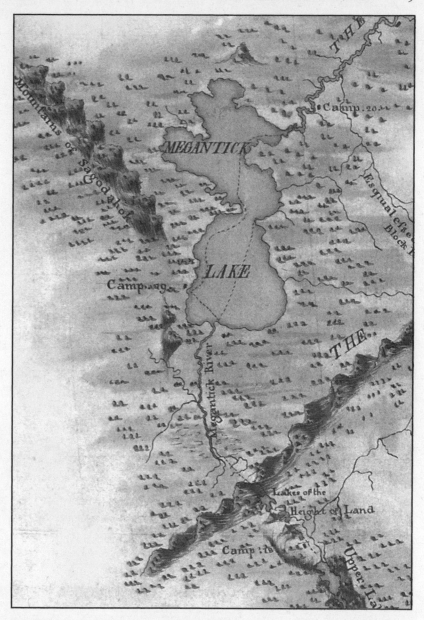

Montressor's 1761 map of the Height of Land and Chaudière Pond (Megantick Lake) showed no evidence of Rush Lake, Spider Lake, or the swamps that lay around them. The expedition's only map, it offered no sign of the impending danger east of Megantick River.

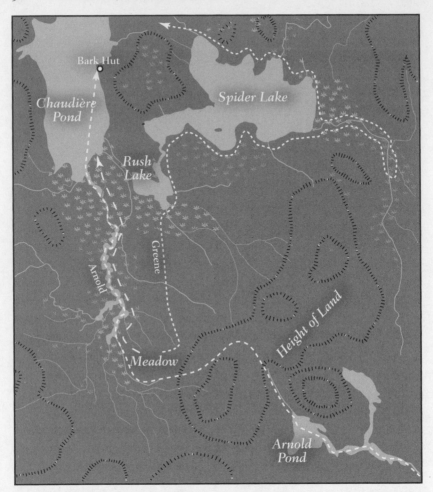

By boat, Arnold (and Morgan's company) traveled easily from the meadow to Chaudière Pond (Lake Megantic). Unaware of the presence of Rush and Spider Lakes, Arnold sent back instructions for his men to move north by northeast in order to stay out of the swamps. Only Greene's division got these instructions, and followed them into a desolate trap. The balance of the expedition followed the river on foot and descended into a swampy mess of their own.

Informing the remaining rifle companies of the good news from the settlements, Hull gave Morgan the directions from Arnold before moving farther to the rear in search of the remaining companies. The difficult labor of carrying the bateaux over the Height would prove a salvation to Morgan and his men, for they avoided the swamps by traveling down the same stream that Arnold had used, arriving at Chaudière Pond with the same relative ease.[16]

Hull came to Greene's division last and personally guided them back toward Arnold and the Chaudière. Greene's men seemed to be in the direst of circumstances, having borne the harshest part of the flood after wasting nearly a week lying idle back on the Dead River, prior to Enos's departure. Simeon Thayer, one of the captains, noted how deeply hunger had set in among his men, when he recorded: "It is to be observed here, with such horror, that the most ferocious and unnatural hearts must shudder at." The men had taken to consuming things that bore an even slight resemblance to food, "taking up some raw-hides, that lay for several Days in the bottom of their boats. . . ." Trying to chomp on them in their natural condition was apparently beyond even these voracious appetites, so the men made them palatable by "chopping them to pieces, singeing first the hair, afterwards boiling them and living off the juice or liquid that they soaked from it."[17]

It was afternoon when Hull reached the division with news from Arnold that the Québécois inhabitants on the Chaudière had pledged their friendship to the men of the expedition. Arnold promised to reach the inhabitants within three days and send provisions back to the divisions in six. This news resounded "to the unspeakable joy of the whole camp" and quickly spread, though somehow it was converted to a prediction that food would *arrive* in three days. The officers decided to distribute the remaining provisions so that each soldier would know how much he would have to carry him the hundred miles they estimated lay between them and relief when they reached the inhabitants. Each share consisted of four or five pints of flour, and several of the men ate the whole at once, so as to have a "full" meal, should it prove to be their last.[18]

Adding to its inadvertent treachery, Arnold's message also informed the troops that they should abandon their boats, because they would make much better time in this wild country on foot, carrying what they could on their backs. For many of the men, this last piece of information created as much pleasure as the news that food was a few days' march away. In many ways, the bateaux had become a symbol of the difficulty of the expedition. As one soldier described it, "The oppression of carrying them was becoming absolutely intolerable." Thus, when Arnold sent word to leave them behind, no one had to repeat the advice. "With inexpressible joy we dropt those grievous burthens."[19] All but one of the companies happily dropped the insufferable boats, saving one per company, which they kept to transport the heavy military stores, particularly the powder and lead. Captain Morgan's rifle company was the exception: since they possessed a large quantity of military stores, they carried all seven of their remaining boats over the Height. Soldiers in other companies took pity on Morgan's men. "Some of them, it was said, had the flesh worn from their shoulders, even to the bone." The sight of these men only added to a growing feeling that Morgan was "too strict a disciplinarian." Despite Arnold's instructions, Morgan apparently held to his decision to carry the seven boats onward; within a few days, his men would see the great value of these boats and the exertions that had borne them across the Height.[20]

THE FOUR COMPANIES WHO HAD LEFT THE MEADOW AHEAD OF ARNOLD'S instructions—those of Dearborn, Goodrich, Smith, and Ward—had moved forward on foot, simply following the path made by Pierce and Handchett, right into the same miserable predicament. Before long, they entered "an ocean of swamp" that reached in front of them as much as seven miles. "We soon entered it and found it covered with a low shrubbery of cedar and hackmetack, the roots of which were excessively slippery, that we could hardly keep upon our feet. The top of the ground was covered with a soft moss, filled with water and ice." Unaware of the danger that lay ahead, they continued in the path of Pierce and Handchett, heading northward in search of the pond. "After walking a few hours in the swamp we seemed to have lost all sense of feeling in our feet and ankles. As we were constantly slipping, we walked in great fear of breaking our bones or dislocating our joints. But to be disabled from walking in this situation was sure death."[21]

Captain Dearborn, in a birchbark canoe, came upon a small island and found Captain Goodrich with a few of his men trying to dry out. Goodrich was not well. In search of a way for his men to cross the river, he had been wading through the icy water, sometimes up to his chest. Now he was inadvertently staking his life on the return of a bateau that he had sent forward on the same errand. The boat did not return, but fortunately Dearborn took him into his canoe at about dusk, when the growing darkness revealed a light on the eastern shore of the pond about three miles ahead of them. On reaching the light, they discovered a bark hut occupied by a man from Handchett's advance party who had fallen so short of provisions that they had left him behind, believing his company would come up and provide for him. While they warmed themselves by the fire, Dearborn and Goodrich sent the canoe farther forward in hope of locating the bateau. After ninety minutes, the canoe returned, having found no sign of the bateau; the two captains spent an uneasy night at the bark hut, fretting over the fate of their men scattered throughout the swamps.[22]

While their captains slept in the relative comfort of the bark hut, the men of the companies gave up hope of making it out of the swamp in the dark and found the driest place available to camp. As one among them described it, "I thought we were probably the first *human* beings that ever took up residence for a night in this wilderness." On a little knoll of land, the group made as much of a camp as the landscape allowed. The only wood available for fires would have to come from dead trees still standing in the water, so, in the dark, soldiers waded back into the icy streams, chopped them down, and dragged them to the knoll. They spent a troubled night, fearing not only the exertions the following day might bring, but whether the rain would submerge their small campsite. As one of them put it, "The water surround[ed] us close to our heads; if it had rained it would have overflown [sic] the place we were in."[23]

It took Dearborn and Goodrich all day to gather what remained of their men and move the two companies a total of four miles, from the depth of the marshes to the bark hut, but, exhausted from their bout with the swamps, they all rested through the night. As one of the riflemen later described the sight, "Never perhaps were a more forlorn set of human beings collected together in one place:—every one of us shivering from head to foot, as hungry as wolves and nothing to eat."

On the following day, Dearborn and his men marched several more miles before they encamped at a waterfall where they found the wreckage of every boat that the men had carried with such difficulty over the Height of Land, except Arnold's canoe and Dearborn's bateau, which had avoided destruction. The falls claimed ten boats in all, including what meager provisions remained in them, along with powder, guns, and the life of a rifleman in Morgan's company named George Innis, who drowned in the rough water.[24]

WITH ALL OF THE DIFFICULTY THAT MEIGS'S AND MORGAN'S DIVISIONS had encountered on their way to the Chaudière, the suffering among the men of Greene's division was even greater. Ironically, their greater share of misery was the result of the apparent advantage of following Arnold's instructions. While trying to avoid swamps "out of which it will be impossible for you to get," they ventured instead into even greater danger. The expedition surgeon described the circumstances that soon confronted the division as "hideous swamps and mountainous precipices, with the conjoint addition of cold, wet, and hunger, not to mention our fatigue—with the terrible apprehension of famishing in this desert."[25]

Arriving at what they thought must be a small lake adjacent to Chaudière Pond, Greene's division turned to the east, hoping this course would bring them shortly to the shoreline of their destination. What they did not know was that this turn to the right was the worst possible choice, leading to the longest route to their goal. Though it did not show on their maps, just east of the southern end of Chaudière Pond there are two lakes: a smaller one now known as Rush Lake, connected by a wide stream to its larger neighbor, Spider Lake. The latter is aptly named for the many legs that stretch out from its main body, making a walk around its circumference a long, tedious journey. Had the division waded the wide stream between these two lakes, they would have joined the rest of the army at the bark hut within about an hour of marching on dry ground. With no way of knowing this, however, they began to skirt the southern shore of Spider Lake, believing it would soon lead them to Chaudière Pond.

Surgeon Senter described the ground here as "the most execrable bogmire, impenetrable *Pluxus* of shrubs, imaginable." He also remembered reaching the shore of Rush Lake and the connecting stream, and then being flummoxed by Spider Lake. "This pond we pursued till coming to an outlet rivulet, we followed to a lake much larger than the first, and notwithstanding the most confident assertions of our pilot, we pursued this pond most of the day, but no Chaudière." After a day of grueling work, Greene's men were at their physical limit, and though they were still in the midst of a great swamp, they had little choice other than to stop and camp as comfortably as they could on the frozen boggy ground.[26]

The following morning—October 30—they woke to find that nature had added insult to their misery. As the men sat up from their resting place on the ground, they discovered that a blanket of snow four inches thick had fallen on them through the night, and so began another day of miserable, exhausting walking. Every step dropped them a half-leg deep into the swamp floor; the wet surface of the moss had frozen overnight to the thickness of a pane of glass. After a half-dozen miles of this wretched struggle, they came to a creek that they surmised must lead out from Chaudière Pond. It was too wide to cross here, so they aimed southward along its banks, in search of a narrower place to wade across. Three miles upstream, the water only widened to a river more than sixty feet across, and since the shores held no timber large enough to use as a bridge, they still had no means of crossing. In despair, they pressed on until they reached a point where the river was about fifty feet wide and four feet deep, and crossed it the only way they could, by wading up to their chests in the near-frozen water. Some of the men even stripped off their clothing so as to have it dry when they reached the far shore, rather than walking in wet clothes freezing stiff from the cold. A little farther on, they reached another stream, though this one at least had a narrow log to convey them across. Still, weary from the march and lack of food, many of the men slipped on the icy banks or the frozen log and fell into this stream as well.[27]

By now it was clear that their guide, Isaac Hull, had no better knowledge of the route than those who were passing over it for the first time, and the weary soldiers directed their wrath toward him. "The pretended pilot was not less frightened than many of the rest; added to that the severe execrations he received from the front of the army to the rear, made his office not a little disagreeable." The knowledge that they could be miles from the Chaudière, and dozens more from any food or comfort, led to a feeling of desperation. "Several of the men towards evening were ready to give up any thoughts of ever arriving at the desired haven. Hunger and fatigue had so much the ascendancy over many of the poor fellows, added to their despair of arrival, that some of them were left in the river, nor were heard of afterwards." Some men, such as Samuel Nichols of Topham's company, simply fell out of the line of march and vanished, never to be seen again. "In this condition, we proceeded with as little knowledge of where we were, or where we should get to, as if we had been in the unknown interior of Africa, or the deserts of Arabia."[28]

The men, soaked from wading streams and frozen from the cold, now discovered that there was a native among them. With more apparent confidence than Isaac Hull, he led the march for the balance of the day. As darkness approached, those at the head of the column finally emerged from the swamp and came upon the tracks of others in the expedition who had already passed by from another direction. Though it was a small sign of hope, Captain Thayer, who had become gravely concerned for his comrades, noted that it "rejoiced our men so much, that they shuddered at the thoughts of the long and painful march which they sustained with becoming courage." It had taken three full days of marching to reach the lake that had been just seven miles from them when they left the meadow and the Height of Land with seemingly clear directions from Arnold.[29]

The following day, Greene's division finally rejoined the rest of the expedition on the banks of the Chaudière River. Their relief at what seemed like deliverance was short-lived, however: they were out of the swamps but not out of danger. Many of Greene's men had now gone at least "two days and nights without the least nourishment," and Captain Topham marveled at how the remaining men continued on. "It is an astonishing thing to see almost every man without any sustenance but cold water which is more weakening than strengthening." Those whose bodies somehow pushed on found their spirits failing and thoughts of death almost comforting. "The universal weakness of body that now prevailed over every man increased hourly on account of the total destitution of food; and the craggy mounds over which we had to pass, together with the snow and the cold penetrating through our death-like frames, made our situation completely wretched, and nothing but death was wanting to finish our sufferings." Survivors of the march later recalled their feelings on this, the most difficult day of the march. "Our spirits were so depressed by the occurrences of this day that death would have been a welcome messenger to have ended our woes." Others even contemplated the notion of bringing the relief to themselves. "My privations in every way were such as to produce a willingness to die. Without food, without clothing to keep me warm, without money, and in a deep and devious wilderness, the idea occurred, and the means were in my hands, of ending existence."[30]

COLD, WET, AND thoroughly exhausted, Captains John Topham and Simeon Thayer were marching in the rear of their companies, doing what they could to keep them moving and alive. After a while, they saw ahead of them a sergeant and a dozen or so men huddled around a fire. As they drew nearer, they realized that the encircled men were eating Henry Dearborn's Newfoundland dog. "They ate every part of him," Dearborn later recalled, "not excepting his entrails; and after finishing their meal, they collected the bones and carried them to be pounded up, and to make broth for another meal." This was one of three dogs devoured in these desperate days. When the dog meat was gone, "old moose-hide breeches were boiled and then broiled on the coals and eaten. A barber's powder-bag made a soup." At this same time, Dr. Senter noted that men resorted to eating pomatum (hair grease), lip salve, and the leather from their shoes, cartridge boxes, and any other item made of hide they could acquire. One soldier considered himself lucky to get a share of broth made from dog meat, a squirrel's head, and some candle wicks, "wich made very fine Supe without Salt."[31]

Unpleasant as it may have been for some to digest, the dog meat provided the men at least some strength to face the work ahead. Leaving two quarters of the meat tied in a tree for those who would follow them, they got back to their marching. Aaron Burr's chum Mathias Ogden remembered the struggle that followed. "We then traveled on a verry bad road sometimes over shoes in mire, sometimes climbing on all fours and at others scarcely able to see for all the thickness of the bramble and small fir."[32]

When they arrived at the falls on the Chaudière River, the survivors of the swamps came upon the scene of John McClellan, first lieutenant in Hendricks's company. The wading and marching in cold weather on the Dead River had brought the poor lieutenant down with pneumonia, until he could no longer walk on his own. His brother Daniel and other soldiers in his company transported him by boat to the Height of Land, where they crafted a litter and carried him over the Height while others bore the bateau in which they hoped to carry him to the inhabitants once on the Chaudière. With great effort, both burdens reached the river safely, and they again placed McClellan inside the boat for the downriver journey north. Because the men were unaware of the presence of the falls, they drifted into the current's pull, and only saved themselves from capsizing by steering into a fortuitously placed midstream rock. Somehow they managed to get McClellan ashore before the bateau disintegrated, but not without worsening his condition. With the boat now a wreck and the men in haste to reach survival among the inhabitants, they had to leave the officer behind. Dr. Senter did what he could for him, despite having lost his box of medicines and equipment in his own wreck at the falls, and two men stayed behind to care for McClellan, while others promised to return from the villages with food as soon as they were able.[33]

NOVEMBER 2 PROVED FOR MANY THE SUMMIT OF THEIR SUFFERING. "When we arose this morning many of the company were so weak that they could hardly stand on their legs. When we attempted to march, they reeled about like drunken men, having been without provisions for five days." The expedition had lost all semblance of military bearing, and the only goal left was simply to keep as many of the men alive as long as possible. "It was therefore given out this morning by our officers," George Morison recorded in his journal, "for every man to shift for himself, and save his own life if possible." Those who were "much beat out with hunger and fatigue," a rifleman recorded, "were not able to keep up with the main body. It was thought best to leave them behind to the mercy of the woods." This meant that the weakest, who had thus far found aid in getting along, would be unable to keep up with the rest, if they could carry on at all. As their comrades abandoned them in the midst of the swamps, they begged not to be left behind. "Never," recalled one of those able to continue, "will that heart-piercing interrogatory forsake my memory." This particular experience was seared into the memories of a number of the men. "I passed many sitting," another wrote, "wholly drowned in sorrow, wishfully placing their eyes on every one who passed by them, hoping for some relief. Such pity-asking countenances I never before beheld. My heart was ready to burst and my eyes to overflow with tears when I witnessed distress which I could not relieve."[34]

At midmorning, a struggling group of men led by Lieutenant Simpson halted at the edge of an "appalling" marsh. "It was three-fourth's of a mile over, and covered by a coat of ice half an inch thick." Here they waited for stragglers from Hendricks's and Smith's companies of riflemen to catch up with them. After a brief pause, they were about to journey into the marsh when someone called out, "Warner is not here." In reply, another soldier explained that he had last seen Private Warner, a rifleman, as he sat down sick beneath a tree a few miles behind them. Remarkably, Warner's wife, "a large, virtuous and respectable woman," had kept up on the march with her husband all the way from Cambridge, and she begged those now with her to wait while she went to get him. "With tears of affection in her eyes, she ran back to her husband." The group waited for the Warners to return, but after an hour had passed they started into the marsh without them.[35]

Some distance behind this group, Abner Stocking, a private in Handchett's company of musketmen, came upon a tragic scene, which he later described as follows.

My heart was ready to burst and my eyes overflow with tears when I witnessed a young Dutchman, and his wife, who followed him through the fatiguing march, particularly excited my sensibility. They appeared much interested in each other's welfare and unwilling to be separated, but the husband, exhausted with fatigue and hunger, fell a victim to the king of terrors. His affectionate wife tarryed by him until he died, while the rest of the company proceeded on their way. Having no implements with which she could bury him she covered him with leaves, and then took his gun and other implements and left him with a heavy heart.[36]

Private Warner's fate was by no means unique. As they overtook men in divisions ahead of them, soldiers scrambling forward came upon those who had fallen out of the march. "They had not when we came up with them a mouthful of provisions of any kind, and we were not able to relieve them as hunger stared us in the face. Some of us were entirely destitute and others had but a morsel of bread, and we now supposed ourselves 70 miles from the nearest inhabitants." Destitute as they were, even the strongest among them must have doubted their survival. In boats, they might reach the settlements and salvation within a day, but the boats were gone, and only their feet could carry them now. "The land was now much descending," one soldier recalled, "yet very difficult traveling. The spruce, cedar and hemlock were the chief growth of the earth, and these were in terrible plenty." Through this knotted woodland they reckoned that they might have as many as one hundred more miles to walk.[37]

7

THE QUÉBÉCOIS

With his men toiling desperately behind him and dangerous water ahead, Arnold pressed on toward the inhabitants as fast as he could. Recovering from the spill at the falls, he climbed back into the now repaired canoe and challenged the Chaudière again. Stopping occasionally, when underwater rocks forced his crew ashore to patch the birchbark walls of their craft, he discovered that the river widened and became more shallow, though no less dangerous. With snow falling and the air cold, one of their encounters with the rocks filled the canoe with water, and even after they patched it, the rapids forced the party to wade the stream, holding the sides of the canoe and dragging it along. On Monday, October 30, while Greene's men struggled with the worst of the swamps, Arnold's group came to yet another set of falls, where they met two natives—the first human beings outside of the expedition they had seen in nearly three weeks—"who appeared friendly and helped us over the portage." Four miles farther, they passed the mouth of the River du Loup where it meets the Chaudière, and another four miles brought them at last to the first house they encountered in Canada.[1]

TWO DAYS LATER, CAPTAIN DEARBORN WAS WAGING HIS OWN STRUGGLES with both the Chaudière and his health. Now at the front of the marching divisions, he was still making use of what remained of a birch canoe, but, as with Arnold's, the rocks were slowly shredding it. When the boat was finally beyond repair, he made camp on the shore. As he did so, the first of the riflemen walking along the river reached the same point, and Dearborn lost his dog to their hunger. Suffering from a growing illness, he set off on foot the following morning and had gone about four miles when he suddenly beheld a welcome but amazing sight. Coming toward him on his side of the river were eighteen Québécois with five oxen, two horses, two sheep, and eleven bushels of flour, a sight of relief that "caused the Tears to Start from my Eyes." Not only was the arrival of food a cause for celebration, but also the knowledge that Arnold must have reached the inhabitants and indeed found the Québécois at least somewhat sympathetic to their cause. Knowing his men would soon be eating beef, Dearborn pressed on and met up with two natives who were also bringing provisions back for the expedition. These natives gave their stores to Dearborn's men and took the captain into their canoe, heading down the treacherous river. After only a few miles, Dearborn saw a house; within another hour, the men of his and Captain Smith's companies began to reach the settlements "in poor circumstances for Travelling, a great Number of them Being barefoot, and the Weather Cold and Snowy, many of our men died within the last three days."[2]

Close behind Dearborn, the men of the rifle companies came within view of the cattle. "At this sight we made a halt and silently gazed upon each other as if doubting our senses; until we were roused from our stupor by the shout of our deliverers." In a few minutes, two of the cows were slaughtered and ready for cooking, though few men waited for such formality and instead ate the meat raw. With part of their stores thus distributed, the Québécois relief party continued on in search of those suffering farther behind, as the cry of "provisions in sight" rang back among groups of weary men. By nightfall, they had reached the men of Meigs's division, who were no less thankful for the relief.[3]

Colonel Greene's men were stretched out over a line some twenty miles long, and as the Québécois drove the sheep on toward the sick and fallen in the rear, more people arrived from the inhabitants, in canoes, carrying "a coarse kind of meal, mutton, tobacco." Hearing that they had but twenty more miles to walk before reaching the villages, the men camped where they had stopped. "We sat down, eat our rations, blessed our stars, and thought it a luxury."[4]

For those of Greene's division who were farther behind, the bout with the swamps had left them so ravenous that when the cow was butchered men grabbed at its entrails as they were discarded. "I had the good fortune," one soldier recalled, "to get hold of a piece of an intestine five or six inches long; this I washed, threw it on the coals for a short time, and then ate it with a relish." Even more desperate were those who, on discovering that the cow was three or four months pregnant, removed the calf and butchered it as well, considering themselves lucky as they "satisfied with eagerness our drooping stomachs." Some of these men had declined the offer of dog meat just the day before. In addition to the meat, the Québécois offered coarse oatmeal that had yet to be sifted. Despite its rough nature, one officer declared it "as good Bread as I ever ate."[5]

When sixteen-year-old John Henry, whose arrival at the relief provisions meant he had very nearly escaped death by starvation twice on the expedition—so far—came upon the place where the Québécois had slaughtered the cow, one of them told him that the others had consumed the entire beast, including those parts normally discarded. "One of the eastern men, as we came to the fire, was gorging the last bit of colon, half rinsed—half broiled. It may be said he ate with pleasure, for he tore it as a hungry dog would tear a haunch of meat." Since the meat was gone, Henry settled for a small portion of the oatmeal in warm water. His opinion of the roughly ground oats was less favorable than the officer's had been; he even became nauseous, though he later remarked that the sight of a comrade consuming colon may have been the root cause of his queasiness.[6]

In the midst of a snowstorm on November 3, the soldiers of the expedition, reinvigorated somewhat by the relief provisions, continued walking on ground that was "exceedingly miry," until they finally began to reach the inhabitants. One rifleman remembered the event. "About two o'clock we espied a house—then we gave three huzzas, for we have not seen a house before thirty days." One of his comrades recalled the enormous sense of relief at re-entering civilization. "Our joy was inexpressible in breaking out of that dismal wilderness. It was like being brought from a dungeon to behold the clear light of the sun."[7]

As great a relief as it was for the men of the expedition to reach the French villages on the Chaudière, it was quite an unusual event in the lives of the inhabitants as well. "The people looked upon us with

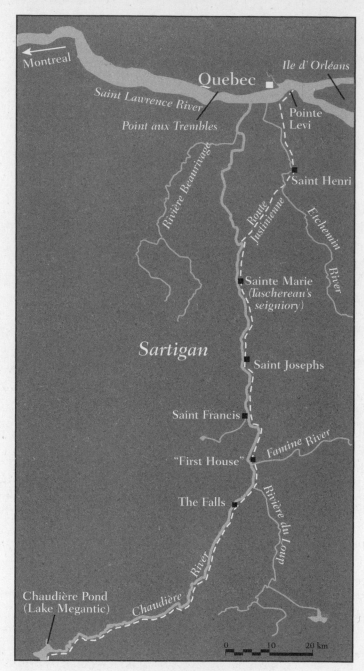

The Chaudière

amazement; and seemed to doubt whether or not we were human beings. To see a number of famished creatures, more like ghosts than
men, issuing from a dismal Wilderness, with arms in their hands, was
the most astonishing site they had ever beheld." Despite their astonishment, however, the villagers "administered to our necessities, and
loaded us with favours."[8]

The first villager greeted the expedition as it arrived on the outskirts
of the settlement, where the Famine River flowed into the Chaudière.
"Here was an old native stationed under a hut built with blankets, in
wait for us with his boiled potatoes, &c, offering them for sale. He was
also the ferryman." As it turned out, the presence of a native in what
they had anticipated was a region full of French settlers was far from
unusual: in the first few settlements, the natives even outnumbered
the French. This peaceful mixture of peoples was the result of a
century-and-a-half-old trading partnership that began when Samuel de
Champlain first sailed to Quebec in 1604. After the British attempted
to infringe on the lucrative fur trade in Canada, the French used this
business relationship to make allies of the natives in the century of
warfare that followed. Though the British had defeated the French at
Quebec in 1759 and signed away their rights to the region in the
Treaty of Paris four years later, many of the French settlers remained,
and the generations-old commerce with the natives continued.[9]

On Saturday morning, November 4, many of the natives in the area
paid Colonel Arnold a call in an effort to learn his intentions, as though
they had no previous knowledge of his coming or purpose—which, of
course, they certainly did. In all, there were "about seventy or eighty
Indians, all finely ornamented in their way with brooches, bracelets,
and other trinkets, and their faces painted." They had brought along an
interpreter, and through him, "They addressed the colonel in great
pomp, and one of the their chiefs delivered an oration with all the air
and gesture of an accomplished orator."[10]

Arnold replied that he was happy to meet "with so many of my
brethren" and that the Americans and natives were "equally concerned
in this expedition." In simplistic terms, and occasionally stretching the
truth a mite, Arnold explained that the King sought to take their lands
and money without their consent, and that the great men from the
Saint Lawrence River to the Mississippi had met at Philadelphia and

asked the King to change his ways. In response, he had sent an army to Boston and "endeavoured to set our brethren against us in Canada." After the King's army came out from Boston, killing many innocent women and children who were presumably minding their own business working their fields, the Bostonians had raised an army of fifty thousand men in six days and drove the King's men back onto their ships, killing and wounding fifteen hundred of them. Arnold's expedition had traveled across the wilderness "by the desire of the French and Indians, our brothers," in order to drive the King's men from this province as well. When that was accomplished, Arnold promised, his army would return to their own country "and leave this country to the peaceable enjoyment of its proper inhabitants."[11]

Though the Continental Congress had decided against the use of Native Americans in the conflict, Arnold offered two dollars' bounty and one Portuguese (about nine dollars) per month to each of them who would join his army, adding that the volunteers would receive provisions and be allowed to choose their own officers. The natives rewarded Arnold's eloquence and exaggeration with the commitment of about fifty men, along with their canoes.[12]

ONE OF THE NATIVES IN THE VILLAGE GREETED LIEUTENANT STEELE, and riflemen Boyd, Cunningham, and Henry, warmly, "and shook hands in the way of an old acquaintance." These were all men who had been among the first scouting party that Arnold had sent off from Fort Western, ahead of the rest of the army. Puzzled by his behavior, the group inquired who he was. Here they learned that this was the infamous villain Natanis, whom they had been ordered to kill on sight as they ascended the Dead River the first time. As it turned out, Natanis was friendly to the Americans and their cause, but had learned that he might not receive such kindness in return. So, rather than risk his life exposing his presence to the scouting party, he stayed hidden but kept a watchful eye on the group until they had safely reached the path over the Height of Land. Among his other benefits to the party, Natanis had left the note for them to find in a forked stick beside the Dead River, which led the party safely up the proper branch.[13]

Bemused by this discovery, the scouts asked him, "Why did you not speak to your friends?," to which he replied, "You would have killed me." None of the expedition journal-writers mentions how Natanis had learned of Colonel Arnold's orders to shoot him, but one of them, at least, left no doubt that they would have. "This was most likely, as the prejudices against him had been most strongly excited, and we had no limit in our orders."[14]

If their stay at the villages of Sartigan altered their feelings toward the natives of the region, it also created a warm bond between the Americans and their French hosts. "They seemed moved with pity for us and to greatly admire our patriotism and resolution, in encountering such hardships for the good of our country."[15] Many of the expedition's members had been soldiers in the colonial wars that had ended just twelve years prior, fighting against French people such as these. Perhaps some of the people who now aided them had been among their enemies on some distant battlefield. With this in mind, many were surprised by their reception among the villagers. "The kindness and hospitality of the inhabitants, was to us very pleasing. After having been lately our enemies, at war with us, we did not expect to experience from them to [sic] much friendship." Now that they were relieved of their desperation and hunger, the feeling among Arnold's men was universal regarding the French. "The politeness and civility with which the poor Canadian peasants received us, added to our joy when we were conducted to our place of rendezvous, and served out firkin butter and hot bread, which we attacked with great spirit."[16]

Religion was at the very center of Québécois life, and the rough frontiersmen of the expedition took peculiar notice of this. "It was very odd to hear them at their devotion," recalled one soldier. "The French People are Very Devout and Religious always at their Prayers Night and morning." Though precious few of these villagers were literate, they were all well versed in their catechism. There was "not one in 400 that could read one word but [all] were very Precise in Saying their Prayers Counting their Beads and Crossing themselves." In their charity toward the men of the expedition, their clergy led the Québécois. "Even the minister was generous eno' to let us have all he could spare."[17]

In general, the Americans were grateful guests in this strange and foreign region. "Had we been in New-England among people of our own nation, we should not, I think, have been treated with more kindness. They readily supplied us with whatever they had to spare, and discovered much tenderness towards those of our company who were sick, or feeble."[18]

A few of the soldiers grumbled briefly about the prices that the villagers asked for their goods. "The people were civil but mighty extravagant with what they have to sell." Some even gently suggested that they were taking advantage of the soldiers' desperation. "The people continued to be hospitable with some few exceptions. Knowing our need of their articles, some of them would extort from us an extravagant price." The members of the expedition had made the same complaint about the frontier settlers on the Upper Kennebec. What they failed to acknowledge, however, was that, unlike the inhabitants of towns and cities in the lower colonies, people in remote areas had to be far more careful with their food supply, for there was often little means of replenishing what they lost or gave away. The Québécois of the Sartigan region relied on their crops and stores to survive the winter, and parting with enough food to feed a starving army of several hundred men was no easy task, given that a trip to the nearest major trading center meant four days of travel. Having to give up such a large share of their own provisions just at the onset of winter—a long season in Canada—might have proved life-threatening to their families before spring arrived, unless they could exchange the money they received for proper replacements.[19]

As they passed through the various villages, the men of the expedition took note of the whitewashed houses with thatched roofs and paper windows, an occasional chapel, and the frequent renderings of the crucifix or the Virgin Mary. They did so partly because these scenes stood in such great contrast to the wilderness from which they had just emerged, but also because the houses differed almost as greatly from their homes in Pennsylvania, Virginia, and New England. To John Henry, they were symbols that ran contrary to his prejudices. "These things created surprise, at least, in my mind, for where I expected there could be little other than barbarity, we found civilized men, in a comfortable state, enjoying all the benefits arising from the institutions of civil society."[20]

Henry's newfound respect for the Québécois was enhanced greatly before the army left the Sartigan region. As the expedition consolidated around Arnold's headquarters beside the Chaudière, the colonel had taken a few of Henry's friends into his confidence as aides, and their comrades wasted little time in taking advantage of the situation. In short order, a group of them had raided a slaughterhouse that had been held for the use of the expedition, and carried off "as many pounds of beef-stakes as we could carry." Henry took part in the impromptu feast that followed and within an hour was regretting his part in it. After days of starvation—and in Henry's case it was the second bout in a month—the human stomach needs to be treated with care and caution. Consuming food too quickly, sometimes even relatively small amounts, can have disastrous, possibly fatal consequences. Henry was aware of this danger but presumed that the few days that had passed since he had reached the settlements and provisions were enough for his stomach to readjust to normal rations. Not long after the feast concluded and the march resumed, a fever set in, and Henry was soon barely able to walk. A warm night by a farmhouse fire found him no better, and before long, "I became, according to my feelings, the most miserable of human beings."[21]

At noon the following day, Henry could go no farther. Dropping out of the line of march, he planted himself on a log and watched as the army passed him by. In time a horse drew up to him; its rider turned out to be Colonel Arnold, who inquired as to Henry's health. Discovering the extent of the soldier's ailments, Arnold dismounted, walked down to the river, and hailed a farmer on the far bank. Soon this Québécois had paddled a canoe across the river. Arnold had him take Henry on board, handing the young rifleman two silver dollars as he did so. Nearly two days in bed with a fever, but without further food, and Henry began to recover. During his brief stay with this industrious family of seven, the soldier from the rough Pennsylvania frontier gained a measure of respect and gratitude toward his keepers. "You might suppose, from their manner of living, that these persons were poor. No such thing. They were in good circumstances. Their house, barn, stabling &c., were warm and comfortable, and their diet such as is universal among the French peasantry of Canada."[22]

By morning of the third day of his respite, Henry had recovered enough of his strength so that he thought it best to pursue the rest of the expedition making its way down the opposite bank of the river. Henry thanked the family and handed Arnold's two silver dollars to the patriarch, who refused, saying Henry would no doubt have need of the currency before he reached his friends, and that his aid to Henry was merely what his religion and humanity required. The Frenchman even escorted Henry as far as the ferry and convinced the operator to give the American free passage across the river. With a newly formed opinion of the papists of French Canada, Henry soon discovered the trail of the army and headed north toward Quebec.[23]

This was but one of the warm experiences that the men of the expedition had while among the Québécois. The group's doctor, Isaac Senter, led a few of the men in a quest for some decent libation downstream from the village of Saint Josephs, a mission that at first resulted only in a quart of expensive and unsatisfying New England rum. In the course of their search they came upon an old peasant's house, wherein they discovered a "merry old woman at her loom, and two or three fine young girls" who were "exceedingly rejoiced with our company." Though he offered few details of their activities in the company of their new acquaintances, aside from buying some food and rum and enjoying the old woman's song-and-dance performance of "Yankee Doodle," Senter did not neglect to add, "We made ourselves very happy." Either Senter was being coy in his journal entries or the entire episode was so innocent it did not require further explanation, for he concluded by saying, "After making the old woman satisfied for her kickshaws, saluted her for her civilities, &c., [and] marched."[24]

Still down with illness, Henry Dearborn lay low through the snowstorm until November 5, when the weather cleared and the temperature warmed considerably. That day, he and Major Bigelow hired horses to carry them downriver, but after only six miles of traveling, they came to a tavern and arranged for the tavernkeepers to serve food to their men. As they observed their new surroundings, Dearborn noted the area's good soil and the thickening settlements on either bank of the river as one moved north. "The People are very Ignorant," he recalled, "but seem to be very kind to us." That evening, one of the men who had enlisted in the expedition back at Fort Western, on the Kennebec, came for Dearborn with horses he had acquired among relatives in the region. Charles Burget was a Québécois who had either settled in or was just visiting the Lower Kennebec when Arnold's army passed by in the fall of 1775. Since he could speak French and knew

well the country and people the expedition would pass, Colonel
Arnold had been wise to hire him on for the journey. Just now his presence paid extra dividends, for Captain Dearborn's fever was rising and
Burget arranged for him to board at the home of one of his relatives, by
the name of Sansoucy. Here Dearborn stayed for more than three
weeks, attended by Burget, his relatives, and another soldier named
Charles Hilton, until he had recovered well enough to follow the army
to Quebec.[25]

Despite the care attending his rank, Dearborn's sickness nearly
proved fatal. For the first ten days, he "had a Violent Fever, and was
Delirious the Chief of the time." Lacking any real medicines or even
garden herbs, the Québécois treated him with remedies such as "a Tea
of Piggen plumb Roots, and Spruce." With a horrible cough, Dearborn
deteriorated until he was "almost Reduced to a perfect Skeleton" and
was unable even to sit up for days. In time, a report reached his company that he had died and that someone had seen Burget and Hilton
making his coffin. Likewise, a report had reached Dearborn that the
expedition had taken possession of Quebec. Anxious for news and
medicine, Dearborn sent Burget into Quebec to get hold of both, but
he returned four days later to report that the Americans were not yet
within the walls of Quebec and he could find no medicine. Despite
the blow to his spirits, the captain slowly regained his strength, until
he felt strong enough to ride in a carriage toward Quebec, where he rejoined his company more than a month after they had left him in the
care of the Québécois.[26]

The kindness shown by the Québécois toward their American
neighbors was not limited to the sick, or even the living. When the rifle
companies first reached the inhabitants, some of the officers hired two
young natives—supposedly nephews of Natanis—to paddle upstream
to the falls and retrieve John McClellan, the sick lieutenant who had
been carried over the Height of Land and placed in a bateau on the
Chaudière only to be wrecked against the rocks at the falls. His
brother Daniel and another Pennsylvania soldier had stayed behind to
care for the ailing and weak lieutenant, and with a skill that impressed
the Americans, the two natives moved their birchbark canoe rapidly to
his aid. Within three days, they had carried McClellan as far as the
first house in the settlements, but to no avail, for he finally passed

away the following day. Extending their customs to a foreigner—and a
Protestant at that!—the villagers buried McClellan in a manner befit-
ting their religion. For at least one member of the expedition, John
Henry, this kind of behavior softened his view of those who belonged
to the Church of Rome. "This real catholicism towards the remains of
one we loved, made a deep and wide breach upon my early prejudices,
which since that period has caused no regret, but has induced a more
extended and paternal view of mankind, unbounded by sect or opinion."[27]

ON NOVEMBER 1, Colonel Arnold wrote again to his contacts in Quebec. The natives who had carried the earlier letter had returned to Sartigan, but had no answer from Quebec, leading Arnold to believe that
they had betrayed him to the British. This time he sent the letter in the
hands of a Québécois named Robichaud, who might raise less suspi-
cion. In this inquiry, Arnold asked about the number of troops both in
Quebec and Montreal, any news of General Schuyler's efforts to the
west, how those who lived within the city might receive the Americans, and whether someone might meet the army with this news along
the road, for which he would gladly pay a reward.[28]

Four days later, Arnold, with 170 soldiers of the expedition, moved
downstream to the village of Saint Mary's. Here he set up headquarters and a rendezvous point at the manor house of the local *seigneur,*
Gabriel-Elzéar Taschereau. When French settlers began colonizing
Quebec in the early seventeenth century, they adopted a system of
land distribution that dated back to medieval France. Under this, the
King owned all of the land but granted control to local lords, or
seigneurs. These landlords then granted the rights to parcels of land
(called *fiefs*) to tenants (*habitants*) who worked and resided on the land
while paying rent and grinding-mill fees in cash, livestock, or crops. As
long as they held up their end of the relationship, the *habitants* virtually owned the land and the rights to leave it to their heirs, though sell-
ing their property rights outside the family required some payment to
the *seigneur.* In return, the *seigneur* built and maintained a grinding
mill, organized a local militia for defense of his *seigneurie,* and settled
minor disputes among his *habitants.* Taschereau had inherited his

lands and title from his father and, at the age of fourteen, had served in the unsuccessful French defense of Quebec against the English in 1759. Arnold was able to occupy the seigneurial manor house because it was vacant: Taschereau had fled to Quebec City in order to serve as colonel of his militia battalion, a position to which Governor Carleton had just appointed him.

At Saint Mary's, Arnold began to receive intelligence from Quebec, and the news was mostly bad. The governor had thrown in jail the spy that Arnold had sent to Quebec, and there were two hundred British regulars on the march to thwart the expedition. Now the news reported that Robichaud and his letter were taken into custody, and this caused great alarm in the villages. Rumors traveling the countryside held that the British authorities intended to burn and destroy all of the villages near Quebec if the inhabitants did not come in and join in the city's defense, though this last rumor had more to do with Québécois fears of British authority than reality. Even if the British did not come out and burn their villages, failing to serve in the region's defense, much less joining with the colonial expedition, might become grounds for forfeiture of their rights as *habitants*. Cautious of these reports, Arnold had sent a lieutenant and twenty men forward to scout out the last few miles to the Saint Lawrence River. Trailing him, he ordered that meat and potatoes be set up every ten or twelve miles for the rest of the men as they came up. He reached Pointe Levi safely, encountering no sign of a British assault force, but it was clear that the authorities in Quebec were aware of his approach—every canoe and boat on his side of the river was gone.[29]

Though the expedition had found relief from starvation at the villages, there was still little comfort to be had against other deprivations. The days that followed brought miserable weather and horrible traveling conditions. "The roads were very bad by means of the great rains and snows that had fallen—we most of the way waded half leg deep in the mud." More and more men were arriving at the more thickly settled portions of Sartigan, though many were in very poor shape. One Rhode Islander walked barefoot on the frozen ground for days before he reached the villages and finally bought a pair of sealskin moccasins from a French family dwelling there. His situation was hardly unusual.

John Pierce, the expedition's surveyor, noted that most of the army was in a similar state. The expedition's doctor noted that, "as fast as the beefs were killed, the hides were made into savage shoes." Their clothes were no better. A Connecticut musketman described them as "torn to pieces by the bushes, and hung in strings—few of us had any shoes, but moggasons made of raw strings—many of us without hats—and beards long and visages thin and meager. I thought we much resembled the animals which inhabit New Spain called the Ourang-Outang."[30]

During the afternoon of November 6, the army had gathered and recovered enough to continue the march. A few miles onward, the road and the Chaudière parted company, heading off in opposite directions. The road northeastward led to Pointe Levi and was called the Justinian Road, after a French priest who had been the first missionary in the region. Though the road had been in place for some time, it was of little service to the marchers. The rainy season followed by snow had turned it into a quagmire in which they sank to their knees as they walked along. Passing through a forest for a dozen miles, their passage must have reminded them of the swamps this side of the Height of Land. It was midnight before they finally emerged from the woods and reached the village of Saint Henri, on the Etchemin River. In ten hours, they had covered just twenty miles. The following morning, in another snowstorm, they took to the march again, though this time on the Route du Pavé (Pavement Road), a thirty-year-old road that was of a corduroy style, meaning it was covered with logs laid across the roadway in a perpendicular fashion to provide stability and prevent knee-deep marching. After traveling only a few miles, Arnold realized that they were within eight or ten miles of Pointe Levi with no real knowledge of what the British might be up to there. Mathias Ogden, among others, had encountered two Québécois on horseback near Saint Andrew the day before, traveling down the road in search of the rumored army of colonials. Today the Americans became convinced that these two had been spies, reminding them of the dangerous situation that they had marched into. As it turned out, Ogden was right about the spies. Two days after he encountered these men, Lieutenant Governor Cramahé wrote to General Howe in Boston, "The advance guard of the body come by the Chaudière was last night I am informed, within two leagues and a half of the St. Lawrence." Searching to gain what knowledge he could, Arnold again pressed Frederick Jaquin into scouting service, sending him back to Quebec City with two natives; in the evening, he sent ahead a lieutenant with twenty or thirty men to scout out the road. A few hours later, the bulk of the army followed.[31]

Before dusk, the snowstorm finally slackened and a messenger from Pointe Levi brought news that a mill along the river held a store of flour and wheat, guarded by a few local inhabitants on word that the British intended to burn it if the local villagers did not surrender it. They also brought word of the British frigate *Lizard*'s arrival in the basin, joining a number of other British sloops and cutters anchored there, but had no useful information on the number of defenders within the walls. Mathias Ogden described the discomfort that many of the men began to feel: "Our situation now seem'd somewhat ticklish yet we had no certain intelligence of the strength of the enemy at Quebec, nor had we heard a word from Genl. Scuyler or his army. Our whole num[ber] not exceeding six hundred and they not all effective, the most of us naked and barefoot and verry illy provided with ammunition, the winter approaching in hasty strides." With a perseverance that was fast becoming the trademark of the expedition, however, Ogden ended his daily entry with a resolute thought: "We determined however to make a bold push for Quebec at all events."[32]

And so it was on November 8, the fifty-first day since they had sailed from Newburyport, that the men of the expedition at last beheld the city of Quebec with nothing but the Saint Lawrence River between them. A Pennsylvania rifleman undoubtedly spoke for many of his comrades when he wrote, "We were filled with joy at this event, when we saw ourselves at the end of our destination; and at length freed from the misery we endured in the woods." They had accomplished one of the most remarkable military expeditions ever undertaken, but all of their suffering and exertion had brought them only to the vicinity of their goal. They were now less than half the number who had sailed from Newburyport six weeks earlier, and those who remained hardly resembled the physical model of soldierly bearing. With little food, scarce clothing, virtually no gunpowder, and without enough guns to arm each man, for the first time the men could see how daunting a fortress they had come to assault. They had survived their terrible wilderness journey, but for what? As they gazed across the river at the solid rock mountain on which the city sat, they were faced with the stark reality that they might have come all this way, through all of their pain and suffering, only to reach Quebec without the means necessary to seize it, and a long, cold Canadian winter almost upon them.[33]

8

QUEBEC AT LAST

There are about five hundred Provincials arrived on *Pointe Levi* opposite to the Town, by way of the *Chaudière*, across the woods. Surely a miracle must have been wrought in their favor. It is an undertaking above the common race of men, in this debauched age. They have traveled through woods and bogs, over precipices for the space of one hundred and twenty miles, attended with every inconvenience and difficulty, to be surmounted only by men of indefatigable zeal and industry.[1]

With these words, a disgruntled British citizen in Quebec marveled at the will of the colonists who had just endured the march through Maine in defense of whatever it was they held dear enough to do so. In stark contrast, on that same day, Roger Enos wrote a letter from Brunswick, Maine, to inform General Washington that he had abandoned the expedition to Quebec and was on his way back to Cambridge with nearly half of Arnold's force.[2]

Though the men of Enos's division had experienced great hardships on their return trip downstream toward the Kennebec settlements, their exertions and suffering were of no comparison with those who had chosen to continue on toward Canada. At the first falls they encountered on their return journey, one of their bateaux hit the rocks and came apart. The men on board survived, but a conspicuous report of the incident shed light on Enos's assertion that before turning back he had given up all of the stores he could spare: "Part of a barrel of flour lost, and a box of lead." On the fourth day of the journey, the Connecticut private named Ephraim Squier reported that his company "took two days provisions for each man." The following day, he and his comrades passed over the Great Carrying Place and reached the Kennebec River, only to cross back over it the next day to retrieve a supply of flour on the far side. There was enough flour in this cache alone that twenty men went to fetch it. After only five days of traveling—moving the bateaux *with* the current—Squier and his company reached the Kennebec inhabitants below Norridgewock Falls. Not counting the flour lost in the first set of falls and the supply that took twenty men to carry, Squier and those with him were limited to the same allowance of a half-ration per day that had sustained the rest of the expedition for two weeks.[3]

At three in the afternoon on October 30, just about the time that the men of Greene's division who had chosen not to turn south with Enos finally emerged from the swamps of Spider Lake, Squier and his companions reached the first of the settlements on the Kennebec. Here they found a supply of bread and flour that had been forwarded to them from Fort Halifax, and they slept in front of a fireplace at the first house for three nights, doling out provisions to the men who came on behind them. Miles to the north, the men of Greene's division who could stomach the idea ate a broth made of dog meat and slept on the snow-covered ground, still dozens of miles from the Québécois villages.[4]

Enos's men had encountered some danger—a Connecticut man in Captain Scott's company drowned when his bateau failed to pass over the rapids above Skowhegan Falls—and struggled against the cold, snowy weather that now held them in Brunswick for more than four days. For reasons unknown, Colonel Farnsworth had not carried out Arnold's orders to forward the emergency provisions from Fort Halifax to the Kennebec side of the Great Carrying Place, but this added only an extra day's travel on the half-rations before Enos and his men reached the safety and provisions of the inhabitants. The returnees would march for twelve more days before completing their return to Cambridge, along the way staying in the homes of settlers—one night in those of Falmouth abandoned by the townspeople when the British put the rest to the torch.[5]

At the end of the long march back to the army at Cambridge, Ephraim Squier closed his journal with a puzzling entry. "To-day went to [my] company at Dorchester, having taken a long and wearisome journey, returned abundantly satisfied." He made no mention of what it was that he had to be satisfied about.[6]

On November 3, authorities within the city of Quebec issued detailed instructions on how they would signal the city's residents "upon the first discovery of an Enemy's approach." The following evening, two ships arrived in the basin in front of Quebec, carrying about seventy recruits from other British outposts to support the defense of Montreal and Quebec. A day later, more recruits arrived, along with the British naval frigate *Lizard*, which had accompanied a supply ship into the province. Within the city walls, morale among the civilians was rapidly depleting. Virtually all of the regular British troops, including Governor Carleton, had gone upriver to defend Montreal, assuming that direction was the only logical approach for the colonials. These soldiers had taken part in the failed defense of Saint Jean and Chambly, both of which were now in the hands of colonial troops under General Montgomery, and it was becoming clear that Montreal would fall prey shortly. One British citizen in Quebec lamented to a friend in England, "Our friends above [in Montreal] will inevitably fall a sacrifice to a Rebel banditti, being unable to withstand such powerful opponents." Each of these losses involved the surrender of their British defenders, so that nearly one thousand soldiers were already lost to the defense of the province, and now another army of colonials had appeared out of the wilderness in Carleton's rear, ready to seize a city nearly devoid of defenses.[7]

A British naval officer from the *Lizard*, who had entered the city walls in order to aid in its defense, found it difficult to describe the situation inside. "It is not easy to form an adequate idea of the deplorable situation of the Town of Quebec at this time," he wrote. "There were no troops to make any defence; all the artillery mounted on the Ramparts consisted of seven pieces of cannon; and the Inhabitants were in a state of despondency." Making matters worse, in Carleton's absence the city was under the command of a career civilian. Lieutenant Governor Cramahé was "a feeble old man [who] was diffident and uncertain what measures to pursue."[8]

According to a British citizen within the walls, Arnold had succeeded in sending messages into the city that grew into rumors and gossip. These held that the "Congress Troops" under Benedict Arnold—who had formerly traded goods in the city—had reached the outskirts of Quebec with a huge force that would starve the residents out or batter the city to the ground if the inhabitants did not surrender. Within the walls, citizens held raucous meetings to discuss the best course of action, and it soon became clear that a large number of them were "in the rebel interest." So much so, recorded Thomas Ainslie, the collector of customs, that "if the report speaks truth some people had actually drawn up a sketch of the articles of Capitulation." Another Brit was more optimistic. "The only thing we want is men, there being no regulars in the Garrison. However, what with sailors, *British* settlers, and *French* (though the latter cannot be much depended on,) we nearly muster two thousand five hundred." Perhaps to bolster his own confidence, he was overstating the number of defenders by nearly one thousand. The lack of personnel was so grave that Captain John Hamilton of the *Lizard* offered to tie up his ship and leave it defenseless so as to allow his men to go onshore and join the forces in the town.[9]

ON NOVEMBER 11, WITH MONTGOMERY'S MEN ON THE VERGE OF ENtering Montreal, Carleton ordered his men to spike all of the cannons that he could not get aboard ship, and throw all of the powder and shot into the river. That evening, he boarded his flagship, *Gaspé*, and fled downriver in hopes of reaching Quebec and staging one last resistance. The following evening, as the small fleet reached the narrow river channel at Sorel, a storm front moved in, and the wind turned to the northeast, directly in the face of their sails. Here the fleet sat at anchor for three days, exposed and awaiting a change in the wind. Finally, on November 15, a loud thudding sound in the distance startled Carleton, but it was not thunder: rather, it was something more ominous. Colonel James Easton, at General Montgomery's behest, had led a force to Sorel—the same group of men that Arnold had led in the capture of Ticonderoga months prior—and cut off Carleton in the channel. The governor's fleet had no choice but to retreat out of range back upriver. Easton sent a messenger out to the now entrapped fleet demanding that it surrender, and confronting Carleton with a difficult problem. If he were to surrender his fleet and fall into the hands of the colonials, Quebec would certainly capitulate soon after, and the province would be lost to the British Crown, who had entrusted him with its care, even to the extent of allowing the unusual provisions of the Quebec Act. His alternative, to fight the colonials from mid-river, would inevitably result in his capture as well. The following evening, Carleton chose a third option. Donning the plain dress of the Québécois, he took a small group of men into the *Gaspé*'s launch boat and slid quietly downriver, his men occasionally using their hands as paddles to avoid making any noise.

Two DAYS BEFORE CARLETON ABANDONED MONTREAL, "THE CANADIans declared that the noblesse had no manner of authority over them, and that even their *seigneurs* had no right to command their military service. They acknowledged that they owed them respect, as their lords of the manor; but they insisted that when they had paid them their rents, and all their other just dues, together with certain compliments which were customary at different seasons, they owed them nothing further." When the colonials had first invaded Quebec Province months earlier, one of the tenants in the *seigneurie* around Pointe Levi refused to join the militia, to which Monsieur Taschereau responded by having him confined. It was not long before he thought better of his actions and released the man, but the incident reflected an increasingly desperate problem for the governor.[10]

The Quebec Act was at the root of Carleton's problems. Though it had pleased the French noblesse in the province—indeed, they had lobbied for it—most of the English settlers and virtually all of the Québécois—the "lower sort," as Carleton described them—found little good in the measure. English Canadians resented the leniency with which the act treated Catholicism and granted an undue political status to the French *seigneurs;* the French peasantry decried it as holding them under the domination of the same. Carleton had thus placated the French noblesse while alienating the masses. Now that the military support of the Québécois and the English settlers was essential to the salvation of British rule in the province, he found himself the victim of his own political success. Even when the Québécois agreed to participate in the defense of Montreal, when the danger was at its greatest, they did so only with a promise from Carleton, in person, that he would do his best to see the Quebec Act repealed. Writing to Lord Dartmouth, the British secretary for colonial affairs in London, just days earlier, Carleton blamed the loss of British outposts at Chambly and Saint Jean directly on "the corruption, and I may add by the stupid baseness, of the Canadian peasantry who not only deserted their duty but numbers of them have taken arms against the Crown."[11]

Though they had quietly begun to agitate against the new form of government in the province, the emergency created by Arnold's seizure of Ticonderoga the previous summer had left the Québécois in no position to assert their feelings individually. When Carleton declared martial law, it naturally became dangerous to speak out against the government, for even meetings on such a topic were illegal. Thus, the French people of the province were caught between the two opposing forces, colonial and British. Were they to take up arms under Carleton, they might win favor with him, but only while helping to sustain a form of government that they believed would raise taxes excessively, among other grievances. If, on the other hand, they fought alongside the colonials in an effort to rid themselves of the noblesse and perhaps win ownership of their property rather than tenancy, they would surely feel the wrath of both their governor and their *seigneurs*. If the colonials failed to end British rule in the province, the *habitants* who fought with them would surely lose their rights to the land that their families had worked for generations. So, while happily willing to provide food, guidance, and supplies to Arnold and his men, particularly when their *seigneur* was away defending the city, they stopped short of picking up their muskets and throwing in with the Americans, preferring to wait until their success was a more certain outcome. Occasionally, some would act more assertively in the colonials' favor, such as when the *habitants* in the village of Sainte Anne, below Quebec, threatened to shoot at those in a neighboring village if they answered the governor's call for troops, but throughout the province, a relative few actively engaged in fighting with the colonials against the British.[12]

This may have disappointed Arnold in his hopes of recruiting them, but it angered supporters of Carleton even more. One English Canadian expressed shock at the news that some of the Québécois had taken that risky step. "Indeed, would you believe it, the *French,* whom the government has done so much for, and relied so much upon, have taken up arms against us, several of whom are now prisoners amongst us."[13]

Informing the Crown's advisers back in England, Governor Carleton blamed much of his failure to defend the province on the Québécois. He would have succeeded, he wrote, "had not this wretched people been blind to honour, duty, and their own interest." As examples, the governor explained that great desertions had occurred among his recruits after a series of incidents involving Québécois resistance. *Habitants* at Berthier, near Montreal, had confined a *seigneur* named Lanaudière after he had raised seventy recruits who then scattered. Another *seigneur*, Rigouville, had gathered a force of 140 at Verchères when the *habitants* sent word to General Montgomery's troops. The colonials responded with a force of men who joined the villagers in attacking their loyal counterparts, capturing Rigouville and putting his soldiers to flight. Looking at the final stronghold he had left to defend, Carleton also lamented the state of affairs in Quebec City. "We have not one soldier in the town and the lower sort are not more loyal than here [Montreal]."[14]

The disposition of the Native Americans in the region was similarly muddled. In October, Carleton had summoned all of the area natives to his aid "except the Caghnawagas"; about sixty "savages," as Carleton described them, came into Montreal in the last week of the month. "I expect many more soon," he informed Lord Dartmouth in England, "but they are as easily dejected as the Canadian peasantry, and like them choose to be of the strongest side, so that when they are most wanted they vanish." The region from Sartigan to Montreal was the domain of the Saint Francis Indians and five other tribes, some of them remnants of the Norridgewock village on the Kennebec, and these had long fought against the British during the century of warfare with the French. With the defeat of their French allies at Quebec in 1759, the natives had largely settled into villages and mixed with their long-time trading partners, the Québécois. It was from these villages that Chief Swashan had taken some of his warriors down the Kennebec in August, contacted Reuben Colburn, and then offered his services to General Washington. The general then sent four of these Saint Francis natives with Arnold as guides and messengers, instructing the colonel to do all he could to convince the natives of Quebec Province of the good intentions of the colonials. This led to the aid and cooperation of the forty natives that Arnold recruited at Sartigan.[15]

With the fall of Saint Jean, the last major British outpost near Montreal, Carleton reported to England that nearly all of the province's "lower sort" had abandoned their governor. "The Indians who remained with me till this event have since taken their leave, the remains of the militia from the parishes deserted." Writing to the same superiors, Lieutenant Governor Cramahé had little better news about the "lower sort" in Quebec City. The Crown would get no aid from "Canadian peasants, whom neither the zealous exertions of the gentry, clergy or *bourgeoisie* could not prevail upon to do their duty, and for want of a force we could neither awe nor compel them to it." The failure of the Québécois to support the Crown's forces, Cramahé added, had already rendered Quebec Province a lost cause. "Two battalions in the spring might have saved the province," he wrote. But now "I doubt whether twenty would regain it." Those observing this cultural tug-of-war from within the walls of Quebec City agreed with Cramahé's bleak assessment, and began to see the question of loyalty among the lower sort as moot, one citizen commenting, "Now all of these considerations are at an end as we are likely to have new masters shortly."[16]

THE PRESUMPTIVE NEW MASTER TO WHICH HE REFERRED WAS AT THAT moment within view of the high rock cliffs upon which sat the sole remaining British holding in Canada. Every decision that Arnold made now was crucial. The desertion of Enos, the loss of provisions to the resurrection of the Dead River, the swamps of the Height of Land, disease, drowning, even falling trees—all had depleted his expedition to a force of barely 550 men at arms, to which he had added about four dozen natives and precious few Québécois. Now he learned with certainty that his messages to allies in Quebec had fallen into the hands of the lieutenant governor. Writing to warn General Montgomery of his circumstances, Arnold was apologetic, though not defeated. "I think you have great reason to be apprehensive for me, the time I mentioned to General *Washington* being so long since elapsed. I was not then apprised, or, indeed, apprehensive of one half the dif-

ficulties we had to encounter." He told the general that he had written
to General Schuyler weeks before, enclosing the letter within a note
to a friend in Quebec—John Mercier, who was now in irons—and
sending it by a native who claimed to have taken sick in the city. Having no answer from Mercier or Schuyler, "I make no doubt," Arnold
lamented, that the native messenger "has betrayed his trust." Before
he could send off this letter telling Montgomery of his position, word
came to him that two transports and a frigate—the *Lizard*—had arrived
in the basin, carrying 150 recruits from Newfoundland. The information concluded that there were now three hundred men to defend the
citadel, including those whom the lieutenant governor had compelled
to take up arms. Further, both the Québécois and the English settlers
were "on [the colonials'] side," and the city was already low on provisions.[17]

Along with this dispatch to Montgomery, Arnold enclosed a letter to
General Washington advising him of his current situation. In this he
was much more forceful about the settlers' idea of defending the city.
"Very few of whom have taken up arms," he wrote, "and those by com-
pulsion, who declare (except a few *English*) that they will lay them
down whenever attacked." Outlining his plans for the immediate future, Arnold also gave his commander a summary of the last of his
tribulations on the Chaudière, adding only a brief mention of Colonel
Enos and his division, "who I am surprised to hear, are all gone back."[18]

It is difficult to say what emotions Arnold masked while reporting
to his commander-in-chief, but he could at least take solace that, in
spite of all the obstacles, his dogged tenacity had brought him 320 tor-
tuous miles to within striking distance of the fortress city and the martial glory that had been his goal through these last two horrible
months. Reaching Pointe Levi, one of his men had written in his journal, "We now arrived before the city of Quebec, to take which by surprise was the great object of our expedition." Taking the city from the
British might still be a possibility, but Arnold now realized that doing
so by surprise was clearly a lost cause. Not only had the British gotten
hold of his messages, but Monsieur Taschereau, now among the defenders within Quebec's walls, certainly had lines of communication
with loyal *habitants* back in the villages on the Chaudière.[19]

On November 9, when Arnold had arrived at Pointe Levi and begun setting up camp around a gristmill on its banks, he began to gain better intelligence. He had been sending messages to John Halstead, a New Jersey native and the primary business partner of John Dyer Mercier. Halstead, who among his other endeavors was managing the mill, confirmed Arnold's suspicions that the lieutenant governor had arrested Mercier after intercepting two of the letters. Halstead and Mercier had just finished construction of a 130-foot wharf on the Quebec waterfront, below Cape Diamond, and had yet to complete the framework for a three-story warehouse on it, when Arnold's messages revealed their "Rebel" sympathies. When Mercier went into irons on board a British ship in the basin, Halstead fled downriver to Ile d'Orléans, where days later he heard of Arnold's approach. Having been out of the city for a time, he could provide no recent intelligence, but he confirmed the capture of the messages and British awareness of the expedition, which was useful to Arnold nonetheless.[20]

Most of the expedition had reached the Saint Lawrence, but groups of soldiers were still making their way northward from the villages. A Pennsylvania rifleman recalled, "They informed us that a number of musketmen, and some of the Riflemen had perished in the woods." Major Meigs met Captain Thayer at Saint Mary's with ninety-six invalids and money to purchase canoes from the Québécois or the natives. When he had bought twenty of them, he ordered Thayer to transport them to Pointe Levi to be used in crossing the Saint Lawrence. For some reason, he had the men carry the boats by land rather than paddling downstream with the current. With four men under each canoe, the group walked more than two dozen miles in two days to deliver their cargo. The bulk of the expedition waited for the stragglers and the sick to reach Pointe Levi, but as soon as enough of them were in place, the weather interfered with their plans to cross the Saint Lawrence—one more in a long line of setbacks and delays. A Connecticut soldier lamented that "all had arrived who were to be expected; many we learnt, to our great sorrow, had perished along the way."[21]

The day the bulk of Arnold's men reached Pointe Levi and began setting up camp near the gristmill, Captain McKenzie of the British sloop-of-war *Hunter,* then anchored in the river, had sent a boat ashore to collect oars and flour. As the boat reached the riverbank, some of

Morgan's riflemen opened fire, and the Brits at the oars began rowing madly for the safety of their ship. In the confusion, the sailors had failed to retrieve their captain's brother, fifteen-year-old Midshipman McKenzie, whose feet were both on the bank when the shooting began. In a rush to save himself, the young man dove into the river and swam toward safety. The riflemen on shore had little bragging to do at their campfire that evening, because the best their expert marksmanship could do was make a few holes in McKenzie's clothes, none in his person. Recognizing his plight, the midshipman had turned back toward shore so as to surrender when suddenly the native Sabatis leapt into the water after him, "scalping knife in hand, seemingly intending to end the strife at a single blow." One of the captains—it was either Morgan or Captain William Humphrey—saw the situation and reacted so swiftly that he reached the sailor just ahead of Sabbatus and thus saved his life. This disturbance alerted the sloop, which fired a few cannon shots toward the mill, doing no damage to the colonials. Back at Arnold's headquarters, McKenzie, "a genteel and well behaved young lad," would offer no useful intelligence. "He is strictly adhered to the old doctrine of war," noted one officer who was present, "never to discover their weakness." Though it had done them little good, and the young Brit was probably more of a burden then a trophy, the expedition had inflicted its first casualty on the defenses of Quebec—one teenaged midshipman captured.[22]

While he waited for his stragglers to arrive, and for conditions to align in favor of a crossing of the river, Arnold sent guards and sentinels up and down the riverbank, and also employed some of the local villagers to help make scaling ladders, spears, canoes, and hooks. With men still staggering in from the villages, Captains Topham and Thayer set out to add to the twenty canoes they had carried from the Chaudière. Rumors now held that the confusion within the city walls was very great, but Arnold could not rely on rumors when the lives of his men and the fate of Quebec hung in the balance. This same day, however, things were happening inside Quebec that began to sway the advantage toward the British.[23]

BEGINNING IN THE 1760S, TENS OF THOUSANDS OF PEOPLE FROM THE Scottish Highland regions fled their homeland as victims of the

Highland Clearances, when British landlords displaced tenant farmers to create grazing land for sheep. Many thousands of these Gaelic-speaking people immigrated to Canada and settled the northeastern portion of it, particularly in Nova Scotia and Prince Edward Island. When unrest became a concern in the colonies, General Thomas Gage, commander of British forces in North America, granted Allan MacLean, a fifty-year-old former British officer with extensive combat experience, permission to raise a regiment among these immigrants to be known as the Royal Highland Emigrants. With fifty shillings and a promise of bounty land as enticement, MacLean enlisted these volunteers from "such Highlanders or other such Loyal Subjects, as you may be able to procure," and commanded the regiment as a lieutenant colonel. On the door of a chapel at Pointe Levi, Colonel Arnold's men got a sense of MacLean's recruiting efforts when they found a "pompous proclamation to ensnare the ignorant." Dated August 3, it was a statement from MacLean on the "conditions to be given such soldiers as shall engage in the Royal Highland Emigrants." In it, he promised those who volunteered "to engage during the present troubles in America only" a bounty of two hundred acres of land anywhere in British North America, rent-free for twenty years; married men got an additional fifty acres for a wife and each child.[24]

Three months later, the enticements had yielded only small success. When the defense of the province from Montreal collapsed, Carleton sent MacLean to Sorel with sixty British regulars, the 120 remaining men of his emigrant regiment, and whatever Canadian militia he could raise. When the colonials approached Sorel with a larger force, the Canadians abandoned MacLean as well, forcing him to board ships with his small remaining force and flee downriver; on November 12, he reached Quebec City with the remnants of his regiment. This was apparently a great relief to the lieutenant governor, for, according to Henry Caldwell, an officer in the city, "Cramahé gave up his share of the command of it never making his appearance out of doors the whole winter." Shortly after his arrival, MacLean gave orders that every "Brittoner" in the city meet with him that evening and, with all the military efficiency he could summon from a city full of civilian defenders, began shoring up the military situation. Among MacLean's defensive improvements was the formation of a battalion of four hundred men, made up of sailors from the ships in the basin. Taking Captain John Hamilton up on his offer, MacLean converted all available seamen into a new "Marine Battalion" and put them to work clearing ditches, constructing barricades in the streets, mounting artillery on the walls, and engaging in any other activity that might prove useful in defending against the impending colonial attack. Despite all that contrived against it, the number of men accounted for as defenders of the city was steadily growing and becoming more prepared to resist an assault. How many of these men would fight, and how many would drop their arms to welcome the colonials, remained to be seen.[25]

MacLEAN BEGAN TO ORGANIZE A DEFENSE WITHIN THE WALLS JUST AS the colonials' expedition finally reassembled with nearly enough equipment at hand to cross the river. That afternoon, still unaware of MacLean's arrival, Arnold called a council of war at which he asked his officers whether they should cross and assault the city after dark that evening. Arnold, Greene, and the Rhode Islanders were in favor, since the British still had "no canon mounted, cartridges made, and even the Gates of the City open." But the same weather that was holding Carleton's fleet at Sorel made crossing the Saint Lawrence a risky chore, so, much to their consternation, the other officers voted against attacking, and the vote failed. Instead, the soldiers continued their preparations for another day.[26]

The following morning, one *habitant* came into camp with news that three armed ships upriver had seized one of the natives who carried Arnold's letters to Montgomery. The other, knowing the contents of the letter, managed to escape and continue toward Montreal. Shortly thereafter, a letter arrived from Colonel Easton at Sorel inquiring about Arnold's progress, thus confirming that news of Arnold's arrival at Pointe Levi had not yet reached the colonial forces to the west. That same morning, three vessels sailed out of the basin toward the Atlantic Ocean, indicating that Cramahé was sending articles and papers of value out of Quebec before the colonials could seize them. In the afternoon, more good news arrived from the west—two of the Saint Francis natives brought a letter from General Montgomery stating that he was on the verge of entering Montreal. As the expedition surgeon noted, "This gave us new spirits, being in hopes to have as good intelligence to communicate to the General." With his camp suddenly brimming with optimism and the weather slightly improved, Arnold assembled his officers for another council, and this time they agreed not only to cross the Saint Lawrence, but that evening, they would go and take Quebec at last.[27]

9

THE FORTRESS CITY

On Sunday, November 12, Colonel McLean, having reached the city, called a council of war, and those present—all officers—agreed that they would defend the city "to the last." Realizing that this would likely mean enduring a months-long siege until British troops could reach them from England when the Saint Lawrence thawed in May, they also agreed that Captain McKenzie's sloop *Hunter* and Captain Hamilton's frigate *Lizard* would winter at the docks, so that their crews and cannons could be put to service in the defense. MacLean wrote to his superiors in England the following week, lamenting the desperateness of his situation. Not only had the colonials captured both Governor Carleton and General Richard Prescott in Montreal, he wrote, "but what above all gives me the greatest uneasiness is that the very best train of artillery in Canada fell into the hands of the rebels at St. John. There is not a single piece of brass ordnance in the province that they have not got; and if they have got a ship that lay at Montreal with 2000 barrels of powder, which I am afraid is the case, we shall be undone."[1]

The roster of defenders within the walls of Quebec on November 13 totaled well over one thousand able-bodied men ready for duty, but, as MacLean knew well, "ready" hardly meant "willing." Both Thomas Ainslie, the collector of customs in the city, and another defender recorded these figures in their journals:[2]

Col. Maclean's Royal Emigrants & Capt. Owens' Fusiliers	200
British Militia	300
Canadian Militia	480

Crew of the sloop *Hunter* 24
Emigrant recruits from Newfoundland 90
Artificers from Newfoundland 32
                                                                    1126

Though this is double the number of men with whom Arnold was about to cross the Saint Lawrence, the total includes nearly five hundred Canadian militia of the sort that had abandoned Carleton and MacLean, and in whom the lieutenant governor had no faith. In fact, the possibility that these men would turn their arms in favor of the colonials was a very real concern, though Cramahé made no effort to expel them, "notwithstanding the repeated representations made to him to order them away." As for the more than six hundred remaining, one could hold considerable doubt as to the military ability of sailors, since many of them had been pressed into British service, or of artificers from another province. The Canadians, "very luke-warm" to the idea, agreed that they would defend the town if the English inhabitants did likewise, but the loyalty of any British militia, particularly in light of the impending assault by two colonial armies, was also questionable. Compounding the defenders' weakness was the need to protect every section of the city walls, whereas the colonials could concentrate their force at just one point. Fortunately for the defenders, the *Lizard* carried twenty thousand British pounds in cash, so that paying the troops, at least, was not a concern. After venturing within the walls, however, one of the officers on board the *Lizard* observed, "The inhabitants were in a state of despondency," fully certain that Arnold and his men would enter the city without any resistance, "for such was the consternation that the gates were not shut."[3]

ON THAT SAME SUNDAY, ARNOLD'S MEN MADE LADDERS AND RESTED from their march, while "the French fiddled and Danced all Day." The expedition's surveyor, Jonathan Pierce, marveled at the Québécois celebration, which apparently occurred every seven days. The Sabbath's events included playing cards, games, hunting, and sports. The Almighty may have prohibited work on Sunday, but celebration was apparently another matter altogether. That evening, they held a "fine ball" complete with "musik of Diverse Sorts Such as Bag Pipes fiddle fife German Flute and Some Vocal Musike."[4]

The following morning, while the Québécois recovered from their revelry and the colonials continued to prepare for the coming assault, Colonel Arnold paused long enough to draft a letter to General Washington to send with new copies of the intercepted messages. In it, he explained that the wind had delayed their crossing by three days but the moderating weather, along with news from Montgomery that he had captured Saint Jean and surrounded Montreal, gave his men all the impetus they would need. Though two British ships of war guarded the passage across the river, he said, he was certain he could slip past, and also noted that about fifteen merchant ships were frantically loading on cargo, day and night, and that four had already sailed. This was a sure sign that those who held valuable goods within the city had little confidence in its defenders and were transferring their property out of reach of the colonials.[5]

At seven o'clock, the men of the expedition gathered, as ordered, at the mill with their canoes and scaling ladders. The wind was not as Arnold wanted, and the night air was unusually cold, but this would have to do. With MacLean preparing the city for their arrival, time was more crucial than ever. They would cross the river, easing silently between the two British warships, and glide into the cove, where the British General James Wolfe and his men, on the same errand, had slipped undetected in 1759, finding the easiest slope on which to climb to the Plains of Abraham and seize Quebec from the French. When all were safely across—an ambitious concept in itself—Arnold's men would make use of their ladders to scale the walls and attack the city. Since they had gathered about three dozen canoes, each one would need to make three trips over and back in order to carry the entire expedition across. This meant multiplying the total number of crossings (each way) by five, and increasing the chance of discovery by the British scouts that were rowing along the riverbanks on barges searching for signs of a colonial movement. This process would give the enemy more than 175 chances to encounter a passing canoe and expose the assault in its most vulnerable state—scattered, waterborne, and in range of enemy naval cannons. If just one canoe drifted up- or downriver toward either the sloop or the frigate, the British could quickly wipe out all of the effort and suffering that Arnold and his men had endured these last two months. They would have survived the wilderness only to die a cold, watery death in the Saint Lawrence River.[6]

Working against the darkness, the current of a rapidly falling tide, and the need to remain undiscovered, the canoes slipped into the water and pushed for the northern bank, more than a mile distant. With Halstead as a pilot, Arnold and a few others slid through the gauntlet and eased the first canoe into Wolfe's Cove, ready to pounce on the British sentries as soon as it reached shore. The boat struck land undetected, and its passengers were amazed to find the cove completely unguarded—a huge stroke of luck, for they would not need to fire their weapons while the remaining canoes were still exposed on their first passage over. Given the distance across, the rest of the boats struck the bank of the river in many different locations, though all but one managed to make its way to Wolfe's Cove safely. That one exception was a heavily laden vessel whose birch belly finally gave out on its third crossing; soldiers in a nearby canoe managed to save the passengers from drowning by dragging them ashore, though without their rifles. In a house near the cove, the men built a large fire so as to warm themselves and dry their soggy clothing in the bitterly cold night. As it turned out, the crossing had been so successful that the British were completely unaware, having presumed that the removal of all of the boats from the southern shore would prevent it. As the colonials scrambled onto the banks and waited for their comrades, they could hear the British watchmen in the distance giving their "all's well." As a precaution, Arnold sent Captain Smith with a detachment of riflemen to scout out enemy movements, but these returned without seeing anything of danger.[7]

After the third passage of the canoe fleet, the weather again made the water dangerous, and Arnold decided he had better not press his luck. Ordering the 350 men around the cove up the hill to the plains, he ordered that the crossings stop for the evening, stranding nearly two hundred men, and all of the army's scaling ladders, at Pointe Levi under command of Captain Handchett. Though not complete, the crossing had been a surprising success. But just when all seemed to be going so startlingly well for the expedition, a British patrol barge from the sloop *Hunter* spotted the fire glowing onshore and rowed in near Wolfe's Cove to investigate. Hearing it approach, Arnold ordered the men to take cover behind a banking near the river.[8]

Dr. Senter believed that some of the riflemen had fired against orders; a Rhode Island officer said that Arnold and five others hailed the barge first, but, whatever the means of discovery, the colonials opened fire on the barge with some effect. Captain Thayer recalled that he "perceived by ye screaming and dismal lamentations of the crew that there were some of them killed or wounded." Those who survived the shooting rowed the barge quickly back into the river, away from the cove. Later, another boat approached, this one carrying a carpenter and four other unarmed men who were traveling upriver. A group of colonials under Lieutenant Webb quickly snatched them up and discovered that the men—one Swiss, the other Canadians—had come to retrieve some lumber for the British within the city walls. Webb took them to Arnold, where they helped verify other reports.[9]

Unlike the steep hill that had confronted General Wolfe's army sixteen years earlier, Arnold's men had the advantage of a fairly easy passage over a road cut diagonally into the side. When they had all reached the crest and gathered on the Plains of Abraham, site of the British conquest of the French in 1759, Arnold sent a scouting party to have a look at the city and posted a few guards in various directions. At this moment, a grave decision faced the colonial commander. He had intended when he left Pointe Levi to cross and attack the town, and the crossing had gone remarkably well as long as the weather allowed. But now that he was in position to carry out the assault he had so long planned, he was without the services of two hundred of his men, and the British were fully aware of his approach. Rather than forge ahead into such a risky situation without the full enthusiasm of his officers, the colonel, for whom a bold, aggressive course of action had brought so much success, suddenly became uncharacteristically cautious and decided to call another council of war.[10]

The soldiers of the expedition, who had endured such great adversity to reach the plains that lay below the walls of Quebec, had no idea how close they were to success. With the British alarmed by the shooting in Wolfe's Cove, Arnold's men, still completely unaware of the true state of the still-feeble defenses inside Quebec's walls, began to lose what little hope remained of taking their prize. One of them admitted, "The idea of storming the city was now inadmissible our plight being so bad, and the enemy's much better after the arrival of Colonel MacLean, the city gates were all closed, cannon in order, &c." It was in this state of mind that the officers gathered to meet their commander on the plain. With the city aware of their presence, more than a third of their men still at Pointe Levi, and dawn fast approaching, the officers present voted against attacking that night. One Pennsylvania rifleman recalled that the question of whether to attack "was decided in the negative by a majority, it is said of only one." Those voting against the assault surely cited the absence of the ten score men still at Pointe Levi with all the expedition's ladders, but the question of waiting for reinforcements may also have swayed the decision. George Morison recorded, "The idea of an attack was given up for the present, until we should receive some supplies from General Montgomery, whose arrival we shortly expected."[11]

The realization that they would need to wait for aid from Montgomery must have struck a cruel blow to the men of the expedition, who recognized its irony. They had suffered enormously in conquering the Maine wilderness and the swamps of Chaudière Pond and had reached the very outskirts of their goal. It was a great accomplishment, but the decision to wait for Montgomery made it all for naught. The strain, the physical exhaustion, sickness, starvation, nights of sleeping under the snow followed by long barefoot marches with their clothes frozen to their backs—all of it was now wasted misery. With Montgomery just a few days' march away, every man of the expedition now had to contemplate the fact that they could have avoided all their wretched struggles had they reached Quebec by the same route that the general had taken. A ride up Lake Champlain by boat, then an overland march through populated regions would have led them to an early victory at Montreal—their numbers supplementing Montgomery's—and a march to Quebec that would have been leisurely compared with the bateau-hauling death march they had endured. Had they gone with Montgomery, rather than as a second prong of the invasion of Canada, they would stand before the walls of Quebec today—sooner, more likely—with their numbers swelled by those who instead had gone back to Maine sick or died in the wilderness, and even by the scoundrels of Enos's divisions. Arnold's force alone would be some four or five hundred men stronger, and their presence would likely have reduced Montgomery's losses in the campaign thus far, making his army larger as well. Nevertheless, ultimate success was still a possibility, if barely.

Near dawn, after marching in place to keep warm while their officers debated a course of action, Arnold's men seized a manor house known as Sans Bruit, then under lease to Major Henry Caldwell, commander of the Canadian militia, who had just departed for the city. John Henry described the estate as "a great pile of wooden buildings, with numerous out-houses, which testified to the agricultural spirit and taste of the owner. He, good soul, was then snug in Quebec." Six months later, Caldwell wrote to the manor's true owner, former Quebec Governor General James Murray, that Arnold had marched "directly to Sans Bruit, where he surprised some of my servants, who were busy loading some of my carts and wagons for town. They got there before day, seized on all my working bullocks [oxen], about 20, and 4 or 5 fat ones [bulls], with all my horses; and there they lived on my beef and potatoes."[12]

The expedition's invasion was especially costly to Major Caldwell, because he also owned the mill at Pointe Levi where Arnold's men had encamped before crossing. Months prior, Caldwell had agreed to give John Halstead a share of the profits as payment for his management of the mill, but Halstead gave the flour and two hundred bushels of wheat to the invaders instead. Calling him a "great scoundrel," poor Caldwell added that Halstead "afterwards was appointed their commissary of provisions, and acted in that capacity till the siege or blockade . . . was raised."[13]

Arnold wrote again to Montgomery in order to keep him abreast of the changes. Informing the general that he had safely crossed the Saint Lawrence, Arnold passed on the optimistic intelligence he had gathered on the state of affairs within the walls. The people inside, he reported, were divided such that the inhabitants had laid down their arms and now refused to give food to the British soldiers, who were poorly provisioned and nearly ready to surrender. Their desperate circumstances explained a recent report that MacLean intended to march out shortly with a force of six hundred men and some cannons in an effort to defeat Arnold and thus avoid a siege through which the British could not hold out. Before he had time to dispatch the letter, an emergency distracted him.[14]

While John Henry was sleeping soundly on the floor of Major Caldwell's now ransacked parlor, a loud cry awoke him at noon with news that the enemy was advancing on the colonial camp. Henry and his comrades soon learned that it was not the rumored approach of Colonel MacLean but, rather, a small group of Redcoats who had ventured out and captured George Merchant, one of Morgan's riflemen, whom his captain, Mathias Ogden, had stationed in a thicket just out of sight of the walls. The problem with Merchant's post was that it likewise gave him no view of the walls, so that a British sergeant and a few privates were out of the gate and on him before he could even cock his rifle (or even awake from his slumber). Within a few days, Merchant was aboard a ship sailing for England, "probably as a finished specimen of the riflemen of the colonies."[15]

Inside the city, there was indeed some interest in marching out to meet Arnold's force with something more than a sergeant and a few privates and ending the contest before reinforcements could reach him from Montreal. Major Caldwell, in whose house Arnold was then lodging, "wished for it very much from the idea I had formed of their situation." Desire, however, was not enough to guarantee victory, and Colonel MacLean knew it. He had been in the city less than two days and had managed only to begin preparations for its defense. Circumstances were improving, but the cannons were not yet mounted and the militia was not yet organized. Though not present at the battle, MacLean had been in the British Army in America when his fellow soldiers paraded out onto the Plains of Abraham sixteen years earlier. On that day, much to their delight, they watched as the French army under General Montcalm marched out from behind the walls of their fortified city and onto the open plains to the west, where the British could more easily trounce them—and did just that. Shortly afterward, the French surrendered North America to the British by treaty. Thus, the sallying out of an army from Quebec had been the stroke that led to the loss of a continent by its previous occupants, and MacLean was not about to repeat his French predecessor's mistake.[16]

Just before the British snatched George Merchant from his hiding place, one of the gunboats in the river began firing on the men left at Wolfe's Cove to guard the expedition's canoes. Coupling the two events, the colonials believed the excitement signaled the approach of British troops coming out to give them battle, and they hastily responded. The colonials clamored to form up in their companies and virtually ran toward Quebec, only to discover that they were the only military force outside the walls. Disappointed that MacLean had not decided to remove these walls from between himself and their army, Arnold had his men drawn up in line of battle so as to challenge the defenders to come out and fight. They halted the line a few hundred yards from the city's western wall and waited, but neither saw nor heard any response from the British. Frustrated, the colonials tried insulting them out with cheers, giving three "Huzzahs" within earshot of the spectators. Some more time passed before the city's response finally came toward them in the form of several cannonballs fired from atop the walls. The colonials waited a short time longer, but, as a Connecticut soldier stated afterward, "We did not choose to stand and merely to be shot at"; instead, they returned disappointedly to their camp.[17]

Later that afternoon, the Americans captured a few cartloads of provisions bound for the city while the nervous British set fire to three houses just outside the Saint Louis Gate, closest to the enemy, along with a pair of blockhouses near the wall. It was difficult for the colonials to watch this "shocking scene," for it drove the inhabitants out of their homes and into the cold Canadian winter, and "we unable to assist them without running in the mouth of their cannon." The intervening hours gave Colonel Arnold ample time to ponder his circumstances and the fact that he did not have the men or ladders to mount an attack. Unwilling to sit idly by while nothing occurred, Arnold decided to test the resolve of those within the city. At sunset, he sent Captain Ogden toward the city with a flag of truce and a politely worded but straightforward note for the lieutenant governor.[18]

Hon. Hect. T. Cramahé,
Lt. Gov. of Quebec.
SIR—The unjust, cruel and tyrannical acts of a venal British parliament, tending to enslave the American Colonies, have obliged

them to appeal to God and the sword for redress. That Being in whose hands are all human events, has hitherto smiled on their virtuous efforts. And as every artifice has been used to make the innocent Canadians instruments of their cruelty, by instigating them against the Colonies, and oppressing them on their refusing to enforce every oppressive mandate; the American Congress, induced by motives of humanity, have at their request sent Gen. Schuyler into Canada for their relief. To co-operate with him, I am ordered by his excellency Gen. Washington to take possession of the town of Quebec. I do therefore, in the name of the United Colonies, demand immediate surrender of the town, fortifications, &c. of Quebec to the forces of the United Colonies under my command; forbidding you to injure any of the inhabitants of the town in their persons or property, as you will answer the same at your peril. On surrendering the town, the property of every individual shall be secured to him; but if I am obliged to carry the town by storm, you may expect every severity practised on such occasions: and the merchants who may now save their property will probably be involved in the general ruin.

I am sir, your most ob't h'ble serv't.

B. ARNOLD.

Observing the customs of war, Ogden took a drummer along on his delivery errand, and as the two crested a hill and came into view of the city walls, the drummer beat a parley while Ogden proceeded forward, waving his flag. When he was about 250 yards from the Saint John Gate, the defenders made their intentions clear by means of an eighteen-pound cannonball that belched forth from atop the walls. The "message" struck the ground so close to the two colonials that Ogden thought it had killed the drummer, though he had only fallen out of fright. Ogden later recalled, "We did not wait for a second [message] but retreated quick time till under cover of the hill." The following morning, to eliminate the possibility that there had been some misunderstanding, Arnold sent Ogden back to the city to make a second attempt to deliver the message. Unable to convince the previous drummer to accompany him, the major found a replacement. This time Ogden had the drummer halt and beat the parley while he advanced slowly and alone, waving his flag. It was not long before the defenders gave the same response as the day previous, the cannonball this time passing just over Ogden's head. He beat a hasty retreat backward and returned to the drummer, finding that his comrade had seen the cannoneers prepare to fire and shouted several warnings that the major had not heard. Ogden had been so focused on the cannon that had fired on him during his last attempt that he failed to notice the activity at another gun.[19]

Safely back at camp, the two heard that a *habitant* who had just left the town had brought word that, in addition to insulting Ogden while he observed the proper customs of war, the British had placed their colonial captive George Merchant in irons, making the expedition's inability to seize the town all the more frustrating. Infuriated by this news, Arnold wrote another message to Cramahé, this one expressing his disgust at the treatment given to Ogden and his message. "This is an insult," he charged, "I could not have expected from a private soldier; much more from an officer of your rank." As to Merchant, Arnold wrote, "I am informed you have put a prisoner taken from me, into irons. I desire to know the truth of this, and the manner in which he is treated." Adding weight to his demand, Arnold added, "As I have several prisoners taken from you, who now feed at my table, you may expect that they will be treated in the same manner in the future as you treat mine."[20]

This controversial issue of placing prisoners in irons dated back several weeks, to the captivity of Ethan Allen, head of the Green Mountain Boys, who had made up the greater part of Arnold's assault on Ticonderoga months before. In late September, while General Montgomery laid siege to Saint Jean, Allen made an ill-conceived attempt to seize Montreal with a relatively small force. For his efforts, the British captured him and sent him to Quebec, where Governor Carleton had him placed in irons aboard a ship in the basin. Word of this reached Montgomery back at Saint Jean, and he responded with a terse letter to Carleton revealing he had heard from numerous sources that the British treated colonial prisoners "with cruel and unnecessary severity, being loaded with irons, and that Colonel *Allen* himself meets with this shocking indignity." Reminding Carleton that he held prisoners of his own, he had threatened to reciprocate. "I shall, though with the most painful regret, execute with rigour the just and necessary law of retaliation upon the garrison of Chambly, now in my possession, and upon all other who may hereafter fall into my hands." Referring to Carleton as "one of the most respectable officers of the Crown," Montgomery nevertheless made clear the possible consequence of the governor's actions. Giving him six days to respond—and probably knowing full well he would not—Montgomery added that, if none was forthcoming, "I must interpret your silence as a declaration of barbarous war." Carleton forwarded Montgomery's letter to his superiors in England, explaining his treatment of the prisoners: "'Tis true the rebels have been in irons, not from choice but from necessity. We have neither the prisons to hold nor troops to guard them."[21]

In December, the issue was still on the minds of colonial leaders. George Washington wrote to General Schuyler at Ticonderoga about the treatment of Ethan Allen, directing the blame at British General Prescott. "From your letter and from General Montgomery's to you, I am led to think he was [poorly treated]." Knowing he addressed the commander-in-chief of all colonial forces in Canada, Washington made an ominous instruction. "If so, he is deserving of our particular Notice, and should experience some Marks of our Resentment for his cruelty to this Gentleman, and his Violation of the Rights of Humanity."[22]

THE DISCOURAGING STANDOFF between the colonials and defenders changed little over the next several days as the men of the expedition alternated between guard duty and rest among their Québécois hosts. Equally aware of the danger of spies and the instructions from Washington to treat the Canadians with care, a Rhode Island rifleman reported, "There are some lurking about Camp whom we suspect, But don't like to take them for fear of aggravating the minds of the People." Though they dreaded the thought of delaying the mission that had driven them for so long now, the wait at least gave the men a chance to bask in relative luxury. "In this delightful encampment we remained," recalled a Pennsylvania rifleman, "living in a sumptuous manner. The houses were close and warm; wood plenty; provisions of every kind in abundance." Though their surroundings had changed drastically from those on the far side of the river, the hospitality of their Québécois hosts did not. As one Pennsylvania rifleman recalled, "The Canadians were highly rejoiced at our arrival among them; they were constantly in our camp, and never failed to bring us a present of some eatables, such as potatoes, turnips, and such things. . . . Our camp furnished a pretty good market." Despite the relative luxury they now found themselves in, however, thoughts of their brush with death in the swamps were not far off. "Our tranquility was disturbed only when those unpleasant recollections of the Wilderness obtruded on our minds."[23]

The soldiers filled the days that followed Ogden's two failed attempts at delivering Arnold's ultimatum with various duties and anxious waiting for word from General Montgomery. The only departure from the daily sameness occurred when an occasional deserter from the city would arrive in camp with some tidbit of news. On their third day since crossing the river, a group of men from Smith's rifle company went in search of a group of cattle that was rumored to be beyond the Saint Charles River from Saint Roque's. As they approached the river near the convent, the defenders on the walls of the city began firing a cannon in their direction. One of their shots struck a sergeant from Lancaster County, Pennsylvania, named Dixon just below one of his knees. After cutting off his leg, the doctor advised the sergeant to drink tea, a product whose taxation had helped launch the sentiments that led to the war, and had, in the words of one of his comrades, "become an abomination" in the colonies. When a woman in the house where Dixon lay brought him a bowl of tea, he refused, saying, "No madam. It is the ruin of my country." The sergeant died the following morning "with great composure and resignation," becoming the first casualty of the expedition to die at the hands of the enemy. His comrades gave him a military burial.[24]

On November 18, two pieces of news forced Arnold to make a hasty and unpleasant decision. After a few days' respite, he received unwelcome news from someone claiming to be a deserter from inside Quebec City. Colonel MacLean, the messenger related, was aware of the weakness of the expedition and had organized his forces to an extent that he now planned to come out and attack Arnold, not only with infantry greater in numbers than the colonials could muster, but also with several pieces of artillery. Arnold had no way of knowing that this first piece of news was untrue and probably the work of a spy, so in response he ordered an inspection of his weapons and military stores. To his surprise, he found that at least one hundred of the guns would not fire, and much of the gunpowder the men had rolled into cartridges was no longer usable. In all, his soldiers had fewer than five rounds of ammunition per man. Capping the avalanche of adverse news, word arrived that a British ship under Captain Napier, carrying two hundred soldiers from Montreal, was nearing Quebec. Arnold knew that, with so few men of his own, he could not mount a formal siege by cutting off every approach to the town, and he respected the threat of an assault by MacLean; he called a council of his officers, who agreed that the men should be ready to march the following morning. The expedition would move up the river, out of MacLean's reach, and wait for reinforcements from Montgomery. Describing his retreat to the general, Arnold explained that the military problems made up only part of his motivation: "Add to this many of the men invalids and almost naked and wanting everything to make them comfortable."[25]

And so, during a brutally cold early morning, completely unaware of how weak the defenses of the city truly were, the men of the expedition made their first movement *away* from Quebec—most on the northern side, while a smaller group under Captain Handchett marched from Pointe Levi on the southern bank. This march must have brought on unpleasant memories of their wilderness trek. One Connecticut private recalled, "Most of the soldiers were in constant misery . . . as they were bare footed and the ground frozen and very uneven. We might have been tracked all the way by the blood from our shattered hoofs." As if timed to add to the feeling of disappointment among the departing colonials, an armed ship—a "snow" christened the *Fell*—moved into view from upriver, and all of the armed vessels in front of Quebec saluted with cannon fire. The demonstration made it clear to the colonials who watched that the salute was directed at a particular passenger on board. The only person in Quebec Province to whom such honors would be extended was Governor Carleton, who had safely reached the city along with his aide-de-camp and several other officers and men. The governor's safe arrival in the provincial capital had the opposite effect on those inside. As a government clerk within the walls described the event, "To the unspeakable joy of the friends of the Government, & to the utter dismay of the abettors of sedition and rebellion; Gen. Carleton arrived. . . . We saw our salvation in his presence."[26]

Despite all of MacLean's preparations and the temporary departure of Arnold's forces, Governor Carleton was convinced he could not save the city. The morning after his arrival, he wrote to the lord secretary in England, "We have so many enemies within and foolish people, dupes to those traitors, with the natural fear of men unused to war, I think our fate extremely doubtful to say nothing worse." This was an ironic message given that he had received upon his arrival the title of commander-in-chief of the Province of Quebec, a military rank to accompany his political standing. No sooner had he been made the highest-ranking military officer in the province than he informed his superiors of the miserable state of military affairs therein. Nevertheless, he told England that he was determined to hold out until spring again thawed the Saint Lawrence and allowed reinforcements to reach the city.[27]

THAT SAME DAY—November 20—with his men now encamped twenty miles upriver at Point aux Trembles, Arnold sent another dispatch to General Montgomery, explaining his new location and situation. He had found leather with which to make shoes for his men, but it was of such poor quality that they would not last long, especially in the midst of a Canadian winter. This, he reported, was "the only article of clothing to be had in this part of the country." The Québécois remained friendly and helpful, but none of them had the three hundred blankets, for example, that he now asked of Montgomery. Arnold also gave the general an assessment of the military situation at Quebec. His intelligence was very good: his estimate of 1,870 defenders was off by only seventy. Reckoning that it would take two thousand men to storm and capture the city, Arnold suggested that, in the meantime, Montgomery send five or six hundred troops if he could spare them, so that he could return to Quebec and resume the siege they had lifted the day before. Captain Ogden took the message toward Montreal with orders to send along all of the supplies, particularly powder and shot, that he encountered along the way.[28]

Along with his message to the general, Ogden carried another letter from Arnold, this one to two Montreal merchants—Prince and Haywood—asking that they bill Arnold's personal business account for any supplies that Ogden could not purchase with the money he carried, "which I will see duly paid." Shortly after Ogden's departure, a message reached Point aux Trembles from General Montgomery informing Arnold that he had, at last, taken Montreal and would move downriver to join the men of the expedition shortly. Four more days passed, however, before Montgomery wrote to General Washington expressing his regrets about the delay in pressing the invasion. "I am ashamed of staying here so long, and not getting to *Arnold's* assistance," he wrote, promising that he would sail the following day with "two or three hundred men, some mortars, and other artillery." The delay, Montgomery explained, was partly the result of his resignation from the army. Three days after Arnold retreated from Quebec, some of his officers began to complain loudly about the good treatment that the general had given to captured British officers, particularly in light of the treatment colonial prisoners were enduring in British hands. "Such an insult," Montgomery wrote Washington, "I could not bear, and immediately resigned." The following day, the disgruntled officers proffered an apology substantial enough that he could honorably resume command of his army.[29]

MONTGOMERY'S FAUX RESIGNATION WAS NOT THE ONLY PROBLEM among the officers of the Canadian invasion forces that confronted General Washington at this time. In a letter to John Hancock, President of the Continental Congress, he wrote, "Colonel Enos is arrived and under arrest. He acknowledges he had no Orders for coming away. His Trial cannot come on, until I hear from Col. Arnold." Washington had heard the news of Enos's actions when he received the letter Enos wrote from Brunswick, Maine, nearly three weeks earlier, but when he reached Cambridge and admitted to the general that he had, indeed, retreated from the Dead River without Arnold's knowledge, Washington must have been as angry as he was disappointed. On the same day, replying to a letter from General Schuyler, he wrote, "Colonel Enos, who had the Command of Arnold's rear Division is returned with the greater Part of his men, which must weaken him so much as to render him incapable of making a successful attack on Quebec." Writing to Arnold, he reported, "You could not be more surprised than I was at Enos's Return with the Division under his Command. I immediately put him under Arrest, and had him tried for quitting the Detachment without your Orders."[30]

Whatever Washington's feelings toward Enos, he would find it very difficult to hold him responsible for abandoning the expedition in the absence of any testimony from his commander, who was then shivering on the Saint Lawrence twenty miles from Quebec and not expected in Cambridge again soon. This was even more significant given that Enos's commission as a colonial officer was due to expire shortly. At first, there was some doubt whether Washington could have Enos tried at all, but he finally agreed to deliver the case to a court-martial, which would have to make the best of whatever information they could obtain. On December 1, General John Sullivan and eleven other officers convened a court-martial in Cambridge to consider the charge of "leaving his Commanding Officer without permission, or orders, and returning to Cambridge."[31]

The court heard testimony from Captains Williams, McCobb, and Scott, along with two lieutenants, Hide and Buckmaster, all of them officers in Enos's division. Knowing that the court would not hear from Arnold, these men apparently conspired to align their stories prior to testifying.

Williams, who had not been present at the decisive council on the Dead River at which Enos's officers decided to abandon the expedition, claimed to have given Major Bigelow a barrel of pork and seven of flour, though Bigelow returned to Greene's division with only two barrels of flour from all of Enos's companies.[32]

The next up was Samuel McCobb, who claimed he was present at a council on the Dead River at which "it was agreed that the whole division under Col. Enos should return," since there was not enough food to supply both his and Colonel Greene's men. His next statement was startling. Though he had been present at the council of war that included Greene and his officers, McCobb now claimed, "Greene's division being some way ahead, it was found that we could save two days' time by letting that division go forward." After thus testifying that Greene's men were a day's travel ahead of his own at that time, McCobb claimed that "we left them with about five days' provisions." The captain apparently never explained how he could leave such a generous donation yet still have it reach the men marching so far away.[33]

Those who followed testified in agreement with the previous statements. So convincing was their testimony that the presiding officer of

the court got the impression that Enos's companies had been so generous in sending provisions forward to other divisions that they had none
left for themselves. Each also added that Colonel Enos had determined to go forward, without his companies if necessary, but that the
disorganized state of the division and the addition of 150 invalids from
other divisions required the presence of a strong commander. Each of
these officers claimed to have contributed to a chorus that demanded
he remain with his men and return to the Kennebec, as they had decided. Enos's only crime, then, was that he acquiesced in the wishes of
his officers. Absent any testimony against Enos, the officers of the
court rendered their decision: "The Court after mature Consideration
of the Evidence, are unanimously of Opinion, that the prisoner was by
absolute necessity obliged to return with his division, and do therefore
acquit him with honor."[34]

Despite the lack of testimony from those who persevered through
the wilderness, soldiers in the army seemed to understand the situation better than the officers of the court-martial. Several months after
he was acquitted of the charges, twenty-five officers of the Continental
Army signed a notice titled "To the Impartial Publick." This lamented
the fact that Enos was "much censured by many persons, for returning
back from the expedition to *Canada* . . . by which Colonel Enos's character greatly suffers," and sought to rectify the situation by claiming
his actions on the Dead River were "justifiable, and conducted as an
understanding, prudent, faithful officer, and deserves applause rather
than censure." Though his peers in the officer corps may have acquitted him of the charge, this formal forgiveness did not dissipate the
cloud of dishonor that followed him well afterward. In May 1776, it
still hung so thickly over Enos that he was reduced to writing letters to
newspapers defending his reputation against ministers who referenced
his behavior in funeral orations as far away as Philadelphia.[35]

IO

SUFFERING AND WAITING

$\mathcal{P}$oint aux Trembles, today the town of Neuville, Quebec, was a riverside village centered, as were nearly all villages in Quebec, on a Catholic chapel. Years later, the survivors of the expedition would remember the welcoming Québécois, the frigid temperatures, and their almost complete lack of winter clothing. "We enjoyed as much comfort as tight houses, warm fires, and our scantiness of clothing would admit." Their quarters may have been comfortable while the soldiers remained inside, but various duties, from gathering wood and provisions to standing guard, kept the men out of doors much of the day, and sometimes portions of the night as well, often on a "two hours on, one hour off" schedule. The soldiers under Arnold were becoming reluctantly accustomed to their somewhat destitute state, eased only by the hospitality of their French hosts. Their stay at Point aux Trembles further diminished the anti-Catholic sentiment felt so strongly back in the largely Protestant colonies to the south. One rifleman remembered, "There was a spacious chapel, where the ceremonies of the Roman Catholic religion were performed with a pomp not seen in our churches, but by a fervency and zeal apparently very pious, which became a severe and additional stroke at early prejudices."[1]

Within twenty-four hours of their arrival at this village, Colonel Arnold received a message from General Montgomery that he was in full possession of Montreal and its shipping, and would join Arnold as soon as he could get organized to move. In the meantime, Montgomery ordered the expedition to await his arrival with reinforcements. The following day, ever mindful of the health of the men, the expedition doctor wrote, "Till now our army had been tolerably healthy since our arrival over the river, but free eating, more than the usually cold weather, &c., produced inflammations . . . some sever 'Peripneumias,' 'Anginas,' &c."[2] If eating too much was outpacing the weather in making them ill, than the men of the expedition were shoving food down their gullets at an alarming rate. Rhode Island Captain John Topham blamed the weather for most of their difficulties: "Our men are reduced to a most distressing Condition, destitute of cloathing shoes & Money, we are Obliged to do hard duty—They must inevitably perish if we cannot Get necessaries for them to screen them from the inclemency of the weater [sic] which begins to be worse still."[3]

Extreme cold had become a regular visitor to the region, especially at night, when the surface of the river froze over. Some of the captains had set men to work making moccasins out of the poor-quality leather they had acquired. Despite all of this difficulty, Captain Simeon Thayer maintained whatever optimism he could muster. "Recruiting fast, and am willing to think, if once cloth'd and refresh'd a little, would be as eager as ever, tho many having their constitutions Racked, are in such a condition as to be capable of enduring half what they have done hitherto." Unlike the Québécois on the Chaudière, significant numbers of French villagers were now coming into camp to volunteer. Colonel Arnold welcomed them as long as they "promised to be obedient faithful soldiers and to be under his Command During the Continuation of the war." The victory of the colonials over British forces at Saint Jean and Chambly, followed by Carleton's swift abandonment of Montreal, was having an encouraging effect.[4]

On November 22, another message arrived from Montgomery. In this one, he reported that he had taken thirteen vessels and a large amount of clothing and supplies at Montreal and was loading provisions, three or four companies of Canadians, and about fifteen hundred Americans onto two small schooners bound for Point aux Trembles. The following day brought another message. Montgomery was on the march for Quebec and had sent ahead clothing, including enough coats, blankets, stockings, mittens, shoes, and caps for each of Arnold's men, along with a large sum of money, flour, pork, cannons, and ammunition. The news that the general would arrive in ten days with all of these spoils of war greatly lifted the sorely tried spirits of Arnold's colonials. Knowing now how long he had to wait for Montgomery, Arnold took time tending to less urgent matters. Among them, he called a council of war at which he appointed a committee of officers to look into the actions of Colonel Enos back on the Dead River.[5]

While they waited at the village, a few reminders of their days in the swamps reached the men in camp in the form of two soldiers they had given up for dead. One was a private named Morse from Captain Jonas Hubbard's company of Massachusetts musketmen. Morse reported seeing eight or ten men starved or starving to death back on the Chaudière and two unburied corpses. In addition, two men from Topham's Rhode Island company—from the division of Colonel Greene, which had suffered the worst in the swamps—along with five riflemen had survived a week in the wilderness this side of the Height of Land, with only roots and birch bark for nourishment. The two Rhode Island men, a private named Burdeen and another named Onely Hart, though sick and left behind by their company, stayed together for six days, wading through rivers and swamps while urging each other on toward the settlements. Soon they discovered the five riflemen, who joined them. On the sixth day, Hart became afflicted with cramps that "continued on him five days when By the violence of the disorder was drawn Out of all manner of shape and died." Burdeen and the others continued on and soon encountered the rotting body of a member of Hendricks's rifle company along the path. The following day, the group had the amazing good luck to encounter a horse that had escaped from one of the Québécois relief parties, days earlier. It took six gunshots to kill the animal, but the resulting meat provided several days' sustenance for the wayward band. During his odyssey, Burdeen claimed to have seen the dead bodies of twelve of his comrades, including Private Warner and his unusually loyal wife, whom he presumed dead as well. Six weeks after Mrs. Warner reluctantly parted with her husband's corpse, however, she reached the expedition's camp, having survived on her own for a time, but successfully reached Quebec, a task in which dozens of her male counterparts failed.[6]

Women were also playing a key role for the colonials in intelligence-gathering, daily smuggling letters out of Quebec and carrying them to the troops at Point aux Trembles. From these, Arnold learned that the defenders had unloaded all of the cannons from the largest ship of war in the basin and were loading two more vessels with valuables, one bound for Boston, the other for London. The letters also brought intelligence from farther away, including news of the burning of Falmouth (now Portland) two months earlier, and that the army at Cambridge had not engaged in battle since they departed.[7]

WITH THE EXPEDITION almost barefoot, Arnold hired all of the shoemakers in the vicinity to make moccasins from a shipment of poor leather the expedition had taken from some Tories. Though this leather was bad and only half tanned, it put something between their feet and the snow-covered ground.[8] Each of these small elements of relief was important to the expedition, for conditions and morale had both deteriorated significantly. One afternoon, two of the volunteers in Morgan's Virginia rifle company walked out of camp at Point aux Trembles toward Montreal, the first leg of their journey home from the war as their period of enlistment expired. Their departure reflected a growing mood among the soldiers that they had done enough. Grumblings among some of the men from New England revealed their intention to return home when their allotted time expired, whether they had taken Quebec or not. During the last few days of November, the issue came to the fore when Arnold placed a private from Captain Hubbard's company, John Dealy, under arrest after he threatened to desert and go into the city.[9]

The expedition surveyor, John Pierce, seemed to be the leading grumbler, making a number of entries in his journal on the subject. Initially, Pierce recorded certain events such as "The men Continue to make Great Complaints with respect to provisions," and "Several Capt and other officers have Possitively Declared that they will go home as Soon as their times are out." In time, however, Pierce became more pointed. "Yesterday a Certain Great Commander [meaning Arnold] was so imprudent and Lost to a Sense of his Duty that none of the army had their allowance till 8 o'clock at night which Should have been drawn at 8 in the morning—the Citizens Declare that they never will Surrender to a Horse Jockey. . . . Many minds Seem to be filled with great Doubts with respect to a Certain man." The disgruntled surveyor claimed that a strong guard had been posted thirty miles above Point aux Trembles and another at Montreal to discourage deserters, and that a large number of the men in Hubbard's company spoke of their intention to march for home a few days later. According to Pierce, Captain Goodrich's company did the same and Handchett's men went so far as to pack up and march into formation before "the General and field officers Purswayed them to Stay till February."[10]

With morale deteriorating, Arnold called another council of his officers, this one to discuss rations. When it was over, the colonel ordered that each man receive a daily ration of one and a quarter pounds of both beef and flour. After this meeting, according to someone in Captain Smith's company, "Altercation and warm language took place. Smith, with his usual loquacity, told us that Morgan seemed at one time on the point of striking Arnold."[11]

IN THE EVENING, Arnold sent a message to any colonial officers on their way from Montreal advising Montgomery of a mistake in reporting that the crews of the two armed ships at Quebec had offloaded all of the cannons. Instead, these vessels and two more were on the move upriver toward Montreal to, Arnold surmised, intercept any troops from Montgomery's force that might be moving by river. The following morning, Arnold wrote again warning of the movement of four ships (two large, two small) upriver as the tide and wind allowed. These spent the night under the watchful eye of the colonials at Point aux Trembles.[12]

Six days after marching to the village, there was still no sign of relief from Montgomery. To be certain this message got through safely, Arnold sent John Halstead to carry it to the general directly. Trying to keep a brave face on the expedition's deteriorating condition, he wrote, "My detachment are as ready, as naked men can be, to march wherever they may be required, but are yet in want of powder, ball, &c. and some arms." He added that the defenders in Quebec were still busy preparing for an assault or siege but seemed less than optimistic, since they were also preparing several more ships to evacuate valuable possessions from the province. Writing to update General Schuyler on his circumstances, Arnold explained, "I am waiting with great anxiety the arrival of Gen. Montgomery, when I expect we shall knock up a dust with the garrison at Quebec, who are already panic struck." He added,

"My brave men were in want of every thing but stout hearts, and would have gladly met the enemy" had they had ammunition and succeeded in drawing them out for a fight.[13]

The next morning, the four British warships from Quebec weighed anchor near Point aux Trembles and sailed upriver about nine miles before one of them ran aground, damaging its hull. The same day, the expedition received news that the ships carrying cannons from General Montgomery had landed upriver, so a party of one hundred men went to help move them. The owners of several merchant ships based in Quebec came to meet with Arnold and brought a copy of a proclamation issued by Governor Carleton. The governor had begun to threaten retribution against any of the "lower sort" who cooperated with the colonials. Among other concerns, French inhabitants sent word to Arnold asking for help in preventing the British from burning and plundering their homes. In response to Carleton's active threats, the colonel sent Captain Morgan and his company back to the outskirts of Quebec to blockade the road leading out of the city toward the expedition. Later, another rumor reached camp that General Montgomery had landed with cannons and ammunition at Saint Anne's, thirty miles upriver, so Arnold sent sixty men to escort him and help with the cannons. After marching most of the thirty miles, the party reached the arms, but the general was not with them.[14]

News also reached camp that Major Caldwell had burned Sans Bruit, the cozy accommodations used by the colonials in the suburbs of Quebec, "in order that we might not have the satisfaction to quarter in it, as we had done before." A Rhode Island officer described this act as "a poor malice tending to his own disadvantage," but it meant that when the expedition returned to Quebec the men would have to sleep in someone else's parlor. The following morning, Morgan's men captured Joshua Wolf, Caldwell's clerk, trying to save whatever he could from the ruins. He confirmed that Caldwell had torched his own home, but the major had a different tale to tell its owner. Though he did not plainly state who had lit the fire, instead writing vaguely on the matter—"Those plunderers came to disturb me" and "The burning of my house . . ."—Caldwell lamented the loss of the home in a letter to his landlord, former Governor Murray, hoping the British government would "take compassion on a poor ruined farmer."[15]

By November 28, the weather had grown colder and the patience of everyone in the expedition was growing shorter. Desperate for relief from Montgomery, Arnold himself went twelve miles upriver to the town of Jacques-Cartier hoping to meet with supplies, clothing, or ammunition coming toward Point aux Trembles. He also returned disappointed. The next day, a foot of snow fell, and the four patrolling British warships returned to Quebec to avoid being frozen into the river for the season. When another group of men that had gone toward Montgomery for supplies returned with Captain Jeremiah Duggan (a former hairdresser in Quebec City), some Québécois, and ammunition, Arnold wrote again to the general, sending Aaron Burr with news that the British ships had returned to Quebec and the river was now safe, hoping this would speed his travel.[16]

At long last, around midday on December 1, four ships arrived from Montreal with General Montgomery and "the York forces" on board. Though this force consisted of only three hundred men, they brought with them artillery, provisions, ammunition, and clothing. On first coming into the general's presence, Captain Thayer took a rather thorough measure of him. "He is a genteel appearing man, tall and slender of make, bald on the Top of his head, resolute and mild, of an agreeable temper, and a virtuous General." When the men of the expedition turned out in order and marched to greet the general formally, he "complimented us on the goodness of our appearance." Given the state of Arnold's men at that time, Montgomery either greeted the men in the dark, without his spectacles, or he made this comment with his tongue planted firmly in his colonial cheek. As one of the officers who appeared before him described the crew, "Were the Cambridge officers to review our men at present, they certainly would sooner prefer the Hospital for them than the field." In front of the village chapel, Montgomery gave the troops "a short but energetic and elegant speech," in which he promised clothing, congratulated the men for their spirit in surviving the wilderness, and expressed a hope that this determination would continue.[17]

In 1775, thirty-seven-year-old General Richard Montgomery somewhat reluctantly found himself in control of an army in a foreign land. A career British officer and son of a member of the British Parliament, he developed a pessimism about the potential opportunities in a peacetime

British army that drove him to immigrate to King's Bridge, New York, in 1772. There he married the daughter of Robert Livingston, a judge and prominent landowner in the region. Within three years of his arrival in the colonies, his name was entered, unbeknownst to him, as a candidate for the New York Provincial Congress. He served in this post out of a feeling of duty to his adopted homeland, and in June 1775 found himself appointed a brigadier general under similar circumstances. When General Schuyler became ill during the invasion, Montgomery was given field command of all the colonial forces in Canada. He succeeded admirably at Saint Jean and Montreal despite the condition of his untrained volunteer force, from which men fled as soon as their short-term enlistments expired—sometimes sooner. Despite his apparent lack of initial enthusiasm for his role, his appearance and manner impressed the men of the expedition. "General Montgomery was born to command," wrote a Pennsylvania rifleman soon after the general reached Point aux Trembles. "His easy and affable condescension to both officers and men, while it forbids an improper familiarity, creates love and esteem; and exhibits him the gentleman and the soldier. He is tall and very well made; and possesses a captivating address. He is a native of Ireland. His recent successes give us the highest confidence in him."[18]

Furthering his reputation among Arnold's men, Montgomery distributed a coat, blanket, vest, and other supplies to each soldier in the expedition, none of whom seemed to mind that many were British Army uniforms. Most of the soldiers now wore new shoddy moccasins stuffed with hay or leaves to keep out the cold. These all became immediately useful, for snow had again begun to fall overnight and continued into the day. With the armed vessels from Montreal finally nearby, the men spent the balance of the day offloading cannons from them, carrying those they could to their encampment, and preparing them for transport to Quebec. They loaded the larger pieces of artillery into bateaux, and Arnold ordered Captain Handchett to take them by water to Quebec. Aware of the recent movement of British vessels up and down the river, and as one of the growing group of disgruntled officers in the expedition, Handchett refused, sending Arnold into a rage. On the march through the wilderness, Arnold had depended on Handchett to lead the advance party to the Québécois villages on the

Chaudière, but because of the poor condition of the expedition, and Arnold's decision to leave his company behind at Pointe Levi when the others crossed, Handchett's opinion of his commander had apparently soured. Swearing he would arrest Handchett, the colonel sent for Captains Topham and Thayer, to whom he said he would consider it a favor if one of them would take on the duty. When both agreed, Arnold flipped a coin that landed in Thayer's favor, "equally to my satisfaction," Thayer remembered, "and vexation of Capt. Topham, who was always ready to Encounter the greatest dangers." Thayer and his crew had to cut through ice for a quarter-mile to reach open water, and then rowed eighteen miles to the suburbs of Quebec. As Thayer recalled, the exertion had its benefits, the night "being so cold we strove with Eagerness to Row, in order to keep ourselves from being frozen with cold."[19]

Before they had covered the distance to Quebec, more snow began to fall, and in the storm the boats got separated. Thayer ordered some of the men to fire a gun so that the other boats could see the flash from the muzzle. With great difficulty, the boats regrouped, and the heavily laden, frozen bateaux headed toward shore, only to run aground on some rocks. Too cold to wait for the boats to work free, some of the men jumped into the river and waded to shore, up to their armpits in the icy water. Once onshore, these men managed to find some horses, which they brought back to the riverbank and put to use hauling the bateaux ashore. After the boat crews had landed the cargo in the suburbs, they tried to pass over to Pointe Levi to retrieve the scaling ladders left behind the night of the crossing, now two weeks past. Ice on the river, however, thwarted their efforts. That night, back at Point aux Trembles, Josiah Carr of Ward's Rhode Island company succumbed to the misery and sickness. The following afternoon, the company held a funeral and, after the chaplain had his say, carried Carr two miles to a local cemetery where the inhabitants had granted permission to bury him.[20]

On December 4, three days after Montgomery's arrival, fifteen after the expedition's retreat from Quebec, and nearly three weeks after crossing from Pointe Levi, the combined forces of Arnold and Montgomery began the march back toward Quebec. Henry Dearborn's company set off at noon, and had traveled as far as the village of Saint

Augustine when they halted for the night. Still fascinated by the habits of these Catholic people, Major Meigs and some other officers joined the parish curate, Michael Barriault, for dinner, and were entertained "with hospitality and elegance."[21]

THOSE WITHIN THE CITY TO WHICH THE COLONIALS AGAIN MARCHED continued preparations to receive them. Colonel MacLean and Captain John Hamilton of the frigate Lizard ordered the four hundred sailors from three British warships—the frigate Lizard, the sloop Hunter, and the schooner Magdalena—to leave their ships and join the defenses, forming them into nine companies under the command of Captains Hamilton (as colonel) and MacKenzie (as major). Since these men had experience with their ships' cannons, they took over the artillery on the city walls. This brought the total number of defenders to eighteen hundred, not quite seven hundred more than had been available the night Arnold crossed the Saint Lawrence, and though half of the defending force consisted of the unreliable "lower sort," the expedition's delay in attacking had allowed both Colonel MacLean and Governor Carleton to re-enter the city and help fortify its defenses.[22]

Despite the superiority in numbers and the aid of a high stone wall between him and the colonials, Governor Carleton was anything but optimistic. He now had an ample force with which to defend Quebec against the colonials and more than enough arms and ammunition, but the question whether or not the defenders would actually fight kept the fate of the city in serious doubt, and the governor began to address this problem. Upon his arrival, Carleton discovered that many in the town refused to join the militia in its defense, others had joined and then refused to fight, and still more were "busy in endeavoring to draw away and alienate the affections of His Majesty's good and faithful subjects." Three days after he reached the city, he issued a proclamation ordering any man eligible for service in the militia but unwilling to bear arms to leave the city within four days, and the Province of Quebec before December 1. This order may have purged some of the less reliable people from the city, but it also proved of service to the colonials. After news of the proclamation reached the expedition's camp, Dr. Isaac Senter noted, "In Consequence of this order, several came out to our army."[23]

The day after Montgomery finally reached Point aux Trembles, Carleton expelled a man from the city "for having industriously made many disheartening speeches concerning the strength of the rebels, & for propagating ridiculous stories to intimidate the country people who will swallow the most absurd things when their fears are awaken'd." Among these tales was a notion circulating among citizens within the walls that the soldiers of the expedition wore suits of metal armor that rendered them musket-proof. This strange belief stemmed from the fact that many of Arnold's men wore a sort of linen frock, which in French is described as *vêtu en toile* (clothed in linen). Somehow in the retelling *toile* (linen) became *tôle* (iron sheet or boiler plate), with the result, as one defender reported, that "the country people absolutely believ'd that Arnolds party were cast in sheet iron." Another peasant alerted the authorities to the approach of a fleet in the river carrying an army of seven thousand Russians! They responded to this by placing the alarmist in prison "until they arrive." Other reports, though more believable, also clearly misled the inhabitants, such as the one claiming that Montgomery led an army of forty-five hundred soldiers with many cannons. One truth was that the former Irish hairdresser Jeremiah Duggan led a group of Canadian militia organized at Chambly, though both the size of his unit and his rank were exaggerated. On hearing that someone practiced in the art of coiffure was somehow qualified to be a military officer, one defender commented to his journal, "If the rebels General gives commissions to such men his army will not be formidable." About Duggan, however, he would prove to be mistaken. When Duggan marched his troops into the suburb of Saint Roque's, the French militia stationed there laid down their arms rather than alarm the city or fight against fellow Québécois—even those led by an Irishman.[24]

ON DECEMBER 5, THE COLONIALS RETURNED TO THE OUTSKIRTS OF Quebec, and Colonel Arnold wrote to General Washington with an update on his circumstances. In this letter, he enclosed a return of the expedition that showed that it now totaled 675 men. One Pennsylvania private, however, painted a less favorable picture of the circumstances in his journal. "Our whole force," he wrote, including the three hundred reinforcements from Montgomery, "amounting only to 800; and 70 of those unfit for duty."[25] This meant Arnold's men totalled just 500.

When Colonel Arnold set about placing companies of men in vary-ing locations to seal off the city from the countryside, he again ran afoul of Connecticut Captain Handchett. Choosing three companies to march forward within a half-mile of the city walls, Arnold selected Handchett's unit among them. Still smarting from Arnold's rebuke over the transportation of the heavy cannon by bateaux, Handchett again refused the order, citing it as too dangerous. Not surprisingly, Arnold reacted in the same manner as at their last confrontation, sum-moning Captains Topham and Thayer, who again agreed to go in Hand-chett's stead, along with another company under Captain Hurlbert. As it turned out, Handchett was right about the danger, at least. For the following three weeks, these companies remained exposed to cannon fire from the city walls. On one occasion, the shelling woke Topham and Thayer in their quarters just moments before a ball passed be-tween them, striking the bed from which they had just risen before it crashed out the other side of the room.[26]

In order to cut off any communication with the city from the east, Arnold and Montgomery sent two companies to the village of Beauport on the opposite side of the Saint Charles River. With Captain Henry Dearborn still recovering among the Québécois on the Chaudière and his men convinced he was dead, his company marched to a building that housed both a general hospital and a convent. Here they set up their quarters, and here Dearborn found them three days later. In this same hospital, Dr. Senter set up his medical practice, since it con-tained a ward of fifty beds and was unusually well fitted to the doc-tor's needs—with one troubling exception. The hospital was within a half-mile of the city walls at St. Roque's Gate, so Senter took up resi-dence at a more comfortable distance, choosing to walk to the hospi-tal. "I was obliged to visit it daily in open view of the enemy's walls," he recalled, "who seldom failed to give me a few shots every time." Fortunately for the doctor and his patients, the cannoneer's aim was poor.[27]

While some of the colonials set up five mortars in the suburb of Saint Roque's and began lobbing shells over the city walls, others be-gan setting up a large battery on the Plains of Abraham, a half-mile from the Saint John Gate, a project that took one hundred men five nights to complete. Before the cannons could be mounted and put

into service, a solid wall had to be constructed around each placement
to protect the men operating the gun. To provide this protection, soldiers and some volunteers from the suburbs had been at work making
what are called *fascines* or *gabions*. These were hollow columns or tall,
bottomless baskets made up of woven sticks that, when completed,
served as a framework for the solid material inside. Earth and gravel
usually made up the inner mass of these creations, though the colonials could scratch precious little earth from the frozen landscape
around them. Instead, they packed layers of snow down inside each,
adding straw for strength, and then poured water on each layer, letting
nature take its course in freezing the whole into a solid mass capable
of withstanding a direct hit from all but the largest British cannonballs. The task of constructing the battery was not only a cold one but
dangerous as well. Several of the builders suffered frostbite, and on
one day alone ten were killed by British cannon fire.[28]

By December 10, with the siege now fully enforced, the defenders
began to make use of some of their plentiful ammunition stores, launching a heavy cannonade toward the enemy throughout the day. At night,
the colonials joined in the bombardment, but despite all of the flying
lead, no one on either side was hurt except an old Canadian woman
who was torn apart by a twenty-four-pound British cannonball. Fearing the colonials would make use of some of the houses near the Saint
John Gate, some defenders ran out through the gate under cover of the
bombardment and set fire to them. In addition to rendering many inhabitants homeless in the dead of winter, the fires incinerated a sick
woman who was unable to flee her home. For the next several days,
each side kept up a fairly continuous fire on the other; one colonial
counted 357 rounds coming from the city in a single day.[29]

With a regular bombardment passing in both directions, the leaders
of each side set about gathering all of the information that they could
about their enemy. One officer inside the walls noted, "There are spies
sent out of Quebec every day, and some taken almost every day, both
men and women." To be sure, the defenders returned the favor as often
as they could, sending their own spies out while the colonials sent messages in by human courier or other means. At one point, the natives
even took part in the propaganda war, as one defender recalled: "This
morning they threw some Letters into the Garrison fixed upon wood

Arrows. They were written in French reflecting upon General Carleton for putting their prison[er]s in Irons and extremely insolent." Still, the most commonly used means of communication were innocent-looking women. A few days after returning to the suburbs of Quebec, the colonials sent a female courier in with letters to some of the key merchants, promising pardon if they were to aid, rather than oppose, the reduction of the city. The same woman carried a message to General Carleton demanding he surrender the city. Carleton simply dismissed the demand and had the woman imprisoned for a brief period before expelling her from within the walls.[30]

Soldiers deserting to one side or the other also carried important information to their new masters. One of these, an Irishman who had previously been a British soldier and was thus familiar with Quebec City, informed his comrades that it would be no easy task to get over those walls. An officer within hearing range immediately chastised him: "You rascal! Do you mean to dishearten the men?" This was apparently enough of a blow to his honor that he soon after made for the walls and gave himself up to the British as a deserter. Naturally, he then explained to the defenders that he "had long intended to join us, as he cou'd not think of drawing his sword against his countrymen. . . . No Gentleman he says wou'd be led by such Officers—they are the greatest part low Mechanics, especially those from New England." This sort of fickleness with which soldiers on both sides treated their commitment to the respective causes, helps explain why Arnold and Montgomery regularly resorted to councils of war before making major decisions, rather than just ordering their men to carry out their will.[31]

Seeking shelter in homes to the north and west of the city walls, many colonials began to develop one or more of the various forms of illness now circulating among them. "The small pox is all around us," wrote a private in Ward's rifle company with alarm, "and there is great danger of its spreading in the army." The discovery of the microscopic organisms that spread disease was still roughly a century away, but even in 1775, one did not have to be Louis Pasteur to realize that people who stayed in close proximity to someone with smallpox most often found themselves suffering from the same affliction in short order. Aware of this, the victims were moved from among their comrades to a separate hospital set up for them, or to houses in the countryside. This horrible disease killed about one-third of its victims, caused a third of all reported cases of blindness, and left deep, pitted scars on most of its victims, as it had with General Montgomery.

The viral infection that had plagued humankind for thousands of years was transmitted from one person to another by face-to-face contact, or by way of bodily fluids left on clothing or bedding. With an incubation period of about two weeks, determining the source of one's infection was impossible. In the third week, high fever and body aches set in, often rendering the victim unable to walk or move about. In a few days, small red spots in the mouth progressed into a rash that covered the body, while the fever often abated. Three days afterward, just when a feeling of recuperation set in, the rash progressed into bumps on the skin, which then filled with fluid. The fever returned and remained for two weeks, while the bumps turned to scabs that eventually fell away. A victim was contagious with the first sign of symptoms, and the contagion reached a peak in the next twenty-four hours but remained until the last of the scabs fell off, weeks after the symptoms first appeared. Despite centuries of experience with the malady, science had developed no cure or even treatment for it, so that it became a dark, mysterious force shrouded in fear and dread. An eighteenth-century French scientist lamented, "No man dared count his children as his own until they had had the disease." Just over two centuries after the expedition, the World Health Organization declared the disease eradicated, but even then medical science had developed no treatment for the infection, other than to try to alleviate a few of the symptoms until the patient recovered. Nearly a quarter-century after the expedition's march through the wilderness, British doctor Edward Jenner used cowpox, a milder relative of the disease, in developing a vaccination against smallpox, the first reliable inoculation used widely by medical science.

Some of the colonials suspected that the British had intentionally set the disease loose among them, but others used it to some advantage. "Great numbers of the soldiers inoculated themselves for this disease," recalled a Pennsylvania private, "by laceration under the finger nails by means of pins or needles, either to obtain an avoidance of duty, or to get over that horrible disease in an easy speedy way." Though it was certainly the most feared, this was not the sole cause of illness among the expedition. In addition to the smallpox, a number of respiratory problems now forced more and more men to the hospital, and Dr. Senter reported that pneumonia, pleurisy, and all manner of lung ailments became prevalent in the army.[32]

Though the smallpox was a concern for the defenders as well, conditions for the soldiers inside the city were far more agreeable, not only because of the abundance of weapons, gunpowder, and ammunition, but also thanks to the warm, snug homes in which the defenders slept while a cast of civilians helped maintain the walkways and roads with relative safety. Outside the walls, however, the danger of well-aimed cannon fire was ever-present, and movements were hindered not just by the long-building fatigue and poor health of the colonials, but also by the footing. As one Pennsylvanian described it, "The snow lay three feet deep over the face of the whole country, and there was an addition to it almost daily."[33]

From their view on the high walls, the defenders could pick their targets, and this, as Topham and Thayer had learned, made even the colonials' quarters unsafe. A Massachusetts private summed up the experience of these days outside the walls of Quebec. "We were considerably annoyed by the British fire. One ball passed through the side of the house in which I was quartered, into the chamber. . . . Another passed into the chimney and fell into the fire. One or two passed into the stoop. Bomb-shells fell near by and burst." When these shells did find their target, the sight was terrible indeed. One member of Captain Lamb's New York artillery "was shot through his Belly and had one of his armes Shot off and all his inwards lay on the Platform which was very awfull to behold." As early as the fifth day after the expedition returned to the suburbs of Quebec, Dr. Senter's hospital ward held 130 soldiers either ill or wounded. There were also many others who suffered without retreating to the doctor. As one soldier recorded, "I remain weak and Low and can get no help we have Lice Itch Jaundice Crabs Bed bugs and an unknown sight of Fleas." Wounds and death supplemented illness; about a half-dozen colonials died each day from the hostile cannon firing on the walls. Disease and enemy fire were not the only causes of death, however. When seven natives in Arnold's force died within thirty-six hours, others in the party surmised that they had gotten poisoned rum from a distillery in Saint Roque's.[34]

As the colonials grew more ill and weary—the defender's cannon fire reducing their numbers daily, and the idea spreading that soldiers planned to abandon the fight on the expiration of their enlistments—a barber came out of the town with word that half of those within the walls would surrender "upon any Terms whatsoever" but the rest were too obstinate to allow it. Shortly afterward, with their cannon fire having little real effect on the defenders, General Montgomery called a council of war to determine whether or not to assault the town. Recognizing the deteriorating morale of his troops, he promised each man who would storm the walls with him two hundred pounds in plunder. The expedition surveyor noted, "There is about two thirds of the officers that Say they are ready and willing to venter [venture] their Lives to Scale the walls and the other third are very unwilling." Captain Smith returned from the council to his men and "was talkative, and what is much worse in military affairs, very communicative." As a result, every soldier who cared to listen knew the plans discussed at the council. The following morning, Major Henry Caldwell's clerk, Joshua Wolf, managed not only to escape from his colonial captors but to take a deserter along as well. The two safely reached the city, bearing ample information with which to warn the garrison. A day later, the general again proposed an assault, until a sergeant named Singleton from Montgomery's army deserted to the city, taking with him knowledge of the attack. Realizing that the defenders were now well aware of his plans, Montgomery again postponed the assault. Inside the now alerted city, the men, including Governor Carleton, slept in their uniforms and equipment, with one thousand of them stationed on the walls and on duty at all times.[35]

The day after Christmas, General Montgomery called another council of war, inviting every officer in the army to attend. A private in Handchett's reluctant company related the effect of the speech the general gave. "But when he stated the great object that would be gained by getting possession of Quebec, and that it would probably lead to peace and the acknowledgement of independence, the fire of patriotism kindled in our breasts, and we resolved to follow wherever he should lead." After the speech, "the question for an assault was put and carried unanimously." All that remained now was to wait for an evening when the weather and the moonlight favored a colonial success.[36]

The following evening, Montgomery ordered the entire colonial force to turn out and divide into two groups. One would attack the upper town with General Montgomery, including four of Arnold's companies, while the remainder feigned an attack on the lower town to distract the defenders. When the troops had assembled, Captains Handchett, Goodrich, and Hubbard, each commander of a company under Arnold, informed their colonel that they were against storming the town, though it was clear the men whom they commanded were ready and willing to do so. On hearing this, General Montgomery declared that he wanted no one with him in the assault who was not fully committed to it. Word of this reached Isaac Senter at the hospital, and the doctor quickly drafted a note to Arnold asking permission to take a place at the head of one of these companies whose men would go, but whose captain would not. Arnold declined, telling Senter that his services as doctor were more valuable to the army and would become even more so shortly.[37]

Before the dissension could be resolved, a bright moon emerged in the night sky, shining too brightly to allow safe conduct of the assault. Regrettably, General Montgomery called off the assault yet again, this time telling the frustrated men he "hoped a more favorable moment should shortly answer, in which he was willing to sacrifice his Life in adding by any means to the honor of his Brother soldiers." This latest postponement apparently did not dampen the spirits of the men who wished to go forward with the attack. The following morning, a party of colonials rounded up four of their comrades who had feigned sickness and failed to turn out for the assault the night before. Binding these men together around their necks with halters, they paraded the shirkers "as a punishment Due to their effeminate courage, who, after suffering in their fatigues to a degree of spirit not as yet known to be equal'd, timorously withdrew from the Laurels they were about to gather."[38]

On December 30, a storm front moved over the region, promising not only a dark nighttime sky, but also a blizzard of snow to help cover the movements of soldiers from guards on the walls. Arnold and Montgomery drafted a new plan of attack, and in the evening made it known to the officers who would carry it out. Colonel Livingston would lead Canadian volunteers and Major Brown a portion of a Boston regiment in a demonstration against the Saint John Gate and the western wall of the city to draw defenders to that area. At five o'clock the following morning, Livingston and his men would fire three rockets to signal the start of the attack. Montgomery with his New Yorkers would march on Cape Diamond and attack the lower town from the west, while Arnold and his "Famine-proof Veterans," as they were now described, along with Captain Lamb's artillery company bearing one cannon, would travel around the northern end of the city to attack the lower town from the east. When Arnold's and Montgomery's forces met in the lower town, they would assault the gate there, force their way inside the walls, and hope that the Canadians would abandon the defense, forcing Governor Carleton to surrender. Since many of the colonials were wearing captured British uniform coats, Arnold ordered his men to fix a piece of a hemlock branch in the front of their hats so that they could recognize one another.[39]

At eight o'clock on December 30, with the snow falling as hoped and the moon hidden well behind the thick cloud cover, General Montgomery delivered orders for the attack to the various groups, with instructions to be ready to march at midnight.[40]

II

❧

STORMING THE WALLS

With only two hours left before daylight on the last morning of 1775, those defending the city of Quebec from within were nearly able to relax after another tense night awaiting the expected attack. Because this was the darkest night thus far, and because the cover of the heavy snow made it more possible to move to the attack unseen, it had seemed all but certain the colonials would soon appear at some perceived weak place along the walls. At five o'clock, Captain Malcolm Fraser of Colonel MacLean's Royal Emigrants made his rounds from post to post, checking with the sentries to ensure that another night had safely passed. When the captain came to these sentries between the Saint Louis Gate and Cape Diamond, they pointed out an unusual flickering of lights out on the Plains of Abraham. The lights themselves seemed fixed, the flickering irregular—as if numerous people were passing between the lights and the walls, each blocking the flames for a moment as he passed. Though Captain Fraser was aware that nervous sentries at their dark posts had awakened and alarmed the city with growing regularity the past several evenings, imagining hundreds, even thousands of colonials arrayed for battle at one corner of the walls or another, something about this sign troubled him. Adding to his discomfort were reports from some of the deserters that General Montgomery viewed Cape Diamond as the weakest and easiest place in the city defenses to surmount with ladders.[1]

On each of the previous few days, deserters or escapees from the enemy had also brought intelligence into the city that the attack was imminent, and that Montgomery had actually gathered his men for the assault on two occasions before changing his plans. The darkness and snow on this night had significantly raised the probability, and though it was nearly daylight, the captain could not ignore such an unusual discovery, or take a chance by failing to raise an alarm. Ordering the sentries and guards on the walls to their arms, Fraser soon had drums beating, alarm bells ringing, and armed men scrambling in every direction to reach their posts. Within minutes, the cathedral bells were clanging and the whole garrison had turned out. "Even old men of seventy were forward to oppose the attackers."[2]

Shortly after Captain Fraser raised the alarm, Colonel Livingston fired the signal rockets from the west of Cape Diamond while his men took cover behind a rise of ground eighty yards from the walls and began firing their muskets. Minding the flashes from their gun barrels, the defenders on the wall began returning fire. In the ensuing confusion, the defenders noticed a body of men moving through Saint John and opened fire on them as well, while colonial artillerymen began firing mortars from Saint Roque's into the city to help foster confusion and fear. This second group of men in Saint John was led by Major Brown, who, along with Livingston, had 160 men with whom to launch a false attack on the western wall and set fire to the Saint John Gate. This action was designed to leave the impression that the colonials intended to attack that part of the city walls. If effective, it would draw the defenders to the corner of the city directly opposite the lower town just as Montgomery and Arnold reached it. Captain Fraser's discovery of this feint before Livingston or Brown was in position thwarted their designs, and though they succeeded in alarming the western end of the city, their maneuver did not lead to a widespread belief that the main attack would fall on that point. Instead, Colonel MacLean ordered Major Henry Caldwell to send some of his British militia to the area, and the resulting cannon fire forced this band of colonials back to camp. The failure of the false attack and the retreat of these forces under Livingston and Brown left the defenders to respond in force to attacks elsewhere in the city.[3]

Though the miserable early-morning conditions gave cover to the attackers' movements, they also complicated them tremendously, for the weather did not play on just one side of the fight. "The storm was outrageous, and the cold wind extremely biting," declared one rifleman, who

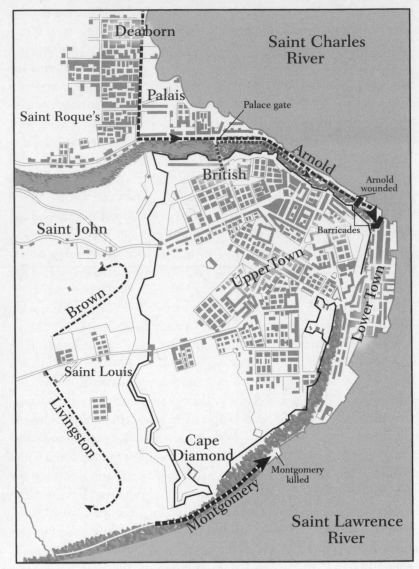

Quebec, 1775

The colonials' attack plan called for a two-pronged assault on the lower town.
Montgomery was killed almost immediately, and Arnold was wounded before his
men began fighting. Arriving late from across the river, Dearborn and his company
were captured when a British force sallied out of the Palace Gate. The same force
cut off the retreat of Arnold's men, forcing them to surrender at the second barricade. Montgomery's men retreated, and the diversionary attempts of Livingston
and Brown failed.

added that the snow blew horizontally into their faces. Before stepping off on the assault, Colonel Arnold declared that no soldier would participate who did not wish to do so. This was welcome news to a handful of men who, according to a Massachusetts musketman, "had got the cannon fever to such a degree that they were excused." Among these, he singled out only Lieutenant Pierce, the expedition's surveyor and an officer in Hubbard's musket company, whose complaints against Arnold had permeated the entries in his diary for the month previous. Pierce's entry for December 30 read, "The Last Day of Service all rejoice—again I Say rejoice. . . . I remain Poorly and unfit for Duty and Determined to Get to New England as Soon as may be."⁴

With only a few men falling out to the rear, Colonel Arnold himself led an advance guard of fifty men out of Saint Roque's and down along the eastern wall. The snow was falling so hard that the balance of the men—three hundred in all—who followed as little as one hundred yards behind, had difficulty finding their tracks. Within minutes of Arnold's departure, Fraser alarmed the city and bells rang, men turned out, and a "horrible roar" erupted from the city's cannons.⁵

With some colonial soldiers now sporting a piece of white paper on their caps so they could identify one another—"Liberty or Death" written on each—they pushed on toward the lower town. They advanced bent forward, since "it was impossible to bear up our faces against the imperious storm of wind and snow." Captain Morgan and his Virginia riflemen led the first body of troops, while Lieutenant Archibald Steele, leader of the scouting party that had been first up the Kennebec and Dead Rivers, followed closely behind in command of Smith's company of Pennsylvania riflemen. Smith's whereabouts were a mystery, though one of his men attributed his absence to "particular causes" that may have been spiritously induced. The balance of the riflemen and musket companies followed—Handchett, Hubbard, Topham, Thayer, Ward, and then Goodrich—as did Captain Lamb's artillery unit, dragging along a single cannon on a sled. Major Meigs commanded the rear of the party, where Captain Hendricks and his company held guard. The attack began around 5:30 a.m., delayed by the effort of Lamb's men to drag their small brass six-pounder through the deep snow. As the column stretched out, the various companies separated and, as Major Meigs would remember, "The main body were led wrong, there being no road, the way dark and intricate, among stores, houses, boats, and wharves, and harassed at the same time with a constant fire of the enemy from the walls." Running single-file along the base of the wall, many of the men fell wounded from British muskets above but were unable to return fire, since all they saw of the enemy was the flash of his muzzle when he fired.[6]

ACROSS THE SAINT Charles River in Beauport, Henry Dearborn heard the ruckus in the city and was surprised to learn that he was supposed to be a part of the attack now clearly begun two miles away, on the opposite shore. He soon discovered that the sergeant major carrying the orders from Colonel Arnold had found the tide unusually high and could not get across the river sooner. Dearborn scrambled to gather his company from their various quarters, some of which were a mile distant in the thick snow; it would take more than an hour.[7]

The first obstacle in the way of the colonials was a barricade placed at Sault au Matelot (Sailor's Leap), which was shielded by a battery of two nine-pound cannons. Knowing of its presence, Colonel Arnold had worked out a careful plan to seize it. When the first group of riflemen reached the barricade, they would halt and divide, moving right or left, allowing a hole to open in the center of their line. Into this breach, Captain Lamb and his men would roll up their cannon and fire it three times directly into the barricade. While Captain Morgan's men slipped around the barrier on a wharf, the rest of the riflemen would rush up to the walls, fire through the holes made by the cannonballs, and scale the wall using their ladders. Morgan would attack the rear of those guarding the barricade, and the rest of the riflemen coming over the top would swallow up the defenders. This plan, however, depended on the brass cannon, which Lamb's men had long abandoned by the time the riflemen reached the barricade. Having no particular backup plan, Colonel Arnold simply led his advance squad in a frontal assault, joined only by Morgan's and Hendricks's companies. With snow swirling in the frenzied darkness, Morgan's men took to the ladders and began scaling the walls, while their comrades held the defending cannoneers at bay by firing their rifles through the portholes. The defenders fired only one cannon shot, killing only one of the attackers, before surrendering the barricade. The whole engagement lasted well under an hour and succeeded even without Lamb's cannon.[8]

In the vicinity, the colonials captured dozens of the enemy, and when the main body of the assault force finally reached the first barricade, the advance group, with Morgan and Hendricks having already secured it, gave a cheer to their comrades, who heartily returned it in congratulations. Pushing on, Captain Thayer led a squad farther up the street, where he discovered some pickets guarded by "a company of the most responsible citizens of Quebec." Apparently, their commander, Captain McLeod of the Royal Emigrants, did not share their sense of responsibility, since he, at this critical juncture, was drunk. In short order, the colonials added these men to their group of prisoners, also confiscating the defenders' dry weapons for their own use. This was important because the colonials had been running along the wall trying to cover their weapons with the flaps of their coats. As the snow fell on them, it was melted by the warmth of their bodies and dripped into the priming powder on their muskets, rendering most unable to fire.[9]

As the confusion waned and officers tried to reassemble their companies, some of the colonials noticed Colonel Arnold on the ground and in pain, red blood dotting the white snow beneath his left leg. A musketball fired from atop the city walls had glanced off of a rock before piercing the leg and passing between the two major bones. Soon the loss of blood forced him to abandon the fight; Reverend Spring and another soldier helped their commander to the hospital as he dragged the damaged leg behind him.[10]

Inside the walls, a messenger reached Colonel MacLean with news that the first barricade on the Sault au Matelot had fallen to the invaders. MacLean sent a group of sailors under Captain Hamilton of the *Lizard* down to the lower town to reinforce the defenders there. When Hamilton arrived, the situation looked chaotic and bleak. Arnold's assault had inflicted casualties and taken a large number of men prisoner, and "there were no proper commanders, at least any whose authority had sufficient weight with the people." This, he added, was especially true among the militia. "This being the situation of things, there was no keeping of any order among either the British or French militia . . . for there were two other attacks made at the same time."[11]

With colonial mortars firing shells into the city from the north, Livingston and Brown making their feint from the west, and Arnold circling along the east wall to the lower town, there was, according to the plan at least, no portion of the town that would not appear threatened by attack save the southern end, along the Saint Lawrence. Now General Montgomery, at the head of two hundred men, remedied this by completing the envelopment. Marching at the foot of the steep walls of the city, this group intended to force its way into the lower town from the west while Colonel Arnold and his men did the same from the opposite direction. Along this path, at a place called the Potash, the defenders had built a barricade with a four-cannon battery. About two hundred paces west of this barrier, they had completed a blockhouse just three days earlier, placing pickets in the ground beyond it to aid in discouraging the invaders. Farther westward, the path narrowed considerably, with a steep cliff on one side mounted by the city walls, and on the other side, close in, the Saint Lawrence River. So close was the water to the base of the cliff that huge blocks of ice, pushed up in the tidal shifts of the river's current, lay along the narrow shoreline. Thus, Montgomery's men moved with great difficulty, even marching single-file. When the head of the column, with the general in the lead, reached the wooden pickets, the carpenters set to work cutting them, and Montgomery helped pull them down with his own hands. As the colonials started pouring through the gap thus created, the Canadian militia stationed in the blockhouse fled without firing their guns, leaving Montgomery an open path to the barricade. Just now, an old woman reached the defenders there, declaring that the attackers had surprised the barricades at Sault au Matelot and gotten into the lower town. When these defenders discovered that the enemy was now behind them, a panic rose up among them, and they began to hide their weapons, some even tossing them into the Saint Lawrence.[12]

Disturbed by this news, the sailor gun crews on the ramparts heard shouting from the western edge of the wall as Montgomery tried to urge his men forward. Many more of the defenders nearby recognized this as a second assault from a separate direction, and so dropped their weapons and deserted their posts. Among the last to do so was a drunken British sailor who had been pressed into service at a cannon. Swearing he would at least fire one shot before joining the retreat, he touched the match to a cannon loaded with grapeshot—a load of several small iron balls designed to shatter and rip apart an enemy vessel's sail and rigging when fired. Forty paces away in the narrow path, a horrific boom and whirring sound preceded a heavy thud as each piece of grapeshot struck rock or earth. Several of these whirrs were followed by an ominous loud groan and the soft dull sound of a body falling into the snow. One piece of the grapeshot had pierced both of General Montgomery's thighs, while another pierced him in the left cheek, then bored into his head, killing him before his body struck the snow. Marching at the general's side were Captains Cheeseman and MacPherson, a sergeant, and a private; they all fell dead as well.[13]

Colonel Donald Campbell, though merely the deputy quartermaster, was nevertheless the senior officer, and thus acceded to command of Montgomery's force. Campbell needed only to push his men onward, seize the now abandoned battery, and march to the lower town to gain possession both of it and the defenders now surrendering in large numbers. Rather than continuing the attack and relieving the pressure on Arnold's besieged force, however, Campbell called for a general retreat, ordering Montgomery's force to abandon the assault and return to camp, leaving nine comrades, including their commander, lying dead on the snow at the barricade. Within minutes, Major Caldwell arrived to reinforce the barricade and found the defenders either in flight or in a state of near panic at their circumstances. Since the attack here had now ceased, however, he managed to regain control before returning to Colonel MacLean with most of his men, in case they were needed elsewhere. Stunned by the death of their general, the attackers had marched away from an important opportunity to seize the lower town.[14]

ACROSS THE WAY, however, Arnold's force was pressing its attack. Having successfully seized the first barricade, Captain Morgan tried to gather the colonials together to continue the assault. Morgan knew almost nothing of the layout of the area except that there was another barricade somewhere between him and the lower town. Where it was and how to reach it in the labyrinth of streets and alleyways was nearly impossible to determine on a dark night in a blizzard, without a guide, and with a hostile enemy potentially around every corner. With his men taking shelter from the storm under the eaves of the buildings and waiting for orders, Morgan had little choice but to remain in place and await the arrival of the main body of the attack force.[15]

The advance group with Morgan and Hendricks, followed closely by Steele, Nichols, and Lamb's artillerymen, pushed on through the alleyways until they reached a second barricade, a few hundred yards from the first. In the snow and darkness, the defenders did not see the attackers until they were right up to the wall, so close that the two cannons on a platform behind and just above the barrier were unable to fire at them. Plucking away at the defenders with rifles aimed through portholes, the colonials could see a large number of them standing with muskets ready to fire when the first head crested the top of the wall. Realizing this, Morgan decided it would be best to seek cover and await the main body of the assault force, still finding their way from the first barricade. Taking up positions in buildings nearby, the colonials could hear heavy musket fire in the distance and took this as a sign that Montgomery's attack was succeeding. Soon a shout of "Quebec is ours!" echoed down the alley.[16]

A MILE TO THE REAR, as Arnold and his two aides passed into Saint Roque's on their way to the hospital, they met Henry Dearborn and his company, finally arriving on the scene of battle. His men were in high spirits, and Arnold briefly described the situation, ordering him to hasten the men toward the barricades. Dearborn urged his company down along the passage between the eastern wall of the city and the Saint Charles River. "We push'd forward as fast as possible, we met the wounded men very thick," he later recalled. But, even though they were led through the snow and darkness by a guide who had lived in Quebec for a numbers of years, Dearborn's company was very soon lost in the streets of the lower town, wasting precious time marching around in confusion. The guide finally announced that he had no idea where he was, and promptly abandoned his post, lest he be found aiding the invaders. Dearborn ordered his men to double back and see if they could find the right path.[17]

At about this time, messengers began to reach Governor Carleton at his palace with reports that the lower town was in serious jeopardy. Coolly reacting to the news, he ordered Colonel MacLean and Major Caldwell to send reinforcements to Sault au Matelot, also sending Captain George Laws of the Royal Engineers to take sixty men out through the Palace Gate on the north wall and circle around behind Arnold's assault force. Shortly after Laws, he sent Captain McDougal of the Royal Emigrants with sixty more. These men had barely descended the hill at the northeast corner of the wall when they began to encounter Captain Dearborn's men, who were stunned by the arrival of enemy troops from their rear. Taking cover around some houses, Dearborn tried to get his bearings, but when a British soldier demanded he identify himself or be shot, the captain discovered that the snow had dampened the powder of his rifle, rendering it useless. He realized that many of his men were in the same state, and instructed them to take cover in the houses and try to get their weapons working again, but it was too late. With his company scattered and lost in the streets, Dearborn urged them to attempt escape, or, failing that, when the British promised "good quarters and Tender usage," to surrender. While Captain McDougal attended to the prisoners, Captain Laws continued on in search of further prey and soon reached the first barricade.[18]

ENDURING THE TREATMENT of his wound at the general hospital, and desperate for news about the progress of his force or Montgomery's at the barricades, Colonel Arnold found the strength to dictate a letter to General Wooster, whom Montgomery had left in charge back at Montreal. Briefly summarizing the attack, Arnold reported that he had already lost two hundred men killed or wounded and that the rest "will either carry the lower town, be made prisoners, or cut to pieces." Having described "the critical situation we are in," Arnold asked Wooster for whatever help he could provide and informed him that his wound had forced him to relinquish command to Colonel Campbell.[19]

WHEN AT LAST the main colonial force, under Colonel Greene, reached the second barricade on Sault au Matelot, their comrades cheered and rushed out of the buildings in which they had taken cover. Approaching the barrier again, they threw ladders against the wall, and the officers led the men up the rungs. The defenders saw that the enemy was about to surmount their barricade, and opened fire from several directions at once. A Massachusetts private later recalled the attackers' plight: "We were surrounded by treble our numbers, [so] that we found it impossible to force it, the enemy being under cover, while we were exposed to their fire." In the chaos, however, despite the absence of Colonel Arnold, the colonials seemed not to lack spirited leadership. "Betwixt every peal the awful voice of Morgan is heard," remembered a rifleman, "whose gigantic stature and terrible appearance carries dismay among the foe wherever he comes."[20]

Into this cauldron rushed reinforcements for the barricade's defenders. On hearing of the danger there, Colonel MacLean ordered Captain John Nairne of the Royal Emigrants to the scene, along with Major Caldwell. As he had on reaching the barricade at Cape Diamond earlier, Caldwell found these defenders seized by "a certain degree of panic." He later recalled, "I found our people, the Canadians especially, shy of advancing toward the barrier." Still, the new troops not only added weight to the defense, but also helped buoy the morale of those already at the barricade. As the defenders began to turn four guns toward their attackers, Colonel Greene ordered the colonials to fire at the cannoneers. Before Captain Hendricks could carry out the order, however, a heavy volley of musket fire erupted from the defenders' side of the barrier. A ball from this firing struck the left side of Hendricks's chest, and he was dead within minutes. Nearby, another ball pierced Captain Lamb's left cheek but did not stop him. He untied a black handkerchief from the stock of his musket and, handing it to Lieutenant Nichols, asked him to tie up the wound. Still another shot removed two fingers from the hand of Lieutenant Steele. Captain Hubbard's wound, in the heel, proved fatal, as did those of Lieutenants Cooper and Humphrey. With the attack disintegrating, the Canadians and natives in Arnold's force fled across the ice toward Beauport, a dangerous undertaking itself. A Pennsylvanian who did not choose this route observed, "Its desperateness consisted in running two miles across shoal ice, thrown up by the high tides of this latitude—and its danger in the meeting with air holes, deceptively covered up by the bed of snow."[21]

The colonials who remained at the now reinforced barricade, taken aback by the renewed defense, sought cover in houses nearby, so they could continue to harass the defenders until some other possibility might present itself. In the confusion, the men in one of these buildings were startled when a British officer suddenly burst in through the front door. Captain Law had so outpaced the British soldiers under his command that he had reached the barricade well ahead of them. Given the confusion, and with soldiers on both sides wearing British uniforms, he decided not to chance exposing himself to his fellow defenders on the opposite side of the barrier, lest he fall victim to friendly fire. Instead, he bolted into the nearest house, where he stunned the colonials inside, both by his sudden appearance and by the fact that he was alone. Before anyone fired a shot, the captain—who apparently thought on his feet as fast as he ran on them—declared that he was there to discuss terms for a colonial surrender. This quick-witted declaration probably saved his life: those in the house took him prisoner rather than shooting him.[22]

Before falling back into the houses near the barricade, the colonials had managed to get a few ladders up against the wall, and even had one fixed on the opposite side to ease their descent once they were over the top. Major Caldwell sent soldiers into the houses accessible from his side of the barricade to return the fire of the enemy in houses in front of it. Looking up, Caldwell noticed a high window in a house with a commanding view of the street beyond the barricade, and he ordered his men to make use of the colonials' ladder to gain access to it. Captains Nairne and Dambourges responded to Caldwell's order and climbed into the window on an upper floor, just as the colonials were entering the same house through the front door. Nairne used his bayonet to advantage and chased the attackers back into the street, securing the house.[23]

Soon the British soldiers who had marched out of the Palace Gate were on top of Arnold's rear guards, who were no match for them. Hemmed in between the second barricade and this new threat, Colonel Greene and his men decided to hold out for hours until nightfall, then try to manage a retreat in the darkness. This hope soon passed, as the reality of their situation set in and more defenders arrived to threaten the scattered colonial force. Soon groups of attackers were surrendering to Captain Nairne, who sent them one by one through the window, down the ladder, and into captivity behind the barricade.

WITH THE ATTACK NOW SUCCESSFULLY REPULSED, CARLETON SENT A force out beyond the city walls to burn Saint Roque's and end, once and for all, the harassing fire of the colonials from its buildings. Beyond that sortie, which collected the five mortars that Arnold's men had been using to lob shells into the city, the governor's only concern was the defense of the city itself, and he made no effort to send out a counterattack. Meanwhile, word of General Montgomery's death reached Colonel Arnold at the hospital, but there was no news at all about his own division. Fearing a counterattack, Arnold sent for help from the local inhabitants, but with Montgomery's death shortening the odds for a colonial success, they refused. He also sent word to the men who had retreated to Montgomery's headquarters, but they provided little aid as well. Dr. Senter and others tried to convince Arnold to let them carry him farther from the town, to a safer location, but he refused. Instead, he chose to sit propped up in his bed with two loaded pistols and a sword by his side, while ordering all of the other sick and wounded men to have loaded guns at their bedsides as well, so that they might put up some resistance if the British came calling.[24]

Just after daylight, Major Mathias Ogden staggered into the hospital and, with blood dripping from his sagging left shoulder, gave a pessimistic opinion of their chances of success. In this tense, uncertain atmosphere, the occupants of the hospital waited until dark, then through the night, the next day, and another night, with no word from the men who had attacked the barricades at Sault au Matelot. The following day was January 1, the dawn of a year that would see an American declaration of independence from Great Britain, but in the general hospital just west of Quebec, the uncertainty hung like a pall over all that the colonials had suffered to accomplish. Starved for news, though beginning to accept the worst, Colonel Arnold allowed a young volunteer named Mathew Duncan to venture into the lower town as a scout in hopes of gaining information. Duncan's failure to return only added to the mystery and their gloomy prospects.[25]

Finally, on the afternoon of January 2, more than fifty hours after the assault had begun, Major Return Meigs, who had been missing nearly all of that time, walked into the hospital. The major explained that he was a prisoner of the British, but that Governor Carleton had allowed him to leave the city on his word of honor to collect the baggage of the surviving colonial officers, all of whom were now in captivity within the walls of the seminary. The surviving enlisted men were held at the Jesuit College, and even Duncan had been captured as well. Meigs gave his best estimate of the killed and wounded as he told the story of the attack at the barricades and how nearly all of the guns the men carried were fouled by the snowfall and would not fire. Despite their overwhelming disadvantages, including the reinforcement of the defenders at the second barricade, Arnold's men had held out for three hours, hoping for General Montgomery to fight his way in behind the enemy, but he did not come. Outnumbered, surrounded, and threatened with annihilation, the men had finally surrendered.[26]

Frustrated and struck low by his failure to seize the object of his agonizing three-month expedition, Benedict Arnold dispatched another letter to General Wooster. In desperation, he pleaded for reinforcements, still not willing to abandon all hope. "For God's sake order as many men down as you can possibly spare, consistent with the safety of Montreal, and all the mortars, howitzers, and shells, that you can possibly bring. I hope you will stop every rascal who has deserted from us, and bring him back again." Suggesting a solution to his predicament, the beleaguered Arnold added, "I hope the honourable Continental Congress will not think of sending less than eight or ten thousand men to secure and form a lasting connection with this country."[27]

As it turned out, Arnold's fears of a British counterattack were unfounded, for Governor Carleton continued to heed the lessons taught by General Wolfe's victory sixteen years earlier. Content to keep the sturdy stone walls between the enemy and his country's last remaining foothold in the province, while waiting five months for the spring thaw that would bring fresh troops from England, Carleton was not coming out. For his part, Colonel Arnold knew the colonials were in no position to make another assault on the walls, even if Wooster brought every man he had in Montreal to his aid. With Lake Champlain frozen and General Washington short of troops as it was, there was also no chance of getting more troops from the south. He had a skeleton force that might be able to maintain a siege by fooling the defenders into believing they were plentiful enough to enforce it, but in doing so his troops on the outside of the city would likely suffer worse than those inside. Unable to attack and unwilling to retreat, Arnold posted his scant troops along the major passages in and out of the city and waited.

INSIDE THE WALLS, the men who had endured one of the most miserable military expeditions in history, only to fail in their one opportunity to achieve the goal for which they had suffered so greatly, now faced a new and different misery. Confined by large numbers in small spaces, the expedition veterans now held in captivity began to realize that their rations would amount to whatever the inhabitants of a city under siege could spare, knowing their provisions would only dwindle until relief arrived with spring—still four months away. With citizens tearing down wood-framed houses to use as firewood, the prisoners' warmth was a low priority; the only luxury came whenever a sympathetic citizen would give or sell some small item to the captives. Those who fell seriously ill—from scarlet fever, smallpox, or a host of other diseases aggravated by the close quarters—often found relief in the Hôtel Dieu, now converted to a hospital staffed by sisters of the convent.

On January 4, after affording General Montgomery's body a proper and respectful burial, Colonel MacLean told all of the prisoners who had been born in Great Britain that they must either join his Royal Emigrants as soldiers, or risk being sent to England and tried for treason, the well-known punishment for which involved a short fall with an uncomfortably tight rope around one's neck. In response to this presentation of choices, nearly one hundred of the "old-country" men obliged the colonel, joined his regiment, and even stood sentry duty on the walls, only to make their escape at the first opportunity. When more than a dozen had thus vacated the city, Carleton had the rest disarmed. Their comrades who remained in confinement endured more than six months as prisoners, plotting failed escapes, serving impressments on board British ships, suffering from illness, and passing many idle hours recalling the horrible march through the wilderness and the failed result. Pondering these thoughts, thirty more men of the expedition died of illness while in captivity.[28]

GENERAL WOOSTER DID not send reinforcements from Montreal until March 18. By April, Arnold was well enough to ride a horse and had received a commission as brigadier general in the Continental Army. Through his recuperation, he managed to see to the construction of batteries across the Saint Lawrence at Pointe Levi and the Saint Charles at Beauport, but with many more cannons opposing him from the city walls, and Captain Lamb, his only artillery officer, captive inside the city, these made little difference. In April, with General Wooster still senior to him in rank and present at Quebec to oversee the siege, Arnold retired to Montreal, where he assumed command of the forces there.[29]

Washington did manage to send more troops to Quebec from New Jersey, Pennsylvania, and the Green Mountains, in an effort to seize the city before the British could reinforce it, but the winter march up Lake Champlain from Ticonderoga was devastating to the soldiers, who arrived weak, their uniforms and weapons in tatters, only to suffer a widespread outbreak of smallpox when they reached Montreal. On May 1, about twelve hundred of these new troops, under the command of Massachusetts General John Thomas, relieved General Wooster at Quebec. Just three days later, a small British fleet sailed into view around the Ile d'Orléans and weighed anchor in the basin before the city. Within hours, the fresh British troops who disembarked marched out of the gates and sent the colonials scurrying westward. The Revolution was still in its first year, the Declaration of Independence had yet to be enacted by Congress, but no American force would ever again threaten the city of Quebec.

EPILOGUE

AMERICA'S HANNIBAL

It was about time for a late breakfast at the Robinson house when two smartly clad officers rode up outside. That summer of 1780, the stately home had served as headquarters for Benedict Arnold, the commanding general of American forces at West Point, since he had taken responsibility for the critical Hudson River defenses a month before. Upon entering, Major James McHenry and Captain Samuel Shaw greeted their superior with news that they would soon have additional company. General George Washington, along with his chief of artillery, Henry Knox, and the Marquis de Lafayette of France were not long behind, and would soon reach the house for a scheduled meeting. Greeting these two officers warmly, their commander asked them to join him for the meal now laid out on the table. It is difficult to say exactly when the idea began to form in his head, or precisely when he began plotting to convert it to action, but the timetable for Arnold's latest military adventure was about to grow tremendously and unexpectedly short. As he sat enjoying breakfast at his headquarters that September morning, another rider approached the Robinson house, entered the room, and handed him some dispatches that would change his life forever. He began thumbing through the usual military correspondence of the day, and none of the others in the room noticed anything terribly out of sorts about Arnold or his demeanor. When Arnold reached a particular dispatch in the pile, Major McHenry thought he noticed a slight embarrassment come to the commander's face, but nothing more. Calmly, Arnold stood up and took the rider aside, whispered something to him privately, and prepared to leave.

The embarrassment that McHenry thought he had noticed turned out to be something far more sinister. In a few moments, Arnold was on his horse riding hard for the river, where his personal boat and the men to handle it were always ready to carry him wherever he ordered them, whenever he desired it. Soon after Arnold's departure, General Washington arrived at the Robinson house, and the officers who minutes before had been enjoying what they believed was a pleasant morning's breakfast with their commander, soon learned that they had been present at one of the most remarkable events in their young country's brief history.

The dispatch that had given Arnold pause was a notice informing him that American soldiers near Tarrytown, New York, had apprehended a British officer named André who, though a major in the British Army, was wearing civilian clothing and carrying the kind of papers no British officer ought to have had. Among these was a pass from Arnold, along with detailed sketches of the American defenses around West Point including troop strengths and positions, all written in Arnold's hand. A courier had taken these to General Washington, and when he arrived at the Robinson house, he was only a few minutes too late to place Arnold under arrest for treason.

Gliding down the Hudson toward British lines, Arnold must have had plenty of time to contemplate the circumstances that had brought him to this point. As the autumn colors along the banks passed by him, his mind must have wandered back through the previous five years, recalling how his once-enthusiastic patriotism and desire to help tear the colonies from the clutches of the Crown had turned to disgust and despair at the hands of conniving comrades-in-arms. Once an ardent patriot, he was now fully convinced that the cause was lost, and that he was not alone in believing so. Somewhere amid his contempt for the American military braintrust—George Washington excepted—and a complete lack of recognition of all that he had achieved for the Americans, Arnold had come to believe that he was not alone in his conviction that the war was a forlorn hope. Soon many leading colonists would began making overtures to the Crown, and in time, as more and more of them saw the reality of the situation, those who believed that prosperity and security lay with the British Empire, and not with foolish notions of independence, would hold sway. Though he may have had good reasons to believe so, he could not have been more wrong.

*   *   *

As soon as word began to spread that Arnold's expedition had penetrated the Kennebec-Chaudière wilderness to stand before the walls of Quebec, its leader became a heroic figure. When General Philip Schuyler received the word, he wrote from Ticonderoga to his commander, George Washington, "Whatever may be Colonel *Arnold's* fate at Quebeck, his merit is very great, marching a body of troops through a country scarcely trodden by human foot." To John Hancock, General Schuyler marveled, "Some future historian will make it the subject of admiration." In a personal letter to Arnold, a delighted George Washington heaped praise as well: "It is not in the power of any man to command success, but you have done more—you have deserved it." Dr. James Warren wrote to Samuel Adams, "Arnold has made a march that may be compared to Hannibal's or Xenophon's," a thought echoed by Thomas Jefferson, "This march of Arnold's is equal to Xenophon's retreat." Jefferson's enthusiasm for Arnold's success in breaching the wilderness with an army had ignited as soon as word reached Philadelphia that the march had succeeded. In late November 1775, he wrote to fellow Virginian John Randolph: "We expect, every hour, to be informed that Quebec has opened its arms to Colonel Arnold." The man who six months later would draft the document that would formally separate the colonies from Great Britain then described the importance of this event: "In a short time, we have reason to hope, the delegates of Canada will join us in Congress and complete the American union as far as we wish to have it completed."[1]

Even after the assault on Quebec failed to seize the city, Arnold's fame and the admiration of his fellow revolutionaries did not diminish. Whatever the outcome, he had shown the British (and, perhaps as important, the French) that American forces could organize, endure, and fight, even on the scale of a coordinated land-and-sea campaign against enemy strongholds. Nevertheless, praise did not quench his desire for victory, nor did failure leave him dejected and defeated. Arnold still wanted Quebec, and his personal duel with Governor Carleton over the control of Canada was far from over.

When the long-suffering Carleton had finally amassed enough reinforcements in Quebec both to protect the city and to begin a campaign
to eject the colonials, he marched toward Montreal with a grim determination not only to seize back his province but to push down Lake Champlain, divide the colonies in half, and join with the British army now
bottled up in New York. Undaunted by their inability to seize the last
British stronghold in Canada, the colonials refused to give back any of
the province easily. Instead, they resisted Carleton's advance doggedly
enough to delay his arrival at Lake Champlain through the summer and
early fall of 1776. This was a critical accomplishment, because it postponed the governor's ability to begin construction of the vessels he
would need to transport his army down the lake to Crown Point and
Ticonderoga. As Benedict Arnold recuperated from his wounds enough
to begin riding, organizing, and fighting, he understood clearly the
need to hold off Carleton so that the approach of winter would force
him to abandon his offensive until the spring. The intervening months
would be crucial to the ability of the colonists to resist this British invasion. If Carleton could reach Ticonderoga, and perhaps Albany, before winter set in, he could deliver a decisive blow to the American
cause. If the colonials could slow him just enough, and winter could
stop him entirely, the intervening months of recruiting and organizing
might preserve their hope for independence.

After weeks of dogged resistance, yielding territory to the British only
with great reluctance, the colonials reached the northern end of Lake
Champlain. Here the necessities of warfare bought them some time to
prepare for Carleton's next step. In order to transport his army of ten
thousand men and all of their equipment and supplies down to Crown
Point and Fort Ticonderoga, the British commander had first to build a
small naval fleet with which to carry it. With ample supplies of wood,
carpenters, and skilled craftsmen from their homeland, and the added
advantage of preconstructed vessels in the form of kits brought over
from England, Carleton felt confident that he would assemble his little
navy and meet with little resistance as he sailed it south toward its intended targets. As he had the previous winter, when he left Quebec City
unprotected from an attack through the Kennebec-Chaudière wilderness, Carleton again underestimated the energy and determination of
his adversary.

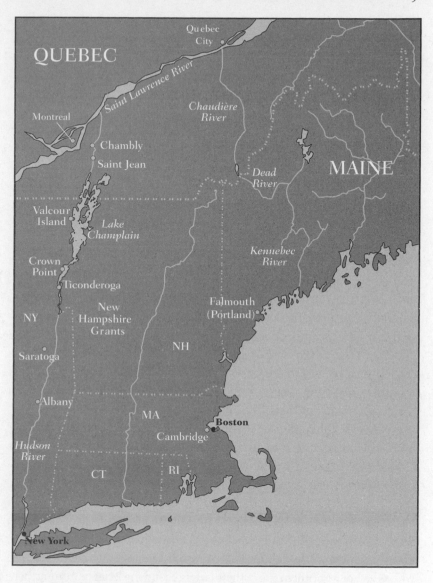

QUEBEC

Quebec
City

Saint Lawrence River

*Chaudière
River*

Montreal

Chambly

Saint Jean

*Dead
River*

MAINE

Valcour
Island

*Lake
Champlain*

Crown
Point

Ticonderoga

*Kennebec
River*

NY

New
Hampshire
Grants

Falmouth
(Portland)

NH

Saratoga

Albany

MA

Boston

Cambridge

*Hudson
River*

CT

RI

New York

Unwilling to see his efforts in Canada completely reversed by a successful British campaign into New York, Benedict Arnold decided he could construct and then command the nation's first navy to resist the Redcoats—and he presently set about doing just that. With wood from the surrounding countryside, iron brought in from Connecticut and the Hudson River Valley, along with rope, sailcloth, and skilled shipbuilders from as far away as the Maine coast, Arnold undertook a task nearly as improbable as his expedition to Quebec. By the time Carleton and Burgoyne assembled their fleet of thirty vessels at Saint Jean and sailed south, the colonials, under Arnold's command and direction, had constructed a small navy in Skenesborough, New York, consisting of thirteen vessels, which, when added to three already on hand, made up just over half the size of the British fleet.

On October 11, anticipating the enemy's arrival, General Arnold readied his fleet in a bay between Valcour Island and the New York mainland, knowing that the British would pass by the colonial position before finding them and would thus have to sail back up the lake to engage the little fleet. This advantage grew considerably when the wind blew from the north, making it difficult for the British fleet to reverse course in that direction. When the British finally struck, Arnold's makeshift navy held them off until dark, then slipped past and through them undetected, to escape down the lake. The following morning, Carleton's fleet was stunned to find that the enemy's ships had vanished, but used the advantage of favorable winds to overtake what was left of Arnold's fleet. The first American navy ran and fought as long as possible, all the while slowing the British advance southward, but in the end, the superior British fleet won out. By the time the engagement came to an end, the British had sunk two of the American vessels and taken two more. When it was clear that they could no longer outrun or outfight the enemy, General Arnold ordered the rearward vessels into a shallow bay, where his men set them afire, their colors flying in defiance. From there he led the remnants of his force over land to Crown Point, where he arrived having not eaten or slept for three days. Hearing of his safe arrival within colonial lines, General Horatio Gates acknowledged, "Few men ever met with so many hairbreadth escapes in so short a space of time."[2]

On October 14, General Carleton dispatched a letter to Lord Germain in London describing what he saw as a decisive naval victory. He ended the letter, however, with a telling and ominous statement: "The season is so far advanced I cannot pretend to inform your Lordship whether anything further can be done this year." In writing this, Carleton realized that Arnold had succeeded in a task thought impossible. He had constructed his country's first naval fleet out of a forest, and used it to slow the British attempt to cut the colonies in half and link up with the other British army at New York. By doing so, he forced Carleton to delay the invasion by several months, until spring, buying the colonials crucial time to build up their defenses and raise militia. More than a century afterward, America's pre-eminent naval historian Alfred Thayer Mahan described the feat in glowing terms. "The little navy on Lake Champlain was wiped out, but never had any force, large or small, lived to better purpose or died more gloriously."[3]

NEARLY A YEAR AFTER THE BATTLE OF VALCOUR ISLAND, GENERAL BURgoyne commanded the British land forces as they approached the region around Saratoga, New York. On September 19, 1777, Burgoyne's army met a colonial force that had taken good advantage of the extra months won by Arnold's fleet the year before. In July 1777, Burgoyne had had little trouble seizing Crown Point and Ticonderoga after only four days' siege. The British plan called for a smaller force, under Colonel Barry St. Leger, to march eastward from Lake Ontario into the Mohawk Valley and support Burgoyne's movements. St. Leger, however, dawdled on his march to besiege Fort Stanwix, one hundred miles west of Albany. South of the fort, his troops stopped a column of colonials at Oriskany and learned that a sizable force under General Arnold was en route. On hearing this news, St. Leger abandoned the siege and retreated toward Canada. When Arnold's men arrived at Oneida Lake on August 24, they could see St. Leger's vessels in the distance, heading back toward Lake Ontario and out of the campaign.

Soon afterward, Burgoyne learned that General Howe's army in New York would not be joining him for their irresistible march through the heart of the colonies to crush the rebellion. Instead, Burgoyne and his army of around ten thousand were left to face the growing colonial threat by themselves. On September 19, Burgoyne's army met the colonial force under General Horatio Gates at the Battle of Freeman's Farm, later recalled as the First Battle of Saratoga by many veterans. This sizable force of colonists was not only a numerical match for their British counterparts, but also considerably well fed, and better equipped than they had been the previous year. When the fighting ended, Burgoyne had driven the colonials back, but only after badly depleting his ammunition and supplies. At the same time, the threat to the colonies helped rouse militia from miles around, strengthening the American cause. Nineteen days later, the two armies clashed again at a place known as Bemis Heights. With the British line resting in woods on either end, the colonials took advantage of the cover to launch surprise attacks, repeatedly breaking the British lines. As General Simon Fraser rode out to rally the faltering Redcoats, Benedict Arnold called on an old comrade to help finish the enemy. Riding up to Daniel Morgan, still in command of his riflemen, Arnold shouted, "That gallant officer is General Fraser; I admire and respect him, but it is necessary that he should die—take your stations in that wood and do your duty." Moments later, Fraser lay dead, his battle lines dissolving in confusion.[4]

The battle was not yet won for the colonials. Smarting from a feud with General Gates, who had ordered him to remain out of the fighting, General Arnold was more brash and daring than usual. General Enoch Poor remembered his presence on the field: "Arnold rushed into the thickest of the fight with his usual recklessness, and at times, acted like a madman. . . . As a prominent object among the enemy showed itself, he would seize the nearest rifle-gun and take deliberate aim."[5]

Arnold had no troops of his own, General Gates having relieved him of command earlier in the day, and at that moment Gates's aide Major John Armstrong was racing to find Arnold so as to deliver Gates's order that Arnold return to his tent immediately, lest he "do some rash thing!" But with General Gates safely in the rear at his headquarters, unaware of the perilously shifting battle, Arnold dashed to the thick of the fighting, leading men in charges upon fortified British redoubts. An American officer in Henry Dearborn's command that day remembered Arnold "riding in front of the line, his eyes flashing, pointing with his sword to the advancing foe, with a voice that rung clear as a trumpet and electrified the line he called upon the men to follow him to the charge, and then dashing forward, closely followed by his troops, he hurled them like a tornado on the British line and swept it away." The targets of Arnold's wrath were two British strongholds that later became known as the Balcarres Redoubt and Breymann Redoubt. After leading colonial troops in a number of attacks on Balcarres without success, Arnold wheeled his horse, galloped through the fire from both sides, and reached the Breymann Redoubt in time to lead the American troops there over the works, routing the German soldiers defending it.[6]

As one American officer later recalled, "Nothing could exceed the bravery of Arnold on this day; he seemed the very genius of war, infuriated by the conflict and maddened by Gates's refusal to send reinforcements, which he repeatedly called for, and knowing he was meeting the brunt of the battle, he seemed inspired with the fury of a demon." As he cleared the crest of the earthworks, however, Arnold finally paid for his brashness and courage. His horse reared and fell on his leg, breaking the bone and adding to the pain caused by a musketball that had hit the leg as well. Henry Dearborn was the first to reach him, and as he helped slide his old Quebec comrade from under the horse, Arnold could only exclaim that it was "the same leg!" and lament that the ball had not pierced his heart.[7]

THE BATTLE OF Saratoga effectively ended when Arnold led the successful charge on the Breymann Redoubt. Ten days later, without further fighting, General Burgoyne surrendered his army en masse to General Gates. The victory showed that an army of Continental soldiers could stand and fight with the British. Thomas Anburey, a British officer who witnessed the battle, indicated that the fighting abilities of the colonials had earned them a large measure of respect. "The courage and obstinacy with which the Americans fought were the astonishment of everyone, and we now become fully convinced they are not that contemptible enemy we had hitherto imagined them, incapable of standing a regular engagement, and that they would only fight behind strong and powerful works." General Burgoyne expressed similar views in a private letter to Lord Germaine.[8]

The surrender of the Crown's northern army, however, was not the only success to which the rebellious colonies could lay claim by the close of 1777. While the colonials in the north had been struggling to take Quebec, General Washington had devised a plan to aid in his efforts against the British forces in Boston. What he needed most was artillery, and there were enough cannons in colonial possession to do the work if he could get them to the heights outside the city. In a journey that nearly rivaled that of the Arnold expedition, Washington sent General Henry Knox and his men to drag fifty-nine cannons and mortars on ox-drawn sleds three hundred miles over snow and ice in the dead of winter to the colonial army at Cambridge. A grateful General Washington placed these guns on Dorchester Heights so as to command the British-held city below. The colonials' siege had bottled the British up there for nearly a year, and the arrival of this artillery now rendered their position completely untenable. On March 17, 1776, all British forces in Boston set sail for Halifax, Nova Scotia. When these ships departed, the Crown's military control over the colonies had dwindled to just one city: Quebec.

For their successes in this first year of warfare the colonies had Benedict Arnold to thank. These victories led directly from his foresight in recognizing the value of Ticonderoga and Crown Point at the outset of hostilities, his efforts to seize, secure, and refortify these important positions, and the pressure he placed on the King's ministers when he nearly seized Quebec. His dogged resistance of Carleton and Burgoyne as they pushed to split the colonies in half through New York, his leadership in building a navy out of the wilderness and commanding it with just enough success to delay the British journey south by one season, and, finally, his impetuous display of courage and skill, which led to the victory at Saratoga, had brought about every success that the colonials could claim against their more powerful foe. All of this should have made Arnold a national hero and won him the highest praise that Congress could bestow, but it did not.

As for the expedition against Quebec itself, hindsight revealed numerous points at which the probability of colonial success was quite high. Most prominently, the wounding of Arnold and the death of Montgomery may have sealed the fate of the assault. Even those inside the city who successfully fought off the attackers later expressed their opinions on how close to success the colonials might have come. Though he was a British sea captain drafted into service as a commander of artillery, John Hamilton had a clear enough view of the attack on the city from the British side of the barricades to offer an opinion on a different possible outcome. "For had the enemy pushed boldly on through our defile," he later wrote, "having got under our last

barrier in the Sault au Matelot they must certainly have carried it."
Major Henry Caldwell, unaware of the confused and piecemeal arrival
of colonial troops on the opposite side of the barricade during the assault, attributed their failure to inadequate determination. "Had they
acted with more spirit, they might have pushed in at first and possessed themselves of the whole of Lower Town, and let their friends in
at the other side, before our people had time to have recovered from a
certain degree of panic, which seized them on the first news of the
post being surprised."[9]

Many of these possibilities must have tormented Arnold in the
months after the failed assault, especially while he lay idly in bed re-
cuperating. Would the outcome have been different if he had not been
wounded or Montgomery not slain at the outset of the fighting? If Colonel Enos had continued on to Quebec with his division, adding a few
hundred men to aid Arnold and Montgomery or to open a third point
of attack? If Arnold had mounted an assault on Quebec as soon as he
reached Pointe Levi, and before Colonel MacLean could help prepare
the garrison's defenders? If Livingston and Brown had successfully
lured defenders to the opposite side of the city with their diversions?
If, if, if. . . . The knowledge of how near he came to success must have
been difficult to abide.

As it turned out, however, the failure of Arnold's men to seize the
citadel at Quebec probably played a significant role in helping the colonials gain their ultimate goal of independence. Had the men of the expedition marched triumphantly through the streets of the lower town
and up to the governor's palace to accept Carleton's surrender, they
might have won the proverbial battle but lost the war. An American victory at Quebec in late 1775 would have greatly altered the response of
the British Crown to the situation in the colonies, forcing George Washington to commit large numbers of troops to the defense of Canada, his
new prize, thus weakening the colonial force near Boston. Ironically, the
expedition's failure at Quebec led directly to the eventual victory at
Saratoga, a battle that not only weakened the British in America but also
convinced the French to offer their support to the fledgling nation. The
British reinforcements that landed at Quebec City in May 1776 became
the army that General Burgoyne surrendered en masse at Saratoga in
October the following year, permanently removing them from the war.

The failure of the colonials to take Quebec, and their stubborn resistance to British counterattacks all the way to Valcour Island, made the pivotal victory at Saratoga possible. As historian Alfred Thayer Mahan noted, "That the Americans were strong enough to impose the capitulation of the British army at Saratoga was due to the invaluable year of delay secured by their little navy on Lake Champlain, created by the indomitable energy, and handled with the indomitable courage of the traitor, Benedict Arnold." The assault on Quebec drew Burgoyne's army to Canada. The homemade American fleet at Valcour Island slowed his approach into the heart of the colonies. The surrender at Saratoga sealed the fate of the British in their attempts to retain their dominance in North America. In each of these pivotal crises, Benedict Arnold was the catalyst.[10]

Had Arnold and Montgomery not threatened Quebec so seriously in the first year of the conflict, the British forces that the Crown diverted to Quebec in response, might instead have reinforced His Majesty's armies at Boston or New York, making it far less likely that General Washington's army could have eventually succeeded. By attempting but failing to seize Quebec, Benedict Arnold led a sizable British force into a trap that he helped spring at Saratoga twenty-two months afterward. French recognition followed, as did several more years of warfare and struggle, but the colonial successes in 1776 and 1777 set the stage for the birth of a nation.

IN THE SPRING that followed the battles at Saratoga, in a speech to his nation's governing body, the general who had commanded the army praised Benedict Arnold as instrumental in the colonial victory. But this was General Burgoyne, the British commander. As for General Gates, Arnold's superior and the general who spent the entire battle within a stone's throw of his own campfire, he chose literally to ignore the man who had won the battle for the colonials in as close to a single-handed manner as such conflicts allow.[11]

Arnold was aware that a combination of conniving former British officers in the Continental Army and some of their supporters in the Continental Congress worked diligently to damage his reputation and career. At nearly every opportunity, as he saw it, these plotters sought to undermine whatever success those fighting in the field might gain. First they turned on his old friend General Philip Schuyler after Ticonderoga, and then they even began to undermine General Washington himself. As he watched all of this unfold from his bed, where the pain of the wounds of Quebec and Breymann's Redoubt held him, Arnold's disgust and contempt boiled. By the time he plotted with Major André to turn the American garrison at West Point over to the British, his disgust, contempt, and anger had driven him to commit the highest crime imaginable to an emerging nation. As reward for his treason, the Crown paid Arnold ten thousand pounds and a commission in the British army. He moved to London where he found a mixed welcome, then returned to the colonies to lead British troops on campaigns in Virginia and against his home state of Connecticut. After the war he was unable to find employment in England, so he returned to British Canada with his family in 1787, settling in St. John, New Brunswick, where he spent four years in the shipping business with his sons, but then returned to London and died there in 1801.

AFTER THE WAR, Aaron Burr became a lawyer in New York, often wrangling in the courtroom with fellow patriot and veteran Alexander Hamilton, though the two were friends outside of their legal debates. In 1791, however, Burr became U.S. senator from New York by defeating General Philip Schuyler, then Hamilton's father-in-law. In the U.S. presidential election of 1800, Burr, a Federalist, ran against Thomas Jefferson, the Republican vice-president. The election ended with each receiving seventy-three electoral votes. As a result, the decision moved to the U.S. House of Representatives, where the deadlock continued through thirty-five ballots. In the end, Burr's former New York friend Alexander Hamilton convinced the Federalists to yield, allowing Jefferson to become the nation's third president. As part of the agreement in the House, Burr became vice-president. Nearly four years later, after Burr blamed Hamilton for his failed attempt at the New York governorship, the ill will between the two men lingered, contributing to a famous duel in which Burr killed Hamilton.

Like his commander on the Quebec expedition, Burr found himself caught up in charges of treason, for which he stood trial in 1807. As Jefferson described it, Burr led a conspiracy aimed at "separating the western states from us, of adding Mexico to them, and of placing himself at their head." Burr's alleged plan called for an assault on Mexico, which would lead to the secession of western states to form a new nation. U.S. Supreme Court Chief Justice John Marshall presided over the trial, which ended in Burr's acquittal. After the trial, Burr traveled to Europe, and remained there in self-imposed exile until 1812, when he returned to the United States and resumed his law practice. Controversy of one kind or another plagued him, and he remained poor, even destitute, and then partially paralyzed by stroke until his death in 1836.

IN 1827, REVEREND William A. Drew produced a newspaper in Gardiner, Maine, and had occasion to pay a visit to one of the town's most prominent citizens. It seems that Henry Dearborn was so smitten with the shores of the Kennebec River during his 1775 passage thereon, that he returned there to settle after the war; but this did not end his long journeys or his military service. Paroled from captivity in Quebec in 1776, when Governor Carleton exchanged him for a British soldier in the captive care of the colonials, he returned to the lower colonies and joined Colonel Alexander Scammell's Third New Hampshire Regiment as its major. After Ticonderoga and Saratoga, Dearborn endured the winter at Valley Forge, fought at the Battle of Monmouth, and was on General Washington's staff at the Siege of Yorktown. When the war ended, he settled on the Kennebec, and represented the District of Maine in the Third and Fourth U.S. Congresses before Thomas Jefferson made him secretary of war for the entire eight years of his term as president. In January 1812, President Madison made him the senior major general in the United States Army in the War of 1812, and he again set out to fight the British in New York and Canada. His performance in this conflict was lacking, however, and after an illness and a term as commander of New York City, then minister to Portugal, he retired to Roxbury, Massachusetts, where he died in June 1829. Dearborn County, Indiana, and Dearborn, Michigan, are named in his honor.

In that visit two years before Dearborn died, Reverend William A. Drew paid a call on the old general at his home in Gardiner, along the Kennebec. Forty years later, Reverend Drew wrote a story about the visit in the pages of the *Maine Standard* built largely on his recollection of their conversation. Among the fascinating anecdotes in this tale was the story of a legendary Indian princess of mixed French and Kennebec ancestry. As the Dearborn-to-Drew story went, the princess, named Jacataqua, lived on Swan Island, in the midst of the Kennebec River, and became smitten with the young Aaron Burr when he disembarked from his ship to spend a night on the island. So taken with him was the princess that she agreed to join the march so as to be with him. Several days later, while the expedition was organizing for the start of the march at Fort Western, the two young lovers became the focal point of a huge banquet for which they combined to kill a bear that became the main course of the meal. One revealing portion of the story recites the supposed details of Burr's clothing at the banquet, right down to his "silver knee and shoe buckles," a description which varies greatly from the picture Burr himself drew in a letter to his sister that same day. Burr's letter describes the rough appearance of a fringed rifleman's outfit, whereas the account that Drew attributed to Dearborn depicts a refined gentlemanly costume.[12]

Not one to let factual details get in the way of a good story, Reverend Drew followed the love story all the way to Montreal, where the princess began to show signs of pregnancy. One night the two young lovers stopped at a spring for a drink and there encountered a British officer on the same errand. The officer agreed to care for Jacataqua and placed her in a local convent until the baby, presumably Burr's daughter, was born. At Burr's request, the officer adopted the child, even taking her back to his home in Scotland at war's end. During the European trip that followed his treason trial, Burr reconnected with the officer and his daughter, who eventually moved to New York and cared for the weak and destitute Burr until his death. Without mentioning Jacataqua directly, Burr biographer James Parton left enough hints in his *Life and Times of Aaron Burr*, published in 1858, to fuel the legend further, recalling conversations between the invalid Burr and his female caretaker that suggest she was his daughter.[13]

In assessing the legend of Jacataqua, it is important to remember that fifty-two years passed between the events described and a seventy-six-year-old Henry Dearborn's narration of them to Reverend Drew, who then wrote them down only after forty more years of fading memories intervened. Further, since Dearborn had served as secretary of war under Thomas Jefferson, and since Burr had nearly prevented Jefferson from becoming president, their rivalry gave Dearborn a vested interested in besmirching Burr's reputation. Part of the campaign to damage Burr politically, involved spreading rumors of his penchant for womanizing, a reputation that fed nicely into the Jacataqua story. Nevertheless, Dearborn's story, with the help of Reverend Drew, found purchase in local tradition and continued to circulate in various forms for decades afterward. The legend persists today, although none of the many journals and memoirs of the expedition mentions either an Indian princess or the elaborate barbecue in which she played a central role.

REVOLUTIONARY WAR HERO GENERAL NATHANAEL GREENE ONCE DEclared, "Great generals are scarce—there are few Morgans around." It was fortunate for the American cause, then, that Daniel Morgan returned from captivity in Quebec, rose to the rank of general in the Continental Army, and proved essential in the colonial victories at Saratoga and Cowpens. In 1797, his fellow Virginians sent him to Congress as their representative. He served one term and declined to run for a second. In 1802, his friends and family laid him to rest in Winchester, Virginia. In his honor, there are Morgan Counties in Alabama, Georgia, Illinois, Indiana, Kentucky, Missouri, Ohio, Tennessee, and West Virginia.

IN 1776, THE Colony of Rhode Island had the largest population of black slaves in New England, and Newport was the largest slave-trading port in the newly forming nation. When the First Rhode Island Regiment dwindled in size that year, the General Assembly voted that "every able-bodied Negro, Mulatto, and Indian man-slave" could enlist for the duration of the war. The colonial government would pay these new recruits the same as freemen in the service. More important, however, was that all recruits held as slaves before enlisting would be declared free once they joined the regiment, and the government would even compensate their owners. In that pivotal year of independence, Rhode Island was home to more than three thousand slaves, but the recruiting scheme bore little fruit. Fewer than two hundred soldiers enlisted under the program. Despite the relatively low number of soldiers with African heritage in the ranks, the newly constituted First Rhode Island became known as "The Black Regiment."[14]

To lead these soldiers into the field, General Washington chose

Colonel Christopher Greene, a veteran of the Arnold expedition, who had recently received his formal parole from Governor Carleton as the result of an exchange of prisoners. On November 4, 1777, Congress ordered the Board of War to present him with an elegant sword in gratitude for his defense of Fort Mercer, in New Jersey. Early in 1781, Greene was at his headquarters, overlooking New York's Croton River, north of Manhattan, when a party of loyalists surprised and surrounded it. In the ensuing fight, they made a widow of Colonel Greene's wife, leaving her to raise their three sons and four daughters alone. With the colonel until his death was another veteran of Arnold's march, Samuel Ward, Jr., who served as major of the regiment.

In August 1776, Ward had returned to Rhode Island from captivity and discovered that his father and namesake, Governor Samuel Ward, Sr., had died of smallpox in March, while "Sammy" was enduring life in Quebec as a guest of Governor Carleton. The following January, Ward became a major, and went on to fight in the battles at Morristown, New Jersey, and Saratoga, New York. He suffered through the following winter with the army at Valley Forge, an experience for which the march to Quebec had suitably prepared him. When the war came to a close, Lieutenant Colonel Ward became a merchant, while expanding the familial relationship to his late brother-in-law and former commander, Christopher Greene, by marrying Greene's cousin Phebe.[15]

Governor Carleton paroled Return J. Meigs in January 1777, which allowed him honorably to resume service of his newly formed country. Four months later, having been promoted to lieutenant colonel, he led a successful raid on Sag Harbor, Long Island. Congress voted him a sword in honor of his actions. After the war, in 1787, the Ohio Company of Associates appointed him one of their first surveyors. After settling in Ohio and Tennessee, he became the U.S. government's Indian agent to the Cherokees. When he was eighty-two years old, he offered his home to a visiting chief and moved his own quarters into a tent. As a result, he contracted pneumonia and died on January 28, 1823. The people of Ohio elected his son, Return, Jr., to the governorship and U.S. Senate.[16]

After the war, young John Henry returned to his native Pennsylvania, where he became a lawyer and eventually the president judge of Lancaster and Dauphin Counties. Decades later, he corresponded with fellow veterans of the Quebec expedition, such as Archibald Steele, John Taylor, and others, and eventually produced the longest, most complete memoir of the expedition written by a veteran. He titled it *An Accurate and Interesting Account of the Hardships and Sufferings of That Band of Heroes, Who Traversed the Wilderness in the Campaign Against Quebec in 1775,* and though it is, in fact, interesting, its accuracy is more than questionable, for it includes numerous contradictions—not unusual for a story written from thirty-year-old memories. Judge Henry died in 1811.[17]

Reuben Colburn never received the pay that George Washington and Benedict Arnold had promised, though he continued to petition the government for payment as late as 1824. He had devised the expedition, provided it with experienced guides, survey maps, provisions, and 220 bateaux. In exchange for his vigorous patriotism, Colburn fell into financial ruin from which it took him years to recover. He did not carry a musket through the blizzard to the walls of Quebec, but his contribution to the expedition was as important as that of anyone else in the American cause.[18]

As FOR THE British who defended Quebec, Allan MacLean was commissioned adjutant general for Canada in 1776 and promoted to brigadier general. At the end of the war, MacLean sold his commission and retired to London, where he lived to the age of seventy-two. For his pivotal role in Quebec's defense, Captain Hamilton was made Sir John Hamilton, First Baronet of Trebinshun, in 1776. Their comrade-in-arms Henry Caldwell received a reward of twenty-five hundred pounds for his part in the defense of Quebec against Benedict Arnold and Richard Montgomery, who used his mansion as their headquarters. He later became receiver general of Lower Canada and a member of the Privy Council. When the siege of the town ended, Governor Carleton chose Caldwell to carry to London the dispatches reporting the victory. His military service earned him the King's praise and five hundred pounds reward. In addition, His Majesty promoted Caldwell to the honorary rank of lieutenant colonel in America and appointed him to Quebec's Legislative Council. Thirteen years after his death, the provincial government discovered that Caldwell had embezzled nearly forty thousand pounds during the exercise of his duties.

Sir Guy Carleton recognized the loyalty of British subjects in the colonies and helped establish new settlements in New Brunswick and Nova Scotia. In 1782, King George recommended him as "the Man who would in general by the Army be looked on as the best officer," and appointed him to succeed Sir Henry Clinton as commander-in-chief in North America. In that role, Carleton became the first major British official to recognize the United States of America. He lived into his eighty-fifth year.

THOSE WHO SUFFERED the most, while gaining the least in glory, promotion, or satisfaction, were the enlisted men who wallowed in their misery as prisoners in Quebec with little hope of freedom. One or two escape plots failed to achieve any success, except that the plotters found themselves with the added discomfort of iron shackles on their wrists and ankles. Private Simon Fobes of Captain Hubbard's company of musketmen was among those who had endured the march through Maine and the cold misery leading up to the assault on the city, only to find themselves held in a virtual dungeon with small rations and little comfort. For these men, filth and disease were especially trying. "When the pock was coming out on seventy or eighty of our number," wrote Fobes years afterward, "our fever very high, with no water to drink, some of the men drank of their own urine, which made the fever rage too violently to be endured." Those not delusional from their fever suffered greatly from the disease and other forms of distress. "The most of us had the small-pox very hard, our flesh seemed a mass of corruption; at the same time we were almost covered with vermin. . . . Our clothes were stiff with corrupted matter." As far as Fobes could determine, the smallpox alone claimed the lives of at least one in twelve prisoners that winter.[19]

Faced with an endless captivity in these horrible conditions, Fobes and two other prisoners agreed to serve as deckhands on a British warship patrolling the river between Montreal and Quebec, hoping the change in their environment would offer a chance at escape. By August 1776, having not yet found an opportunity to slip away from their captors, Fobes and his companions got word that their fellow prisoners back in Quebec were about to board a ship to return them to Boston and freedom, under a parole agreement with Governor Carleton. When their shipboard captors ignored their desperate pleas to return to Quebec and join the others, the threesome finally made a dash for freedom during a brief trip on shore. They managed to reach the southern shore of the Saint Lawrence and eventually the mouth of the Chaudière undetected. Once in this more familiar region, however, the group took stock of their circumstances with apprehension. "Anxiety," recalled Fobes, "as to the final issue of our undertaking, and thoughts of the circumstances we were in—six hundred miles from home, three hundred of which lay through an unbroken wilderness—without food or any means of taking game, bore heavily on our minds. . . ."[20]

Confronting the thought of a second trip through the wilderness that had treated them so harshly the previous fall, the men of the group could see little hope of success in any other course of action, and they pressed on toward the Maine frontier. After passing Chaudière Pond and navigating around the swamps to its south, they were reminded of their previous passage through the region when they came upon human hair and bones, "doubtless the spot where some of our fellow-soldiers perished the Fall before on their way to Quebec." Once they had passed over the Height of Land, they found a bateau they had abandoned on the march northward, and used it to travel down the Dead River to the Great Carrying Place. Thanks to warmer weather and the help of the current that had resisted them on their way to Quebec, the return trip was considerably briefer and infinitely less painful than the trek north had been the previous year. With the help of settlers along the Kennebec, some of whom had struck up small farmsteads in the time since the expedition passed by the year before, the weary band reached the area near what is now the state capitol at Augusta. Here they agreed to help load wood onto a sailing vessel in return for passage to Boston, its destination. It took the ship two weeks to pass down the Kennebec against contrary winds, after which they endured an anxious voyage along the coastal inlets and bays to avoid British warships. After two days of sailing the Maine coast, they passed the small New Hampshire shoreline and came within sight of a lighthouse at the head of Boston Harbor. Onshore, they sought out the military commander there and received enough money to make their way.[21]

After the group divided in search of their respective homes, Simon Fobes took the road toward Worcester, hoping to reach the home of his parents in a few days. He stopped along the way to visit with two of the officers of the expedition who had returned from Quebec sooner than he, under the parole agreement, had begun recovering from their ordeal, and were working their way back into civilian life. Both welcomed their former comrade into their homes, giving him what aid they could to ease the balance of his journey.

On that last day of September, when Fobes surprised his family with his sudden appearance at their home, an ordeal ended for the young farmer, perhaps the last member of Arnold's army to return from the trials and sufferings that had taken them to Quebec and home again. Though he did not yet know it, his fatigues and sacrifices were not in vain. The expedition through Maine to Quebec had contributed mightily to the cause of American independence, though its glory would soon become irreversibly tainted by the treasonous failings of its commander.

When Simon was safely home among his family again, his father thought it best that the family should give public thanks for his son's safe return. Because the local minister had become "a good deal of a Tory, so much so that he frequently prayed earnestly for the success of the British troops," the elder Fobes would not attend, but instead gave Simon a note to deliver to the minister on the Sabbath. "After the introductory service he read the paper I had handed him," recalled Fobes, "and then it seemed to me I never heard a more earnest and appropriate prayer than the one he offered, thanking Almighty God for his special care of me, a youth; carrying me through the dangers of battle, the hardships of a prisoner's life, and bringing me at length safely to my home and parents."[22]

No one could rightly say that Simon Fobes, like hundreds of his comrades on the expedition, had not served his colony and country with sacrifice and honor and had thus earned the right to settle down back home and once again take up the quieter, safer life of a farmer. Despite the hardships he had endured on his way to and from Quebec, however, Fobes chose a different path, which testifies to his patriotism. He recovered fully from his experience in Canada and was soon back in the Continental Army, serving as a lieutenant in Colonel Levi Wells's regiment, even though paper money had so depreciated that his pay would not allow him to buy his own clothes.

NOTES

I. THE FOURTEENTH COLONY

1. Simon Fobes Journal, in Kenneth Roberts, ed., *March to Quebec: Journals of the Members of Arnold's Expedition* (New York: Doubleday, 1938), pp. 612–13.
2. Ibid.
3. Samuel de Champlain, *The Voyages and Explorations of Samuel de Champlain (1604–1616)*, p. 97.
4. Ibid., p. 92.
5. Ibid., p. 97.
6. "Declaration of Colonial Rights by the First Continental Congress, October 14, 1774," *Journals of the Continental Congress, 1774–1789*, (Washington, D.C.: Library of Congress, 1904), vol. 1, pp. 63–73.
7. Ibid.
8. Paul David Nelson, *General Sir Guy Carleton, Lord Dorchester*, p. 11.
9. Ibid.
10. Ibid.
11. Carleton to Lord Dartmouth, Quebec, Oct. 25, 1775, in K. G. Davies, ed., *Documents of the American Revolution, 1770–1783*, vol. 11, pp. 165–66.
12. Carleton to Dartmouth, July 1, 1775, Colonial Office Papers, CO 42/34.
13. Carleton to Lord Dartmouth, June 7, 1775, Colonial Office Papers, CO 42/34.
14. For more detail on Arnold's prewar life, see James Kirby Martin, *Benedict Arnold, Revolutionary Hero: An American Warrior Reconsidered*.
15. Petition of Jonathan Brewer to Massachusetts Provincial Congress of Massachusetts Bay, May 1, 1775, in Peter Force, *American Archives*, series 2, vol. 4, p. 462.
16. Committee of Safety to the Massachusetts Congress, May 25, 1775, in Force, *American Archives*, series 4, vol. 2, pp. 716–17.
17. Benedict Arnold to Continental Congress, June 13, 1775, in Force, *American Archives*, series 4, vol. 2, pp. 976–77.
18. Ibid.
19. Ibid.
20. Ibid.
21. Philip Schuyler to Silas Deane, Albany, July 3, 1775, *Collections of the Connecticut Historical Society*, vol. 2 (1870), p. 252. Schuyler's hope was to get the Continental Congress to appoint Arnold as his adjutant.
22. George Washington to Philip J. Schuyler, Aug. 15, 1775, George Washington Papers, Library of Congress, 1741–99, series 3b, Varick Transcripts. The natives' visit occurred on Tuesday, Aug. 14, 1775.
23. Gerrit Roseboom, Intelligence Report on Indians in Canada, Albany, New York, Corresponding Sub-Committee, July 15, 1775, George Washington

Papers, Library of Congress, 1741–99, series 4, General Correspondence, 1697–1799.

24. George Washington to Philip J. Schuyler, Aug. 20, 1775, George Washington Papers, Library of Congress, 1741–99, series 3b, Varick Transcripts.

25. Philip J. Schuyler to George Washington, Aug. 27, 1775, George Washington Papers, Library of Congress, 1741–99, series 4, General Correspondence, 1697–1799.

26. John Montressor, Journal, in Kenneth Roberts, ed., *March to Quebec*, pp. 5–24.

27. Colburn signed a letter as a member of the Committee of Safety on June 13, 1775, asking the Massachusetts Provincial Congress for aid in defending the province (Massachusetts State Archives). See also *Pennsylvania Gazette*, Aug. 30, 1775; Reuben Colburn to George Washington, Aug. 20, 1775, and Sept. 3, 1775, George Washington Papers, Library of Congress, 1741–99, series 5, Financial Papers, Revolutionary War Accounts, Vouchers, and Receipted Accounts 2.

28. Benedict Arnold to Reuben Colburn, Watertown, Mass., Aug. 21, 1775, in Philander Chase, et al., eds., *Papers of George Washington: Revolutionary War Series*, vol. 1, pp. 409–10.

29. Samuel Goodwin to George Washington, Oct. 17, 1775, in Force, *American Archives*, series 4, vol. 2, pp. 1086–87.

30. George Washington to Reuben Colburn, Cambridge, Mass., Sept. 3, 1775, in Chase, et al., eds., *Papers of George Washington*, vol. 1, p. 409.

31. *Pennsylvania Gazette*, Aug. 30, 1775.

2. TO QUEBEC AND VICTORY!

1. Philip J. Schuyler to George Washington, Sept. 20, 1775, George Washington Papers, Library of Congress, 1741–99, series 4, General Correspondence.

2. George Washington, General Orders, Sept. 5, 1775, George Washington Papers, Library of Congress, 1741–99.

3. George Washington to Canadian Citizens, Sept. 6, 1775, George Washington Papers, Library of Congress, 1741–99, series 3b, Varick Transcripts.

4. Roberts, ed., *March to Quebec*, p. 173. Rick Meigs, *The Meigs Family in America: The First Six Generations* (available at www.meigs.org).

5. Roberts, ed., *March to Quebec*, p. 127.

6. Ibid., pp. 129–30.

7. George Washington to Col. Lewis Morris, Cambridge, Mass., Aug. 4, 1775, Manuscripts Division, Department of Rare Books and Special Collections, Princeton University Library, box 2, f. 37. John Hancock to George Washington, July 19, 1775, in Chase, et al., eds., *Papers of George Washington*, vol. 1, pp. 132–33.

8. Fobes, Simon, Narrative of Arnold's Expedition to Quebec, Mahoning Valley Historical Society Collections, vol. 1, 1876, introductory section.

9. Ibid.

10. John Joseph Henry, Journal, in Roberts, ed., *March to Quebec*, p. 301.

11. George Washington, General Orders, Sept. 8, 1775, George Washington Papers, Library of Congress, 1741–99, series 3g, Varick Transcripts.

12. Joseph Leach, Boston Harbor Shipping Report, Sept. 6, 1775, George Washington Papers, Library of Congress, 1741–99, series 4, General Correspondence, 1697–1799. George Washington, General Orders, Sept. 6, 1775, George Washington Papers, Library of Congress, 1741–99. George Washington to Nicholas Cooke, Sept. 6, 1775, George Washington Papers, Library of Congress,

1741–1799, series 2, Letterbooks. George Washington to Bermuda (British) Citizens, Sept. 6, 1775, George Washington Papers, Library of Congress, 1741–1799, series 3c, Varick Transcripts.

13. Simon Fobes, Journal, in Roberts, ed., *March to Quebec*, p. 581.

14. Isaac Senter, Journal, in Roberts, ed., *March to Quebec*, p. 198.

15. Benedict Arnold, Journal, in Roberts, ed., *March to Quebec*, pp. 44(a–b).

16. For more on the Popham Colony of 1607, see Eliot Tozer, "Maine's Lost Colony," *Yankee Magazine*, May 2001, p. 19; "Finding the Lost Colony," *Early American Life*, vol. 34, no. 2 (2003), pp. 42–45.

17. For background on the possible Viking presence on the Kennebec, see Einar Haugen, "The Rune Stones of Spirit Pond, Maine," *Man in the Northeast*, vol. 4 (1972), pp. 62–79; O. G. Landsverk, "The Spirit Pond Cryptography," *Man in the Northeast*, vol. 6 (1972), pp. 67–75; Edward J. Lenik, "Excavations at Spirit Pond," *Northeast Anthropology*, vol. 9 (Spring 1975), pp. 54–59. Carbon 14 dating of charcoal found in the sod houses dated this material to somewhere between 1335 and 1475 A.D. This excavation was conducted in 1972–73, by the New England Antiquities Research Association, under the jurisdiction of the State Parks and Recreation Commission. Scholarly study of the sod houses has led to a widespread belief that they are colonial in nature, dating from the seventeenth century or later. The origin of the rune stones remains a subject of great controversy, with some arguing they date from 1010 A.D., others from the fourteenth century, and many others that they are entirely a hoax.

18. Return J. Meigs, Journal, in Roberts, ed., *March to Quebec*, p. 174.

19. Parker M. Reed, *History of Bath and Environs* (Portland, Maine: Lakeside Press, 1894), pp. 55–57, reprints the muster roll of McCobb's regiment back in Cambridge on September 7, 1775. This shows only forty-four men detached, meaning that McCobb had done some hasty recruiting to reach his complement of sixty-four.

20. In addition to the Kennebec, Merrymeeting Bay is formed by the confluence of the Androscoggin, Eastern, Abagadasset, Cathance, and Muddy Rivers.

21. Henry Dearborn, Journal, in Roberts, ed., *March to Quebec*, p. 131. Benedict Arnold, Journal, in ibid. (1980 softcover edition, Down East books), p. 44a. Quote from John Pierce, Journal, in ibid., p. 655.

22. Benedict Arnold, Journal, in Roberts, ed., *March to Quebec*, p. 44b.

23. Arnold to George Washington, Sept. 25, 1775, George Washington Papers, Library of Congress.

24. Dennis Getchell and Samuel Barry, Letter, Sept. 13, 1775, Maine Historical Society, coll. S-104, misc. box 2/44.

25. Ibid. The report states that the local natives had "gone to Johnson" to trade. Sir John Johnson was the last Provincial Grand Master of the Province of New York, and coordinated trade with Native Americans in the area around northern New York and Montreal from 1766 until the Revolution.

3. SCOUTING PARTY

1. William Williamson, *History of the State of Maine*, pp. 391, 418. Getchell family data from Everett Lamont Getchell, *The Family of Samuel Getchell of Salisbury, Mass.*; Addison Getchell, *Genealogy of the Getchell Family*. Dennis went on to serve in the American army during the Revolution, eventually achieving

the rank of major. Arnold mentions the guiding work of Nehemiah in his journals. John J. Henry's memoir of the expedition reverses the first names of the guides John Getchell and Jeremiah Horn. There was not a Jeremiah among the Vassalboro Getchells at that time.

2. Benedict Arnold Journal, in Roberts, *March to Quebec*, p. 44b.
3. Paxtang Township was formed in 1729 and named for a stream passing through it known by its native name. By the late eighteenth century, it had been divided into several separate townships, including Upper, Middle, and Lower Paxtang, Susquehanna, Swatara Township, and the borough, now city, of Harrisburg.
4. John Joseph Henry, Journal, in Roberts, ed., *March to Quebec*, p. 313.
5. Ibid., p. 305.
6. Ibid., p. 307.
7. Ibid., p. 309.
8. Ibid., pp. 309–10.
9. Ibid., p. 311.
10. Ibid., pp. 314–15.
11. Ibid., p. 315.
12. Ibid., pp. 315–16.
13. Ibid., p. 316.
14. Ibid., p. 319.
15. Ibid., p. 321.
16. Ibid., p. 323.
17. Ibid., p. 324.
18. Ibid.
19. Ibid., p. 325.
20. Ibid., pp. 325–26.
21. Ibid., p. 326.
22. Ibid.
23. Ibid., p. 327.
24. Ibid., p. 328. In his entry for Sept. 23 (p. 306), Henry described an encounter with McKonkey in which the latter "showed himself as mean in spirit as he was devoid of decency. . . . Many years afterwards at Lancaster, in Pennsylvania, he applied for and received a loan by way of charity from me, which he meanly solicited with the most abject sycophancy."
25. Ibid., Oct. 17, p. 327.

4. CHALLENGING THE KENNEBEC

1. George Washington to Continental Congress, Sept. 21, 1775, George Washington Papers, Library of Congress, series 3a, Varick Transcripts.
2. Arnold to George Washington, Sept. 25, 1775, George Washington Papers, Library of Congress. George Washington to Daniel Morgan, Oct. 4, 1775, ibid.
3. Isaac Senter, Journal, in Roberts, ed., *March to Quebec*, p. 199.
4. Caleb Haskell, Journal, in Roberts, ed., *March to Quebec*, p. 474. Simeon Thayer, Journal, in ibid., p. 249.
5. Simeon Thayer, Journal, in Roberts, ed., *March to Quebec*, p. 249. Isaac Senter, Journal, in ibid., p. 199. Quote from Abner Stocking, Journal, in ibid., p. 547.
6. Simeon Thayer, Journal, in Roberts, ed., *March to Quebec*, p. 249. Ephraim Squier, Journal, in ibid., p. 622. Quote from Abner Stocking, Journal, in ibid., p. 547.

7. Roberts, ed., *March to Quebec*, p. 67. Simeon Thayer, Journal, in ibid., p. 249. Henry Dearborn, Journal, in ibid., p. 132. Isaac Senter, Journal, in ibid., p. 199. Benedict Arnold, Journal, in ibid., p. 44b. Arnold to General Washington, Sept. 27, 1775, George Washington Papers, Library of Congress. Return J. Meigs, Journal, in Roberts, ed., *March to Quebec*, p. 175. Quote from Abner Stocking, Journal, in ibid., p. 547.

8. Arnold to Washington, Sept. 27, 1775, in Roberts, ed., *March to Quebec*, p. 67. Abner Stocking, Journal, in ibid., p. 547. Caleb Haskell, Journal, in ibid., p. 474.

9. Benedict Arnold, Journal, in Roberts, ed., *March to Quebec*, p. 44b. Force, *American Archives*, series 4, vol. 3, p. 763. George Washington to Continental Congress, Sept. 21, 1775, George Washington Papers, Library of Congress.

10. Arnold to George Washington, Sept. 25, 1775, George Washington Papers, Library of Congress.

11. Ibid. Isaac Senter, Journal, in Roberts, ed., *March to Quebec*, p. 200.

12. Aaron Burr to Sally Burr Reeve, Sept. 24, 1775, in Mary-Jo Kline, ed., *Political Correspondence and Public Papers of Aaron Burr, 1756–1836*. 2 vols. (Princeton: Princeton University Press, 1983).

13. Arnold to George Washington, Sept. 25, 1775, George Washington Papers, Library of Congress. Isaac Senter, Journal, in Roberts, ed., *March to Quebec*, p. 200. Benedict Arnold, Journal, in ibid., p. 45.

14. Laurel Thatcher Ulrich, *A Midwife's Tale: The Life of Martha Ballard, Based on Her Diary, 1785–1812*, p. 173; Martha plied her trade in the area around and south of Fort Western. John Henry, Journal, in Roberts, ed., *March to Quebec*, pp. 14, 305. John Pierce, Journal, in ibid., p. 656. Pierce mentions "one Bollard a Tory lived there."

15. John Pierce, Journal, in Roberts, ed., *March to Quebec*, softcover edition (Camden, Maine: Down East Books, 1980), p. 657.

16. Arnold to Capt. Farnsworth, Sept. 29, 1775, in Roberts, ed., *March to Quebec*, p. 69.

17. Jouise Helen Coburn, *Skowhegan on the Kennebec*, vol. 1, pp. 140–44.

18. Simeon Thayer, Journal, in Roberts, ed., *March to Quebec*, p. 250.

19. Benedict Arnold, Journal, in Roberts, ed., *March to Quebec*, p. 46. Coburn, *Skowhegan on the Kennebec*, pp. 79, 144. J. W. Hanson, *History of the Old Towns Norridgewock and Canaan*, p. 127.

20. Simeon Thayer, Journal, in Roberts, ed., *March to Quebec*, p. 250. Abner Stocking, Journal, in ibid., p. 548.

21. Hanson, *History of the Old Towns Norridgewock and Canaan*, pp. 179–80. Nathan Parlin of Norridgewock was among those who joined Arnold's group, probably to help carry baggage as a paid laborer. He contracted smallpox on the trip.

22. George Morison, Journal, in Roberts, ed., *March to Quebec*, p. 519.

23. Abner Stocking, Journal, in Roberts, ed., *March to Quebec*, pp. 511, 548.

24. George Morison, Journal, in Roberts, ed., *March to Quebec*, p. 520.

25. Isaac Senter, Journal, in Roberts, ed., *March to Quebec*, pp. 202–3. Henry Dearborn, Journal, in ibid., p. 133.

26. George Morison, Journal, in Roberts, ed., *March to Quebec*, pp. 511–12. Simeon Thayer, Journal, in ibid., p. 251.

27. John Pierce, Journal, in Roberts, ed., *March to Quebec*, softcover edition (Camden, Maine: Down East Books, 1980), p. 656. Simeon Thayer, Journal, in Roberts, ed., *March to Quebec*, p. 250. William Humphrey, Journal, Oct. 2, at Rhode Island Historical Society, Providence, Rhode Island, Manuscripts Division, William Humphrey Diary, 9/9/1775–8/11/1776.

28. Isaac Senter, Journal, in Roberts, ed., *March to Quebec*, p. 203.
29. Ibid.
30. George Morison, Journal, in Roberts, ed., *March to Quebec*, p. 512.
31. Benedict Arnold, Journal, in Roberts, ed., *March to Quebec*, pp. 47–48.
32. Arnold's journal (ibid.) shows that he arrived at the falls on Monday morning, Oct. 2, and departed the following Monday, Oct. 9.
33. With his letter to Congress, dated Oct. 5, 1775 (George Washington Papers, Library of Congress), Washington sent these letters as enclosures. The most revealing was from Captain Thomas Gamble in Quebec to Major Sheriff in Boston, dated Sept. 6, 1775. Washington also passed this intelligence on to Schuyler. See George Washington to Philip J. Schuyler, Oct. 4, 1775, George Washington Papers, Library of Congress, 1741–99. In a letter written as he left Colburn's shipyard (Arnold to George Washington, Sept. 25, 1775, George Washington Papers, Library of Congress), Arnold estimated he would reach Chaudière Pond in twenty days. If we use Montressor's journal as an estimating tool, the trip down the Chaudière to Quebec would then take about eleven days, for a total of thirty-one days. When Washington received the news about Quebec on Oct. 5, there were twenty-one days left of Arnold's estimate.

5. THE RIVER DEAD

1. George Morison, Journal, in Roberts, ed., *March to Quebec*, p. 513.
2. Simon Fobes, Journal, in Roberts, ed., *March to Quebec*, p. 582.
3. George Morison, Journal, in Roberts, ed., *March to Quebec*, p. 521.
4. Ibid., p. 514.
5. John Pierce, Journal, in Roberts, ed., *March to Quebec*, p. 659. "Musquash" is a Native American name for a muskrat.
6. Ibid., p. 655. A perch (sometimes called a rod) is 16.5 feet.
7. George Morison, Journal, in Roberts, ed., *March to Quebec*, p. 514. Ephraim Squier, Journal, in ibid., p. 623.
8. George Morison, Journal, in Roberts, ed., *March to Quebec*, p. 514.
9. Simon Fobes, Journal, in Roberts, ed., *March to Quebec*, p. 582. Benedict Arnold, Journal, in ibid., pp. 49–50.
10. Isaac Senter, Journal, in Roberts, ed., *March to Quebec*, p. 205.
11. Ibid. George Morison, Journal, in Roberts, ed., *March to Quebec*, pp. 533–34.
12. George Morison, Journal, in Roberts, ed., *March to Quebec*, p. 521.
13. Arnold to John Mercier, Oct. 13, 1775, in Roberts, ed., *March to Quebec*, pp. 69–70. There are two copies of Arnold's letter to Quebec in print. The one in Force, *American Archives*, series 4, vol. 3, p. 1061, lists the addressee as "John Manir," but the copy that Cramahé sent to London on Nov. 9 is to John Dyer Mercier. The difference is probably attributable to unclear handwriting, but it was Mercier who ended up in the brig. See Cramahé to Lord Dartmouth, Nov. 9, 1775, in Davies, ed., *Documents of the American Revolution*, vol. 10, pp. 117–18. Information on Frederick Jaquin from Charles Edwin Allen, *Collections and Proceedings of the Maine Historical Society*, vol. 2, no. 3 (1892), pp. 351–79.
14. Arnold to George Washington, Oct. 13, 1775, in Roberts, ed., *March to Quebec*, pp. 71–73. Henry Dearborn, Journal, in ibid., p. 134.
15. Benedict Arnold, Journal, in Roberts, ed., *March to Quebec*, p. 50.
16. Arnold to Col. Farnsworth, Oct. 14, 1775, in Roberts, ed., *March to Quebec*, p. 73. Arnold to Lt. Col. Enos, Oct. 15, 1775 (two messages), in ibid., pp. 73–74.

17. Local legend has it that Bigelow climbed the mountain in order to see the spires of Quebec. This seems very unlikely, since, as a major, Bigelow was fully aware how far the army still was from Quebec and that the exertion needed to climb the snow-covered mountain would have been wasteful for men already stretched physically. In addition, Bigelow was too busy carrying out Arnold's order to retrieve provisions from the rear division to be going on a sightseeing trip.
18. Ephraim Squier, Journal, in Roberts, ed., *March to Quebec*, p. 622. John Topham, Journal, in ibid., p. 253.
19. John Pierce, Journal, in Roberts, ed., *March to Quebec*, softcover edition (Camden, Maine: Down East Books, 1980), p. 660.
20. Return Meigs, Journal, in Roberts, ed., *March to Quebec*, p. 178.
21. Simeon Thayer, Journal, in Roberts, ed., *March to Quebec*, p. 254.
22. John Henry, Journal, in Roberts, ed., *March to Quebec*, p. 330.
23. Benedict Arnold, Journal, in Roberts, ed., *March to Quebec*, pp. 54–55.
24. Isaac Senter, Journal, in Roberts, ed., *March to Quebec*, p. 209.
25. Kennebec County, Maine, Registry of Deeds, 1760–99, book 1, pp. 440–41. Getchell descendants still live in Vassalboro today. According to a personal conversation with Frank Getchell, family tradition holds that John and Nehemiah returned to the Dead River at a later season, when the water was low, and retrieved the barrel of coins. There certainly is no other easy way to explain how the brothers came into such an abundance of coins.
26. Henry Dearborn, Journal, in Roberts, ed., *March to Quebec*, p. 137.
27. Simon Fobes, Journal, in Roberts, ed., *March to Quebec*, p. 583. Lyman Coleman, *Genealogy of the Lyman Family in Great Britain and America*, p. 445. Benedict Arnold, Journal, in Roberts, ed., *March to Quebec*, pp. 55–56.
28. Arnold to Lt. Col. Enos, Oct. 24, 1775, in Roberts, ed., *March to Quebec*, p. 75.
29. Simeon Thayer, Journal, in Roberts, ed., *March to Quebec*, p. 256; Isaac Senter, Journal, in ibid., p. 210.
30. John Pierce, Journal, in Roberts, ed., *March to Quebec*, softcover edition (Camden, Maine: Down East Books, 1980), p. 666; John Topham, Journal, in ibid., p. 258.
31. Simeon Thayer, Journal, in Roberts, ed., *March to Quebec*, p. 257.
32. Isaac Senter, Journal, in Roberts, ed., *March to Quebec*, pp. 210–11.
33. Ibid. Simeon Thayer, Journal, in Roberts, ed., *March to Quebec*, p. 257.
34. Patricia Bigelow, ed., *Bigelow Family Genealogy*, vol. 1, p. 78.

6. THE KING OF TERRORS

1. Washington to President of Continental Congress, Oct. 24, 1775, in Force, *American Archives*, series 5, vol. 4, pp. 1151–52. Committee of Conference to President of Congress, Oct. 20, 1775, in ibid., series 4, vol. 3, pp. 1155–56. Washington to Committee of Falmouth, Oct. 24, 1775, in ibid., series 4, vol. 3, p. 1167.
2. Committee of Conference to President of Congress, Oct. 20, 1775, in Force, *American Archives*, series 4, vol. 3, pp. 1155–56.
3. Schuyler to President of Congress, Oct. 21, 1775, in Force, *American Archives*, series 4, vol. 3, pp. 1130–32.
4. Ibid. Montgomery to General Schuyler, Oct. 20, 1775, in Force, *American Archives*, series 4, vol. 3, pp. 1132–33.
5. *Quebec Gazette*, Oct. 26, 1775.

6. Force, *American Archives,* series 4, vol. 3, pp. 1417–20.

7. Ibid.

8. Arnold to John Manir [Mercier], Oct. 13, 1775, in Roberts, ed., *March to Quebec,* p. 69. On Nov. 9, Cramahé informed his superiors in England that he had "taken up" Mercier after intercepting two letters. Cramahé to Earl of Dartmouth, Nov. 9, 1775, in Davies, ed., *Documents of the American Revolution,* vol. 11, pp. 178–79.

9. Isaac Senter, Journal, in Roberts, ed., *March to Quebec,* p. 213.

10. Henry Dearborn, Journal, in Roberts, ed., *March to Quebec,* p. 137.

11. George Morison, Journal, in Roberts, ed., *March to Quebec,* p. 523.

12. John Pierce, Journal, in Roberts, ed., *March to Quebec,* p. 667. Benedict Arnold, Journal, in ibid., p. 58. Arnold to General Washington, Nov. 27, 1775, in ibid., pp. 77–78.

13. Abner Stocking, Journal, in Roberts, ed., *March to Quebec,* p. 553. Arnold to General Washington, Nov. 27, 1775, in ibid., pp. 77–78.

14. John Pierce, Journal, in Roberts, ed., *March to Quebec,* p. 667.

15. Benedict Arnold, Journal, in Roberts, ed., *March to Quebec,* softcover edition (Camden, Maine: Down East Books, 1980), pp. 58–59.

16. Arnold to "Field officers and captains in the detachment," Nov. 27, 1775, in Roberts, ed., *March to Quebec,* p. 79.

17. Simeon Thayer, Journal, in Roberts, ed., *March to Quebec,* p. 258.

18. Isaac Senter, Journal, in Roberts, ed., *March to Quebec,* pp. 213–15.

19. George Morison, Journal, in Roberts, ed., *March to Quebec,* p. 523.

20. John Henry, Journal, in Roberts, ed., *March to Quebec,* pp. 335–36.

21. Abner Stocking, Journal, in Roberts, ed., *March to Quebec,* p. 554.

22. Henry Dearborn, Journal, in Roberts, ed., *March to Quebec,* pp. 138–39.

23. Abner Stocking, Journal, in Roberts, ed., *March to Quebec,* p. 554. James Melvin, Journal, in ibid., p. 438.

24. James Melvin, Journal, in Roberts, ed., *March to Quebec,* p. 438. George Morison, Journal, in ibid., p. 524.

25. Isaac Senter, Journal, in Roberts, ed., *March to Quebec,* p. 217.

26. Ibid., p. 216.

27. Ibid., pp. 216–17. John Henry, Journal, in Roberts, ed., *March to Quebec,* p. 336. Simeon Thayer, Journal, in ibid., pp. 259–60. John Topham, Journal, in ibid., p. 260.

28. Isaac Senter, Journal, in Roberts, ed., *March to Quebec,* p. 217. Simeon Thayer, Journal, in ibid., p. 259.

29. Simeon Thayer, Journal, in Roberts, ed., *March to Quebec,* p. 260. Simon Fobes, Journal, in ibid., p. 584.

30. John Topham, Journal, in Roberts, ed., *March to Quebec,* in ibid., p. 261. George Morison, Journal, in ibid., pp. 525, 527–28. John Henry, Journal, in ibid., pp. 341–42.

31. James Melvin, Journal, in Roberts, ed., *March to Quebec,* p. 440. Simeon Thayer, Journal, in ibid., p. 259. Henry Dearborn, Journal, in ibid., p. 139. Dearborn to William Allen, quoted in *Proceedings of the Maine Historical Society,* vol. 1 (1831), p. 514. Jeremiah Greenman, Journal, in Robert C. Bray and Paul E. Bushnell, eds., *Diary of a Common Soldier in the American Revolution, 1775–1783: An Annotated Edition of the Military Journal of Jeremiah Greenman,* p. 18.

32. Mathias Ogden, Diary, Oct. 30, 1775, Morristown National History Park (here-after MNHP).
33. Isaac Senter, Journal, in Roberts, ed., *March to Quebec,* p. 218. John Henry, Journal, in ibid., p. 340.
34. Abner Stocking, Journal, in Roberts, ed., *March to Quebec,* pp. 555–56. George Morison, Journal, in ibid., p. 527.
35. John Henry, Journal, in Roberts, ed., *March to Quebec,* p. 337.
36. Abner Stocking, Journal, in Roberts, ed., *March to Quebec,* p. 556.
37. Ibid., p. 555.

7. THE QUÉBÉCOIS

1. Benedict Arnold, Journal, in Roberts, ed., *March to Quebec,* pp. 60–61.
2. Henry Dearborn, Journal, in Roberts, ed., *March to Quebec,* p. 140. John Pierce, Journal, in ibid., p. 670. Isaac Senter, Journal, in ibid., p. 219.
3. George Morison, Journal, in Roberts, ed., *March to Quebec,* p. 529.
4. Isaac Senter, Journal, in Roberts, ed., *March to Quebec,* p. 219.
5. Simon Fobes, Journal, in Roberts, ed., *March to Quebec,* p. 585. Simeon Thayer, Journal, in ibid., p. 231. John Topham, Journal, in ibid., p. 262.
6. John Henry, Journal, in Roberts, ed., *March to Quebec,* p. 343.
7. Caleb Haskell, Journal, in Roberts, ed., *March to Quebec,* p. 478. Abner Stocking, Journal, in ibid., p. 556.
8. George Morison, Journal, in Roberts, ed., *March to Quebec,* p. 531.
9. Isaac Senter, Journal, in Roberts, ed., *March to Quebec,* p. 220.
10. James Melvin, Journal, in Roberts, ed., *March to Quebec,* pp. 440–41. Isaac Senter, Journal, in ibid., pp. 220–21.
11. Isaac Senter, Journal, in Roberts, ed., *March to Quebec,* pp. 220–21.
12. Ibid.
13. John Henry, Journal, in Roberts, ed., *March to Quebec,* pp. 344–45.
14. Ibid.
15. Abner Stocking, Journal, in Roberts, ed., *March to Quebec,* p. 557.
16. Isaac Senter, Journal, in Roberts, ed., *March to Quebec,* p. 220. Abner Stocking, Journal, in ibid., p. 557. Return J. Meigs, Journal, in ibid., p. 181.
17. John Pierce, Journal, in Roberts, ed., *March to Quebec,* softcover edition (Camden, Maine: Down East Books, 1980), p. 671. Return J. Meigs, Journal, in ibid., p. 181.
18. Abner Stocking, Journal, in Roberts, ed., *March to Quebec,* p. 557.
19. Simeon Thayer, Journal, in Roberts, ed., *March to Quebec,* p. 262. Abner Stocking, Journal, in ibid., p. 557.
20. John Henry, Journal, in Roberts, ed., *March to Quebec,* pp. 346–47.
21. Ibid.
22. Ibid.
23. Ibid.
24. Isaac Senter, Journal, in Roberts, ed., *March to Quebec,* p. 222.
25. Henry Dearborn, Journal, in Roberts, ed., *March to Quebec,* pp. 140–41.
26. Ibid., pp. 145–46.
27. John Henry, Journal, in Roberts, ed., *March to Quebec,* pp. 345–46.
28. Benedict Arnold to unknown, Nov. 1, 1775, in Roberts, ed., *March to Quebec,* pp. 80–81.

29. John Pierce, Journal, in Roberts, ed., *March to Quebec,* p. 671. Isaac Senter, Journal, in ibid., p. 222. George Morison, Journal, in ibid., p. 531.
30. Abner Stocking, Journal, in Roberts, ed., *March to Quebec,* pp. 557, 558. Jeremiah Greenman, Journal, in Bray and Bushnell, eds., *Diary of a Common Soldier,* p. 19. John Pierce, Journal, in Roberts, ed., *March to Quebec,* p. 671. Isaac Senter, Journal, in ibid., p . 223.
31. J. M. LeMoine, *Album du Touriste,* p. 162. Mathias Ogden, Journal, Nov. 6–7, 1775, MNHP. Cramahé to Howe, "Quebeck, November 8, 1775," in Davies, ed., *Documents of the American Revolution,* vol. 11, pp. 175–76.
32. Mathias Ogden, Journal, Nov. 7, 1775, MNHP.
33. George Morison, Journal, in Roberts, ed., *March to Quebec,* p. 531.

8. QUEBEC AT LAST

1. Letter, "Quebeck, November 9, 1775," part of "Extract of Letters received in England," in Force, *American Archives,* pp. 1417–20.
2. Enos to Washington, Nov. 9, 1775, in Force, *American Archives,* series 4, vol. 3, p. 1610.
3. Ephraim Squier, Journal, in Roberts, ed., *March to Quebec,* pp. 624–25.
4. Ibid.
5. Ibid., p. 626. According to Pierce, the drowned man was named Seabrid Fitch.
6. Ibid., p. 628.
7. Extract of letter to gentleman in London, "Quebeck, November 7, 1775," in Force, *American Archives,* series 4, vol. 3, p. 1396.
8. "The Case of Lieutenant John Starke of His Majesties Navy," Archives of the National Maritime Museum, Greenwich, England, MS 149/129, BGR/9.
9. Vialar/Lester, "Orderly Book," in Fred C. Würtele, *Blockade of Quebec in 1775–1776 by the American Revolutionists (Les Bastonnais)* (Quebec: Daily Telegraph Job Printing House, 1905–06), pp. 176–77. *Quebec Gazette,* Nov. 9, 1775; Nov. 16, 1775. Ainslie, *Canada Preserved,* p. 93. Ainslie, *Canada Preserved,* p. 21. Extract of letter to gentleman in London, "Quebeck, November 7, 1775," in Force, *American Archives,* series 4, vol. 3, p. 1396. On Dec. 1, the number of defenders stood at eighteen hundred, including 230 Royal Emigrants who had yet to arrive when this letter was written. See Ainslie, "Journal of the Most Remarkable . . . ," p. 24.
10. Extracts of letters received in England, "Quebeck, November 9, 1775," in Force, *American Archives,* series 4, vol. 3, pp. 1417–18.
11. Ibid. Carleton to Lord Dartmouth, Quebec, Oct. 25 and Nov. 5, 1775, in Davies, ed., *Documents of the American Revolution,* vol. 11, pp. 185–86.
12. Hugh Finlay to Anthony Todd, "Quebeck, November 1, 1775," in Davies, ed., *Documents of the American Revolution,* vol. 11, pp. 170–71.
13. Extract of letter to gentleman in London, "Quebeck, November 7, 1775," in Force, *American Archives,* series 4, vol. 3, p. 1396.
14. Carleton to Lord Dartmouth, Quebec, Oct. 25 and Nov. 5, 1775, in Davies, ed., *Documents of the American Revolution,* vol. 11, pp. 165–66, 172–73.
15. Carleton to Lord Dartmouth, Quebec, Oct. 25, 1775, in Davies, ed., *Documents of the American Revolution,* vol. 11, pp. 165–66. "Questions asked the Indians of the St. François Tribe," Aug. 17, 1775, in Force, *American Archives,* series 4, vol. 3, pp. 339–40. George Washington, "Instructions to Colonel

Benedict Arnold," in Chase, ed., *Papers of George Washington: Revolutionary War Series,* pp. 457–59.
16. Carleton to Lord Dartmouth, Quebec, Nov. 5, 1775, in Davies, ed., *Documents of the American Revolution,* vol. 11, p. 173. Cramahé to Lord Dartmouth, Quebec, Nov. 9, 1775, in Davies, ed., *Documents of the American Revolution,* vol. 11, pp. 178–79. Extracts of letters received in England, "Quebeck, November 9, 1775," in Force, *American Archives,* series 4, vol. 3, pp. 1417–18.
17. Arnold to General Washington, Pointe Levi, Nov. 8, 1775, in Force, *American Archives,* series 4, vol. 3, pp. 1635–36.
18. Arnold to Montgomery, Sainte Marie, Nov. 8, 1775, in Force, *American Archives,* series 4, vol. 3, p. 1634. Mathias Ogden reported in his journal on Nov. 6 that he had encountered two Québécois on horseback on the road to Pointe Levi, who had said that the French inside Quebec intended to throw down their arms on Arnold's arrival.
19. Abner Stocking, Journal, in Roberts, ed., *March to Quebec,* p. 558.
20. Isaac Senter, Journal, in Roberts, ed., *March to Quebec,* p. 223. Würtele, *Blockade of Quebec,* pp. 5–7. Henry Caldwell, "The Invasion of Canada in 1775." In Historical Documents of the Literary and Historical Society of Quebec, series 2, (1867).
21. Simeon Thayer, Journal, in Roberts, ed., *March to Quebec,* p. 262. Abner Stocking, Journal, in ibid., p. 558. George Morison, Journal, in ibid., p. 531.
22. John Henry, Journal, in Roberts, ed., *March to Quebec,* pp. 349–50. Simeon Thayer, Journal, in ibid., p. 263. Ainslee, *Canada Preserved,* pp. 21–22.
23. Simeon Thayer, Journal, in Roberts, ed., *March to Quebec,* p. 263. Ebenezer Tolman, Journal, in ibid.
24. Isaac Senter, Journal, in Roberts, ed., *March to Quebec,* pp. 223–24. "George R." (King George) to William Tryon, April 1775, in E. B. O'Callahan, ed., *Documents Relative to the Colonial History of the State of New York,* pp. 562–63.
25. Carleton to Lord Dartmouth, Quebec, Nov. 5, 1775, in Davies, ed., *Documents of the American Revolution,* vol. 11, p. 173. Caldwell, "Invasion of Canada," (Historical Documents of the Literary and Historical Society of Quebec, series 2, 1867), p. 5. "The Case of Lieutenant John Starke of His Majesties Navy," Archives of the National Maritime Museum, MS 149/129, BGR/9.
26. Simeon Thayer, Journal, in Roberts, ed., *March to Quebec,* p. 264.
27. Isaac Senter, Journal, in Roberts, ed., *March to Quebec,* p. 224.

9. THE FORTRESS CITY
1. Henry Caldwell, "The Invasion of Canada in 1775." In Historical Documents of the Literary and Historical Society of Quebec, series 2, (1867), p. 5. MacLean to Viscount Barrington, Nov. 20, 1775, in Davies, ed., *Documents of the American Revolution,* vol. 11, pp. 189–90.
2. Ainslie, *Canada Preserved,* p. 23.
3. Henry Caldwell, "The Invasion of Canada in 1775." In Historical Documents of the Literary and Historical Society of Quebec, series 2 (1867), p. 5. "The Case of Lieutenant John Starke of His Majesties Navy," Archives of the National Maritime Museum, MS 149/129, BGR/9.
4. Jonathan Pierce, Journal, in Roberts, ed., *March to Quebec,* pp. 674–75.
5. Arnold to Washington, Nov. 13, 1775, in Force, *American Archives,* series 4, vol. 3, p. 1636.

6. Jonathan Pierce, Journal, in Roberts, ed., *March to Quebec,* p. 676. The number of canoes that made the crossing varies by report. For example, Arnold said forty (Arnold to Washington, Nov. 13, 1775, in Force, *American Archives,* series 4, vol. 3, p. 1636), but Dearborn and Meigs, who had been in charge of gathering them, said thirty-five (Return J. Meigs, Journal, in Roberts, ed., *March to Quebec,* p. 183; Henry Dearborn, Journal, in ibid., p. 142). James Melvin, Journal, in Roberts, ed., *March to Quebec,* p. 440.
7. Isaac Senter, Journal, in Roberts, ed., *March to Quebec,* pp. 224–55.
8. Ibid. Simon Fobes, Journal, in Roberts, ed., *March to Quebec,* p. 587.
9. Return J. Meigs, Journal, in Roberts, ed., *March to Quebec,* p. 182. Isaac Senter, Journal, in ibid., p. 225. Simeon Thayer, Journal, in ibid., p. 264.
10. John Henry, Journal, in Roberts, ed., *March to Quebec,* p. 352.
11. Simon Fobes, Journal, in Roberts, ed., *March to Quebec,* p. 587. George Morison, Journal, in ibid., p. 533.
12. Henry Caldwell, "The Invasion of Canada in 1775." In Historical Documents of the Literary and Historical Society of Quebec, series 2, (1867), p. 5.
13. Ibid.
14. Arnold to Montgomery, Nov. 14, 1775, in Roberts, ed., *March to Quebec,* pp. 87–88.
15. John Henry, Journal, in Roberts, ed., *March to Quebec,* pp. 353–54.
16. Caldwell, "Invasion of Canada," p. 6.
17. Abner Stocking, Journal, in Roberts, ed., *March to Quebec,* pp. 559–60.
18. Jacob Danford, "Quebec Under Siege, 1775–1776," p. 70. Mathias Ogden, Journal, MNHP. Henry Dearborn, Journal, in Roberts, ed., *March to Quebec,* p. 142. Isaac Senter, Journal, in ibid., p. 226. Arnold to Cramahé, in ibid., pp. 89–90.
19. Mathias Ogden, Journal, MNHP.
20. Ibid. Arnold to Cramahé, Nov. 15, 1775, in Roberts, ed., *March to Quebec,* pp. 88–89.
21. Montgomery to Carleton, Oct. 22, 1775, in Force, *American Archives,* series 4, vol. 3, pp. 1138–39. Carleton to Lord Dartmouth, Oct. 25, 1775, in Davies, ed., *Documents of the American Revolution,* vol. 11, pp. 165–66.
22. Washington to Philip Schuyler, Dec. 18, 1775, in John C. Fitzpatrick, ed., *The Writings of George Washington from the Original Manuscript Sources, 1745–1799.*
23. Simeon Thayer, Journal, in Roberts, ed., *March to Quebec,* p. 265. George Morison, Journal, in ibid., p. 533.
24. Isaac Senter, Journal, in Roberts, ed., *March to Quebec,* p. 226. Simeon Thayer, Journal, in ibid., p. 265. John Topham, Journal, in ibid., p. 265. John Henry, Journal, in ibid., p. 359. Caleb Haskell, Journal, in ibid., p. 480. Return J. Meigs, Journal, in ibid., p. 183.
25. Arnold to Montgomery, Nov. 20, 1775, in Roberts, ed., *March to Quebec,* pp. 90–91.
26. Ainslie, *Canada Preserved,* p. 22.
27. Carleton to Lord Dartmouth, Nov. 20, 1775, in Davies, ed., *Documents of the American Revolution,* vol. 11, pp. 185–86. Arnold to Washington, Nov. 20, 1775, in Force, *American Archives,* series 4, vol. 3, pp. 1695–96.
28. Arnold to Montgomery, Nov. 20, 1775, in Force, *American Archives,* series 4, vol. 3, pp. 1696–97.
29. Henry Dearborn, Journal, in Roberts, ed., *March to Quebec,* p. 143. Arnold to "Messrs. Prince and Haywood, Merchants, Montreal," Nov. 20, 1775, in Force,

American Archives, series 4, vol. 3, p. 1697. Montgomery to Washington, Nov. 24, 1775, in ibid., p. 1695.

30. Washington to John Hancock, Nov. 28, 1775, George Washington Papers, series 2, Letterbooks, Library of Congress. Washington to Philip Schuyler, Nov. 28, 1775, George Washington Papers, Library of Congress. Washington to Arnold, Dec. 5, 1775, George Washington Papers, Library of Congress.

31. Washington to John Hancock, Dec. 11, 1775, George Washington Papers, series 2, Letterbooks, Library of Congress. General Orders, "Head Quarters, Cambridge," Dec. 4, 1775, in Fitzpatrick, ed., *Writings of George Washington.*

32. "Proceedings of a General Court-Martial of the Line, Held at Head-Quarters, at Cambridge, by Order of His Excellency George Washington, Esq., Commander-in-Chief of the Forces of the United Colonies, December 1, A.D. 1775," in Force, *American Archives,* series 4, vol. 3, pp. 1709–10.

33. Ibid. John Sullivan, Letter, New York, April 28, 1776, in ibid., p. 1710.

34. "Proceedings of Court-Martial," pp. 1709–10. General Orders, "Head Quarters, Cambridge," Dec. 4, 1775.

35. "To the Impartial Publick," in Force, *American Archives,* series 4, vol. 3, pp. 1710–11. "New-London," May 31, 1776, in ibid., p. 1711.

10. SUFFERING AND WAITING

1. John Henry, Journal, in Roberts, ed., *March to Quebec,* p. 361.
2. Isaac Senter, Journal, in Roberts, ed., *March to Quebec,* p. 227.
3. Ibid. Henry Dearborn, Journal, in Roberts, ed., *March to Quebec,* p. 143. Caleb Haskell, Journal, in ibid., p. 481.
4. Henry Dearborn, Journal, in Roberts, ed., *March to Quebec,* p. 143. Caleb Haskell, Journal, in ibid., p. 481. Isaac Senter, Journal, in ibid., p. 227.
5. John Pierce, Journal, in Roberts, ed., *March to Quebec,* p. 682. Henry Dearborn, Journal, in ibid., p. 143. John Topham, Journal, in ibid., p. 268.
6. Return J. Meigs, Journal, in Roberts, ed., *March to Quebec,* p. 184. Simeon Thayer, Journal, in ibid., pp. 267–68. John Topham, Journal, in ibid., pp. 267–68.
7. John Pierce, Journal, in Roberts, ed., *March to Quebec,* p. 682.
8. Jeremiah Greenman, Journal, in Bray and Bushnell, eds., *Diary of a Common Soldier,* p. 21.
9. John Pierce, Journal, in Roberts, ed., *March to Quebec,* pp. 685, 689.
10. Ibid.
11. Caleb Haskell, Journal, in Roberts, ed., *March to Quebec,* p. 481. Jeremiah Greenman, Journal, in Bray and Bushnell, eds., *Diary of a Common Soldier,* p. 21. John Henry, Journal, in Roberts, ed., *March to Quebec,* p. 356. Henry dates this comment Nov. 15, but the circumstances surrounding it and the lack of any mention of it in any other account on that date make it unlikely, especially since the colonials captured an entire wagonload of flour on that day. Comments in other journals and the supply of provisions neatly fit the Nov. 24 council. Henry had a habit of recording dates that conflicted with his comrades' accounts.
12. Arnold to "Officers of the Continental Army on Their Way from Montreal to Quebec," Nov. 24, 1775, in Roberts, ed., *March to Quebec,* p. 95. Arnold to "Officers of the Continental Army on Their Way from Montreal to Quebec," Nov. 25, 1775, in ibid. Jeremiah Greenman, Journal, in Bray and Bushnell, eds., *Diary of a Common Soldier,* p. 21.

13. Arnold to Montgomery, Nov. 25, 1775, in Roberts, ed., *March to Quebec*, p. 96. Arnold to unknown (probably Gen. Clinton), Nov. 25, 1775, in ibid., pp. 96–97.
14. Simeon Thayer, Journal, in Roberts, ed., *March to Quebec*, p. 269. Jeremiah Greenman, Journal, in Bray and Bushnell, eds., *Diary of a Common Soldier*, p. 21. Henry Dearborn, Journal, in Roberts, ed., *March to Quebec*, p. 143. Isaac Senter, Journal, in ibid., p. 227.
15. Henry Dearborn, Journal, in Roberts, ed., *March to Quebec*, p. 143. Simeon Thayer, Journal, in ibid., p. 269.
16. Jeremiah Greenman, Journal, in Bray and Bushnell, eds., *Diary of a Common Soldier*, p. 21. Arnold to Montgomery, Nov. 30, 1775, in Roberts, ed., *March to Quebec*, p. 100. Henry Dearborn, Journal, in ibid., p. 144.
17. Return J. Meigs, Journal, in Roberts, ed., *March to Quebec*, p. 185. John Henry, Journal, in ibid., p. 363. (Meigs said Montgomery arrived at 1:00 p.m., Simeon Thayer said 9:00 a.m., Henry Dearborn claimed 10:00 a.m., and Isaac Senter said noon.) Journal of Jeremiah Greenman, in Bray and Bushnell, eds., *Diary of a Common Soldier*, p. 22.
18. George Morison, Journal, in Roberts, ed., *March to Quebec*, p. 534.
19. Jeremiah Greenman, Journal, in Bray and Bushnell, eds., *Diary of a Common Soldier*, p. 22. Henry Dearborn, Journal, in Roberts, ed., *March to Quebec*, p. 144. Caleb Haskell, Journal, in ibid., p. 482. Simeon Thayer, Journal, in ibid., pp. 269–71.
20. Arnold to Washington, Dec. 5, 1775, in Roberts, ed., *March to Quebec*, pp. 101–2. Henry Dearborn, Journal, in ibid., p. 144. Simeon Thayer, Journal, in ibid., pp. 269–71. Jeremiah Greenman, Journal, in Bray and Bushnell, eds., *Diary of a Common Soldier*, p. 22.
21. Jeremiah Greenman, Journal, in Bray and Bushnell, eds., *Diary of a Common Soldier*, p. 22. Henry Dearborn, Journal, in Roberts, ed., *March to Quebec*, p. 144. Return J. Meigs, Journal, in ibid., p. 185.
22. Caldwell, "Invasion of Canada," p. 5. "The Case of Lieutenant John Starke of His Majesties Navy, Archives of the National Maritime Museum, MS 149/129, BGR/9. Ainslie, *Canada Preserved*, pp. 24–25. Vialar/Lester, "Orderly Book," in Würtele, *Blockade of Quebec . . .* , pp. 176–77.
23. "A Proclamation," Nov. 22, 1775, in Force, *American Archives*, series 4, vol. 3, pp. 1639–40. Isaac Senter, Journal, in Roberts, ed., *March to Quebec*, p. 227.
24. Anonymous, "Journal of the Most Remarkable Occurrences in Quebec since Arnold Appeared Before the Town on the 14th November 1775," series 7 (1905), pp. 95–96. Ainslie, *Canada Preserved*, p. 25.
25. Arnold to Washington, Dec. 5, 1775, in Roberts, ed., *March to Quebec*, pp. 101–2. George Morsion, Journal, in ibid., p. 534.
26. Simeon Thayer, Journal, in Roberts, ed., *March to Quebec*, p. 271.
27. Henry Dearborn, Journal, in Roberts, ed., *March to Quebec*, p. 144. Simeon Thayer, Journal, in ibid., p. 271. Isaac Senter, Journal, in ibid., p. 228.
28. Henry Dearborn, Journal, in Roberts, ed., *March to Quebec*, pp. 144–45. Isaac Senter, Journal, in ibid., pp. 228–29.
29. Isaac Senter, Journal, in Roberts, ed., *March to Quebec*, pp. 228–29. John Topham, Journal, in ibid., p. 272.
30. Danford, "Quebec Under Siege," p. 71. Caleb Haskell, Journal, in Roberts, ed., *March to Quebec*, p. 482. W.T.P. Short, ed., *A Journal of the Principal Occurrences During the Siege of Quebec*, pp. 57–58.

31. Ainslie, *Canada Preserved*, p. 27.
32. John Henry, Journal, in Roberts, ed., *March to Quebec*, pp. 374–75. Caleb Haskell, Journal, in ibid., p. 482. Isaac Senter, Journal, in ibid., p. 230.
33. John Henry, Journal, in Roberts, ed., *March to Quebec*, p. 364.
34. Simon Fobes, Journal, in Roberts, ed., *March to Quebec*, p. 588. John Pierce, Journal, in ibid., pp. 690, 694, 699.
35. John Pierce, Journal, in Roberts, ed., *March to Quebec*, p. 694. John Topham, Journal, in ibid., p. 272. John Henry, Journal, in ibid., p. 373. To ease the anxiety created by this desertion, Montgomery claimed that Singleton had deserted under orders and would return soon after, though he did not.
36. Abner Stocking, Journal, in Roberts, ed., *March to Quebec*, pp. 561–62. George Morison, Journal, in ibid., p. 535.
37. Simeon Thayer, Journal, in Roberts, ed., *March to Quebec*, p. 273. Isaac Senter, Journal, in ibid., pp. 230–31.
38. Simeon Thayer, Journal, in Roberts, ed., *March to Quebec*, pp. 273–74.
39. Ibid., p. 275. Isaac Senter, Journal, in Roberts, ed., *March to Quebec*, pp. 230–31.
40. John Pierce, Journal, in Roberts, ed., *March to Quebec*, p. 704.

II. STORMING THE WALLS

1. Ainslie, *Canada Preserved*, p. 33.
2. Ibid.
3. Francis Nichols, "Diary of Lieutenant Francis Nichols . . . ," p. 504. Henry Dearborn, Journal, in Roberts, ed., *March to Quebec*, p. 152.
4. John Henry, Journal, in Roberts, ed., *March to Quebec*, p. 375. Simon Fobes, Journal, in ibid., p. 590. John Pierce, Journal, in ibid., p. 790.
5. John Henry, Journal, in Roberts, ed., *March to Quebec*, p. 375.
6. Ibid., pp. 375–76. Henry Dearborn, Journal, in Roberts, ed., *March to Quebec*, p. 152. Return J. Meigs, Journal, in ibid., p. 190. Isaac Senter, Journal, in ibid., p. 232. Nichols, "Diary of Lieutenant Francis Nichols," p. 504.
7. Henry Dearborn, Journal, in Roberts, ed., *March to Quebec*, p. 149.
8. Ibid., pp. 152–53.
9. Danford, "Quebec Under Siege," pp. 72–74. Nichols, "Diary of Lieutenant Francis Nichols," p. 504. Simeon Thayer, Journal, in Roberts, ed., *March to Quebec*, pp. 275–76.
10. Henry Dearborn, Journal, in Roberts, ed., *March to Quebec*, pp. 152–53. Isaac Senter, Journal, in ibid., pp. 233–34. Danford, "Quebec Under Siege," p. 73.
11. Short, ed., *Journal of the Principal Occurrences*, pp. 66–68.
12. Caldwell, "Invasion of Canada," p. 13. Return J. Meigs, Journal, in Roberts, ed., *March to Quebec*, p. 189. Abner Stocking, Journal, in ibid., p. 565.
13. Nichols, "Diary of Lieutenant Francis Nichols," pp. 504–5.
14. Ibid. Danford, "Quebec Under Siege," p. 73.
15. Abner Stocking, Journal, in Roberts, ed., *March to Quebec*, pp. 565–66.
16. Ibid.
17. Henry Dearborn, Journal, in Roberts, ed., *March to Quebec*, pp. 149–51.
18. Ibid. Short, ed., *Journal of the Principal Occurrences*, pp. 66–68.
19. Arnold to General Wooster, Dec. 31, 1775, in Roberts, ed., *March to Quebec*, pp. 102–3.

20. Nichols, "Diary of Lieutenant Francis Nichols," pp. 504–5. George Morison, Journal, in Roberts, ed., *March to Quebec*, p. 539.
21. Nichols, "Diary of Lieutenant Francis Nichols," pp. 505–6. Henry Dearborn, Journal, in Roberts, ed., *March to Quebec*, p. 379.
22. Danford, "Quebec Under Siege," pp. 72–73.
23. Caldwell, "Invasion of Canada," p. 11.
24. Isaac Senter, Journal, in Roberts, ed., *March to Quebec*, pp. 234–35.
25. Ibid.
26. Return J. Meigs, Journal, in Roberts, ed., *March to Quebec*, p. 192. Isaac Senter, Journal, in ibid., p. 235.
27. Arnold to General Wooster, Jan. 2, 1776, in Roberts, ed., *March to Quebec*, pp. 103–6.
28. John Henry, Journal, in Roberts, ed., *March to Quebec*, pp. 390–91.
29. Isaac Senter, Journal, in Roberts, ed., *March to Quebec*, pp. 235–37.

EPILOGUE: AMERICA'S HANNIBAL

1. Washington to Arnold, Dec. 5, 1775, in Force, *American Archives*, series 4, vol. 3, p. 192. Schuyler to General Washington, Ticonderoga, Nov. 22, 1775, in ibid., series 4, vol. 3, p. 1635. Schuyler to John Hancock, Nov. 22, 1775, in ibid., series 4, vol. 3, p. 1633. Warren to Samuel Adams, Dec. 5, 1775, Samuel Adams Papers, Bancroft Collection, New York Public Library. Jefferson to John Randolph, Nov. 29, 1775, in Paul Leicester Ford, ed., *The Writings of Thomas Jefferson*, vol. 1, p. 491.
2. Gates to George Washington, Oct. 12, 1776, in Force, *American Archives*, series 5, vol. 2, pp. 1080–81.
3. Carleton to Lord Germaine, Oct. 14, 1776, in Force, *American Archives*, series 5, no. 2, p. 1080. Alfred Thayer Mahan, *The Major Operations of the Navies in the War of American Independence*, p. 25.
4. William L. Stone, *Campaign of Lieut. Gen. John Burgoyne and the Expedition of Lieut. Col. Barry St. Leger*, pp. 384–86.
5. General Enoch Poor, Letter, quoted in Frank Moore, *Diary of the Revolution*, Hartford: JB Burr, 1875, pp. 497–98.
6. Thomas Wakefield, quoted in W.T.P. Stone, *Visits to the Saratoga Battle-Grounds, 1780–1880*, p. 152.
7. Henry Dearborn, "A Narrative of the Saratoga Campaign, 1815," pp. 8–9. Thomas Wakefield, quoted in Stone, *Visits to the Saratoga Battle-Grounds*, p. 152.
8. Thomas Anburey, quoted in Jackman, ed., *With Burgoyne from Quebec*, p. 175. Davies, ed., *Documents of the American Revolution*, vol. 14, pp. 236–37.
9. Short, ed., *Journal of the Principal Occurrences*, pp. 66–68. Henry Caldwell, "The Invasion of Canada in 1775," in Historical Documents of the Literary and Historical Society of Quebec, series 2 (1867), pp. 12–13.
10. Mahan, *Major Operations of the Navies*, p. 25.
11. John Burgoyne, *A State of the Expedition from Canada as Laid Before the House of Commons*, p. 17.
12. Account reproduced in Charles E. Allen, *History of Dresden, Maine*, pp. 304–5. Aaron Burr to Sally Burr Reeve, Sept. 24, 1775, in Mary-Jo Kline, ed., *Papers of Aaron Burr, 1756–1836*, microfilm ed., reel 1.
13. James Parton, *Life and Times of Aaron Burr* (New York: Mason Brothers, 1858), see esp. pp. 667–68, 676.

14. Act of Rhode Island Legislature, Feb. 1778.
15. William Gammell, *Life of Ward*.
16. Mark M. Boatner, *Landmarks of the American Revolution*, p. 49. Washington County Historical Society, *History of Washington County, Ohio*, p. 45. B. V. Meigs, *One Man in His Time: Return Jonathan Meigs*, p. 286.
17. "Notes and Queries," *Pennsylvania Magazine of History and Biography*, vol. 12 (1889), pp. 568–71.
18. Annals of Congress, U.S. Senate, 18th Cong., 1st sess., pp. 342–43.
19. Simon Fobes, Journal, in Roberts, ed., *March to Quebec*, pp. 592–93.
20. Ibid., p. 603.
21. Ibid., pp. 608–13.
22. Ibid., p. 613.

BIBLIOGRAPHY

MANUSCRIPT COLLECTIONS

William L. Clements Library, University of Michigan, Ann Arbor
Thomas Gage Papers.
Houghton Library, Harvard University, Cambridge, Massachusetts
Anonymous. "Journal of the Most Remarkable Occurrences in the Province of Quebec, From the Appearance of the Rebels in September 1775 Until Their Retreat on the Sixth of May, 1776, Kept by an Anonymous Defender Under Sir Guy Carleton."
Library of Congress, Washington, D.C.
George Washington Papers, 1741–1799: Series 3–4.
Literary and Historical Society of Quebec, Morrin Centre, Quebec City, Quebec
Anonymous. "Journal of the Most Remarkable Occurrences in the Province of Quebec Since Arnold Appeared Before the Town on the 14th November 1775." Series 7 (1905).
Henry Caldwell. "The Invasion of Canada in 1775." Historical Documents. Series 2 (1867).
Maine Historical Society, Portland, Maine
Collection S-104.
Morristown National Historical Park, Morristown, New Jersey
Mathias Ogden. Diary.
National Maritime Museum, Greenwich, England
Archives. "The Case of Lieutenant John Starke of His Majesties Navy (MS 149/129, BGR/9).
New York Public Library, New York, New York
Bancroft Collection. Samuel Adams Papers.
Princeton University Library, Princeton, New Jersey
Manuscripts Division, Department of Rare Books and Special Collections.
Public Record Office, Kew, Surrey England
Colonial Office Papers. CO 41/1–107—Secretary of State's Correspondence with Governor, Quebec and Lower Canada.

PUBLISHED WORKS

Ainslie, Thomas. *Canada Preserved: The Journal of Captain Thomas Ainslie.* Ed. Sheldon Cohen. New York: New York University Press, 1969.
Allen, Charles Edwin. *Collections and Proceedings of the Maine Historical Society,* 1892.

Allen, Charles Edwin. *History of Dresden, Maine.* Augusta, Maine: Kennebec Journal Printshop, 1931.

Anbury, Thomas. *With Burgoyne from Quebec.* New York: Macmillan, 1963.

Arnold, Benedict. "Arnold's Letters on His Expedition to Canada in 1775." *Maine Historical Society Collections,* Portland: Maine Historical Society, 1831, vol. 1, pp. 341–86.

Arnold, Isaac. *Benedict Arnold at Saratoga.* Philadelphia, 1880.

Bigelow Patricia, ed. *The Bigelow Family Genealogy,* vol. 1., Bigelow Family Society, 1986.

Boatwer, Mark M. *Landmarks of the American Revolution.* Camp Hill, Pa: Stackpole Books, 1973.

Bray, Robert C., and Paul E. Bushnell, eds. *Diary of a Common Soldier in the American Revolution, 1775–1783: An Annotated Edition of the Military Journal of Jeremiah Greenman.* DeKalb: Northern Illinois University Press, 1978.

Burgoyne, John. *A State of the Expedition from Canada as Laid Before the House of Commons.* London: Almon, 1780.

Champlain, Samuel de. *The Voyages and Explorations of Samuel de Champlain (1604–1616).* New York: A. S. Barnes, 1906.

Chase, Philander, et al., eds. *Papers of George Washington: Revolutionary War Series.* 6 vols. Charlottesville, 1985.

Coburn, Jouise Helen. *Skowhegan on the Kennebec.* vol. 1., Skowhegan, Maine, 1941.

Danford, Jacob. "Quebec Under Siege, 1775–1776: The 'Memorandums' of Jacob Danford." Ed. John F. Roche. *Canadian Historical Review,* vol. 50 (March 1969), pp. 68–85.

Davies, K. G., ed. *Documents of the American Revolution, 1770–1783.* 21 vols. Shannon, Ireland: Colonial Office Series, 1972– .

———. "A Narrative of the Saratoga Campaign, 1815." *Bulletin of the Fort Ticonderoga Museum,* vol. 1 (1928–29).

Drake, Samuel Gardiner. *Biography and History of the Indians of North America.* Boston: Benjamin B Mussey, 1851.

Fitzpatrick, John C., ed. *The Writings of George Washington from the Original Manuscript Sources, 1745–1799.* 39 vols. Washington, D.C.: United States Government Printing Office, 1931–44.

Force, Peter. *American Archives.* 9 vols. in 5 series. Washington, D.C.: M. St. Clair Clarke and Peter Force, 1837–53.

Ford, Paul Leicester, ed. *The Writings of Thomas Jefferson,* 10 vols. New York and London, 1892–99.

Gammell, William, "Life of Ward." In Jared Sparks, *Library of American Biography.* series 2. vol. 9. Boston: Little, Brown, 1846.

Getchell, Addison C. *Genealogy of the Getchell Family.* Boston, n.d.

Getchell, Everett Lamont. *The Family of Samuel Getchell of Salisbury, Mass.* Boston: New England Historic Genealogy Society, 1909.

Hanson, J. W. *History of the Old Towns Norridgewock and Canaan* [Maine]. Boston, 1849.

Haskell, Caleb. *Caleb Haskell's Diary, May 5–May 30, 1776: A Revolutionary Soldier's Record Before Boston and with Arnold's Quebec Expedition.* Ed. Lothrop Withington. Newburyport, Mass.: W. H. House, 1881.

Hayden, Horace Edwin. "A Defense of Gen. Roger Enos." *Magazine of American History,* vol. 13, suppl. Extra no. 42.

Henry, John Joseph. *Account of Arnold's Campaign Against Quebec and of the Hardships and Sufferings of that Band of Heroes Who Traversed the Wilderness of Maine from Cambridge to the St. Lawrence in the Autumn of 1775.* Albany: Joel Munsell, 1877. [Originally published as *An Accurate and Interesting Account of the Hardships and Sufferings of That Band of Heroes, Who Traversed the Wilderness in the Campaign Against Quebec in 1775* (Lancaster: William Greer, 1812). Reprinted in *Pennsylvania Archives,* series 2, vol. 15 (1893), pp. 59–191.]

LeMoine, J. M. *Album du Touriste.* 2nd ed. Quebec, 1872.

Lyman, Coleman. *Genealogy of the Lyman Family in Great Britain and America.* Albany: J. Munsell, 1872.

Mahan, Alfred Thayer. *The Major Operations of the Navies in the War of American Independence.* Boston: Little, Brown, 1913.

Martin, James Kirby. *Benedict Arnold, Revolutionary Hero: An American Warrior Reconsidered.* New York: New York University Press, 1997.

Meigs, B. V. *One Man in His Time: Return Jonathan Meigs.* Privately printed, 1981.

Meigs, Return Jonathan. *Journal of the Expedition Against Quebec, Under the Command of Col. Benedict Arnold, in the Year 1775.* Ed. Charles I. Bushnell. New York: Privately printed, 1864.

Moore, Frank. *Diary of the Revolution,* 2 vols. Hartford: J. B. Burr, 1875.

Nelson, Paul David. *General Sir Guy Carleton, Lord Dorchester.* London: Associated University Presses, 2000.

Nichols, Francis. "Diary of Lieutenant Francis Nichols, of Colonel William Thompson's Battalion of Pennsylvania Riflemen, January to September 1776." Ed. Thomas H. Montgomery. *Pennsylvania Magazine of History and Biography,* vol. 20 (1896), pp. 504–15.

O'Callaghan, E. B., ed. *Documents Relative to the Colonial History of the State of New York.* Albany: Weed, Parsons, 1857.

Ogden, Mathias. "Journal of Major Matthias Ogden, 1775." Ed. A. Van Doren Honeyman. *Proceedings of the New Jersey Historical Society,* new series, vol. 13 (Jan. 1928), pp. 17–30.

Parton, James. *The Life and Times of Aaron Burr.* New York: Mason Brothers, 1858.

Reed, Parker M. *History of Bath and Environs.* Portland, Maine: Lakeside Press, 1894.

Roberts, Kenneth, ed. *March to Quebec: Journals of the Members of Arnold's Expedition.* New York: Doubleday, 1938.

———. *March to Quebec.* Camden, Maine: Down East Books, 1980. This softcover reprint includes the journal of John Pierce, which did not appear in the original hardcover edition (1938); it was first published in the third edition (1940).

Short, W.T.P., ed. *A Journal of the Principal Occurrences During the Siege of Quebec.* London, 1824.

Stone, William L. *Campaign of Lieut. Gen. John Burgoyne and the Expedition of Lieut. Col. Barry St. Leger.* Albany: J. Munsell, 1877.

———. *Visits to the Saratoga Battle-Grounds, 1780–1880.* Albany: J. Munsell's Sons, 1895.

Ulrich, Laurel Thatcher. *A Midwife's Tale: The Life of Martha Ballard, Based on Her Diary, 1785–1812.* New York: Knopf, 1990.

Unknown. "A Journal of the March of a Party of Provincials from Carlisle to Boston and from Thence to Quebec, 1775." *Pennsylvania Archives,* series 2, vol. 15, pp. 23–58.

Ware, Joseph. "A Journal of a March from Cambridge on an Expedition Against Quebec, in Col. Benedict Arnold's Detachment, Sept. 13, 1775." Ed. Justin Winsor. *New England Historical and Genealogical Register,* vol. 6 (April 1852), pp. 129–145.

Washington County Historical Society. *History of Washington County, Ohio.* Marietta, Ohio, 1881.

Wild, Ebenezer. "A Journal of a March from Cambridge, on an Expedition Against Quebec, in Colonel Benedict Arnold's Detachment, Sept. 13, 1775." *Proceedings of the Massachusetts Historical Society,* vol. 22 (April 1886), pp. 265–275. [Series 2, vol. 2.]

Williamson, William. *History of the State of Maine.* Hallowell, Maine: Glazier, Masters and Smith, 1832.

Würtele, Frederick Christian, ed. *Blockade of Quebec in 1775–1776 by the American Revolutionists (les Bastonnais).* 2 vols. Quebec: Daily Telegraph Job Printing House, 1905–6.

INDEX